Philanthropy and American
Higher Education

Philanthropy and Education

Series Editor

Marybeth Gasman, Professor of Higher Education, Graduate School of Education, University of Pennsylvania, USA

This series highlights first-rate scholarship related to education and philanthropy, attracting the top authors writing in the field. Philanthropy is broadly defined to include time, talent, and treasure. In addition to traditional forms and definitions of philanthropy, the series highlights philanthropy in communities of color as well as philanthropy among women and LGBT communities. Books in the series focus on fundraising as it is an integral part of increasing philanthropy and has an ever-increasing market.

Philanthropy in Black Education: A Fateful Hour Creating the Atlanta University System
  By Vida L. Avery

Saving Black Colleges: Leading Change in a Complex Organization
  By Alvin J. Schexnider

Philanthropy and American Higher Education
  By John R. Thelin and Richard W. Trollinger

Philanthropy and American Higher Education

John R. Thelin and Richard W. Trollinger

PHILANTHROPY AND AMERICAN HIGHER EDUCATION
Copyright © John R. Thelin and Richard W. Trollinger, 2014.

First published in 2014 by
PALGRAVE MACMILLAN®
in the United States—a division of St. Martin's Press LLC,
175 Fifth Avenue, New York, NY 10010.

Where this book is distributed in the UK, Europe and the rest of the world,
this is by Palgrave Macmillan, a division of Macmillan Publishers Limited,
registered in England, company number 785998, of Houndmills,
Basingstoke, Hampshire RG21 6XS.

Palgrave Macmillan is the global academic imprint of the above companies
and has companies and representatives throughout the world.

Palgrave® and Macmillan® are registered trademarks in the United States,
the United Kingdom, Europe and other countries.

ISBN: 978–1–137–31996–8

Library of Congress Cataloging-in-Publication Data

Thelin, John R., 1947–
    Philanthropy and American higher education / John R. Thelin,
    Richard W. Trollinger.
        pages cm
    Includes bibliographical references and index.
    ISBN 978–1–137–31996–8 (hardback)
        1. College benefactors—History—United States. I. Trollinger,
    Richard W., 1949– II. Title.

LB2336.T47 2014
378.1'06—dc23   2014009003

A catalogue record of the book is available from the British Library.

Design by Newgen Knowledge Works (P) Ltd., Chennai, India.

First edition: August 2014

10 9 8 7 6 5 4 3 2 1

Multum Donavit... They Gave a Lot

To the philanthropists whose gifts, large and
small, support higher education

Contents

Preface   ix

Acknowledgments   xi

About the Authors   xv

Introduction   1

1   Connecting Past and Present: Historical Background on
    Philanthropy and American Higher Education   9

2   Giving and Receiving: Major Philosophical Concepts and
    Theoretical Issues in Philanthropy   35

3   Philanthropists and Their Foundations   67

4   Endowments: Colleges and the Stewardship of Good Fortune   95

5   Government Relations and the Nonprofit Sector: Legislation
    and Policies in Philanthropy and Higher Education   119

6   Professionalization of Philanthropy: Fund-Raising and
    Development   145

7   Colleges and Their Constituencies: New Directions in
    Philanthropy   167

Notes   193

Bibliography   215

Index   231

Preface

In 1994, as a graduate student at Indiana University, I enrolled in John Thelin's Philanthropy and American Higher Education course. From that point forward, I have been captivated by the role that philanthropy plays in our nation's colleges and universities. John's depiction of philanthropy's role was riveting and he was able to make the various stories and individuals involved, jump out of the texts we read in class. When I envisioned this new series for Palgrave Macmillan, the first person I thought of to write a seminal piece of work on philanthropy and American higher education was John Thelin. I was happy to have him oblige along with his coauthor Richard Trollinger.

Together, John and Richard have produced the most comprehensive piece of writing on philanthropy and higher education. Their depiction of the influence of philanthropy in the development and growth of higher education helps the reader to better understand how higher education operates in the current day. John and Richard examine large-scale philanthropy and its role in changing the direction of higher education or keeping it the same. In addition, the authors explore smaller examples of how individual philanthropy shaped individual institutions.

Perhaps the most interesting aspect of the book is the way it is organized—a hallmark of Thelin's past work. The authors use both a vertical and horizontal approach to looking at philanthropy. The vertical approach gets at the heart of philanthropy in colleges and universities whereas the horizontal approach explores the many organizations that touch higher education, including nonprofits, churches, foundations, and government entities. By viewing philanthropy from various directions and angles, the reader gets a comprehensive picture of its influence and development rather than the flat portrayal, which is the typical view that readers have had in the past.

Thelin and Trollinger are also cognizant of their audiences. Rather than writing only for a traditional academic audience, they are mindful of the various audiences that can benefit from this work, including fund-raising practitioners, students, those working in philanthropic organizations, those leading colleges and universities, and even donors to higher education. Given the increasing role of philanthropy, a deeper knowledge of its history, how it works, and how it is changing is essential to all of these constituents.

Readers will be pleased to read *Philanthropy and American Higher Education* because it gives an understanding of the topic from multiple vantage points and perspectives. It will make their understanding of higher education richer and deeper whether they are scholars or practitioners.

MARYBETH GASMAN
University of Pennsylvania
Series Editor, Philanthropy and Education

Acknowledgments

We are indebted to our colleague Professor Marybeth Gasman of the University of Pennsylvania for her suggestion and then insistence that we write this book. Given that we have relied mightily on her own scholarship about philanthropy and higher education her invitation inspired both optimism and pressure that we show the right stuff as we filed the write stuff with our editors at Palgrave Macmillan.

As prelude to our book we benefitted from the support and endorsement of several national groups who have serious, enduring commitments to sound policy and informed discussion about philanthropy and education. The Aspen Institute awarded us a generous major research grant in 2008 for our in-depth policy analysis of how foundations and all nonprofit organizations deal with the important topic of endowments. We were pleasantly surprised that the Aspen Institute's program on social policies and philanthropies took seriously our concerns about the potential dysfunctions of having boards of trustees assume that perpetual endowments were as a matter of course a good thing and sound long-term policy. The culmination of this cooperation was their 2009 publication of our monograph, *Time Is of the Essence: Foundations and the Policies of Limited Life and Endowment Spend-Down* in which we used case studies of selected foundations to prompt a reconsideration of perpetual endowments as a conventional and widely used sound policy.

Whereas our study for the Aspen Institute dealt with contemporary nonprofit organizations and philanthropic foundations, we then shifted gears to focus on the historical study of endowments at colleges and universities. This resulted in publication of our article, "Forever Is a Long Time: Reconsidering Universities' Perpetual Endowment Policies in the Twenty-First Century," published originally in the journal, *History of Intellectual Culture* (2010/2011) vol. 9, no. 1, pp. 1–17. We thank editor P. J. Stortz for kind permission to draw from this article as a central part of our chapter 4 of this book. The capstone for this line of research came in 2013 with the news that the Council for the Advancement and Support of Education (CASE) had selected our article for its annual John D. Grenzebach Award for outstanding published work on philanthropy and education. We appreciate and take seriously CASE's support and acknowledgment as impetus for continuing our research on these topics.

The growing interest in the serious study of philanthropy and higher education has been characterized by development of an informal, essential network of scholarly colleagues at numerous colleges and universities. Central to these collaborations and exchanges have been the research paper sessions and symposia at the Association for the Study of Higher Education and the History of Education Society. Professor Andrea Walton of Indiana University, whose own original scholarship has included the historical study of women and philanthropy along with other significant themes, warrants special thanks. Dr. J. Travis McDearmon, now established as a director of Development for the School of Dentistry at Indiana University-Purdue University, made stellar contributions to the field of philanthropy with his PhD dissertation research on profiles of recent alumni as donors—as part of his graduate studies at the University of Kentucky's Educational Policy Studies and Evaluation departmental program. Professor Stanley Katz of the Woodrow Wilson School of Public Affairs at Princeton University has been influential in his analyses of philanthropy, with particular attention to higher education, both in his published scholarship and his thoughtful conversations. Noah Drezner, professor at Columbia University Teachers College and formerly at the University of Maryland, has published recent works that have been significant for fusing philanthropy and fundraising with underserved constituencies. Amy Wells Dolan, professor and associate dean at the University of Mississippi, has been generous and influential with her scholarship dealing with philanthropy and higher education in the South.

We are among many who read and write about the philanthropy associated with colleges and universities who are fortunate to have access to excellent articles from noteworthy higher education publications: *Inside Higher Ed*, *The Chronicle of Higher Education*, and *The Chronicle of Philanthropy*. Doug Lederman and Scott Jaschik, editors of *Inside Higher Ed* have written frequently and insightfully on foundations and higher education philanthropy—and also have provided us a good forum for our own op-ed essays. Dianne

Donovan, senior editor of the Commentary section of the *Chronicle of Higher Education* sponsored an excellent special issue on the Bill and Melinda Gates Foundation—from which we learned a lot—and to which we were invited to be contributing authors in July 2013. For over two decades we have relied on the astute reporting about philanthropy and higher education provided by our colleague and friend, Goldie Blumenstyck.

Systematic and serious study of philanthropy is inseparable from Indiana University's Lilly Family School of Philanthropy. We are grateful to our many colleagues there, especially Eugene Tempel and Dwight Burlingame for contributions to our own thinking and analyses in research and scholarship associated with public policies.

For one of us—John Thelin—special gratitude goes to Sharon Thelin Blackburn for her editorial excellence. Her perspectives acquired from her own professional work in development at the Colonial Williamsburg Foundation along with serving as a consultant to numerous nonprofit organizations have been essential. Virginia Fadil Hodgkinson, in her work at the National Institute of Independent Colleges and Universities and, later, with the founding of Independent Sector, has been our model and inspiration of sound public policies for philanthropy and the nonprofit sector. The late Kenneth Beyer, vice president of Claremont University Center, has been influential in his insistence on educational values as the enduring principle for philanthropy and higher education.

For the other one of us—Richard Trollinger—special gratitude goes to Patsi Barnes Trollinger for teaching the meaning of loving kindness by her example and for improving the quality of my writing with her capable editing. An author of children's books, when she is not writing, she is tirelessly researching future topics. I also am grateful to work with inspiring and supportive colleagues at Centre College. Traci Wilson is due special thanks for the many ways she assists me in making my work more effective. Having had the good fortune to be in attendance in the summer of 1974 when the American Alumni Council and the American College Public Relations Association united to form CASE, I have long been inspired by the people who devote their life's work to advancing higher education. Participating as a speaker at the 2010 Global Philanthropy Forum, organized by Jane Wales of the World Affairs Council, gave me a new perspective on and renewed appreciation for the philanthropists who are determined to make the world, not just our country, a better place for all of its inhabitants.

We have been fortunate to have Palgrave Macmillan as our publisher. In particular, Burke Gerstenschlager worked with us in the early stages of discussing themes and drafting the book proposal. In completing the finished manuscript we wish to thank editor Sarah Nathan and editorial assistant Mara Berkoff for their support, expertise, and patience in helping us bring our book to press. Susan Eberhart, production assistant at Palgrave Macmillan, made certain that production went well. We also wish to thank Deepa John, project manager for Newgen Knowledge Works, for thoughtful oversight of the copyediting of our manuscript. David M. Brown, PhD candidate in Studies in Higher Education at the University of Kentucky, took time from his own research to draft the index for us and to work on editing the manuscript and proofing galleys. The Educational Policy Studies Department of the University of Kentucky kindly provided generous financial support for the index project.

About the Authors

John R. Thelin and *Richard W. Trollinger* have collaborated since 2009 on projects about higher education and philanthropy. In 2013 the Council for the Advancement and Support of Education (CASE) awarded them the Grenzebach Prize for outstanding published research on philanthropy and education. In 2009 they received a research grant from the Aspen Institute that resulted in publication of their monograph, *Time Is of the Essence*. They have presented their papers at the Association for the Study of Higher Education (ASHE) and the Chicago Donors Forum.

John R. Thelin is a professor of Educational Policy Studies at the University of Kentucky. At Brown University he concentrated in history and was elected to Phi Beta Kappa. He received his MA and PhD from the University of California, Berkeley. He has been president of the ASHE and received the ASHE outstanding research award in 2011. In 2007 he received the American Educational Research Association award for outstanding research on higher education. Since 2006 he has been a member of the American Enterprise Institute's higher education group. John was Chancellor Professor at the College of William & Mary from 1981 through 1993 and was president of Williamsburg United Way. As a professor at Indiana University he was a member of the Center on Philanthropic Studies.

Richard W. Trollinger is vice president for college relations at Centre College. He is an alumnus of Emory & Henry College, where he formerly served as vice president for development and external affairs. He received his MEd from Vanderbilt University, MA from Indiana University, and PhD from the University of Kentucky. An educational fund-raiser for four decades, he also studies the role of philanthropy in shaping higher education. His doctoral dissertation, "Philanthropy and Transformation in American Higher Education," was awarded the 2009 CASE Grenzebach Prize for outstanding doctoral dissertation.

Introduction

A front-page story in the *New York Times* on December 24, 2012, brought attention to an unusual occurrence: in France officials for famous museums and cultural institutions were seeking private donors. It was hard for curators and boards to engage in what they called "begging," simply because the nation had a long, universally accepted tradition of government support for spending on cultural institutions.[1]

Readers in the United States found the French response curious. What was all the hand-wringing over handouts? Going hat in hand was old hat in the United States of America. More important, for Americans there was no stigma associated with "begging" for worthy institutions and causes. In the late nineteenth and early twentieth centuries the pioneers in large-scale philanthropy, who served as middlemen between such great donors as Andrew Carnegie and John D. Rockefeller and worthy institutions, were proudly known as "Honorable Beggars."[2] The tradition and titles endured. Indeed, in March 1996 the president of Cornell University told an audience of fellow university presidents at a conference held at Princeton University that college presidents in the United States were "beggars who lived in big houses."[3] His statement was good-natured and matter of fact, indicating the essential and ongoing need for presidents to make a good case for supporting the cause of higher education.

In contrast to France, giving and receiving are seen as part of the American Way. They are a source of pride in US national culture and its institutions. It is a fundamental lesson that is passed on with pride and enthusiasm in what has been—and continues to be—a nation of grateful newcomers. For example, on January 9, 2013—also on the front page of the *New York Times*—headlines announced that affluent Asian immigrants were showing their gratitude and generosity to America and as Americans by willingly donating to prestigious universities, museums, concert halls, and hospitals. The newly affluent donors understood and eagerly sought to be part of the "journey of becoming American." As the president of the India Foundation—a Citibank executive, himself an immigrant from India, commented, "They see their mainstream American peers giving and they say, 'I'm going to do that.'"[4]

This living tradition of American philanthropy has been well documented in a flow of outstanding scholarship pioneered over a half century ago by such historians as Robert Bremner, Merle Curti, and Roderick Nash.[5] Furthermore, it is a vital heritage that continually resurfaces in the public forum and popular celebrations. For example, on October 7, 1998, the United States Postal Service issued a first-class stamp celebrating "Giving and Sharing: An American Tradition." The official proclamation noted "Charitable giving in the U.S. exceeded $150 billion in 1998. While some of the money came from corporations and foundations, the overwhelming majority—about $120 billion—was given by individuals...Americans contribute to charitable causes through their workplaces and religious institutions. Telethons raise large sums and containers placed in stores collect money for neighbors in need. The national organization for a larger number of groups raising money for health, re-creation and welfare agencies is the United Way of America, which marked its 80th anniversary in 1998."

The vitality of philanthropy as celebrated by the commemorative stamp in 1998 has continued into the twenty-first century. Total charitable giving for 2012 was $316 billion. Gifts to higher education constituted a substantial portion of this—about 10 percent among all received donations. So, the legacy is that philanthropy—defined as "voluntary giving for the public good"—runs deep in the American grain and national character. It is an American saga in which colleges and universities have been center stage since the establishment of colonies in the New World more than four centuries ago.

Most important is that these customs and commitments pioneered at such colleges as Harvard, William & Mary, Princeton, Brown, Columbia, and Yale did not fade. Rather, they accelerated with the creation of a new nation in the late eighteenth century. Today higher education in the United States stands out globally as a success story. The skeletal statistics indicate that in Fall 2013 more than 2,000 degree-granting nonprofit colleges and universities enrolled 16 million students. In 2012, a total of 1,650,000 undergraduates received their bachelor's degrees and 500,000 graduate degrees. Central to this record is that philanthropy in the form of voluntary donations totaled

$31 billion for the fiscal year 2012. To flesh out these statistics, what one finds is a remarkable, enduring commitment of donors who think that going to college is important—and that it should be excellent, accessible, and affordable.

Beneath the campaign totals and final reports one usually finds interesting stories of individuals and their families whose financial support is buoyed by a strong sense of commitment to campus and community over time. Consider the case of the city of Baltimore and the Carey family to exemplify the enduring relation of private wealth promoting civic welfare in large measure through gifts to local higher education.[6] The family elder, William Polk Carey, told reporters in 2011, "It's time to think about the future of Baltimore, a great city with a great history." His approach was to first give $30 million to the University of Maryland School of Law, which is located in Baltimore, and would be renamed as the Francis King Carey School of Law, in honor of his grandfather. The grandson, William Polk Carey, then planned to follow with establishing a joint JD-MBA program with the Johns Hopkins University's School of Business (which is also the Carey School of Business, named after his *great-great*-grandfather). Taking stock of this tradition of family giving to Baltimore that has spanned six generations and well over a century, Carey said he planned to give the bulk of his fortune to his family foundation for philanthropic purposes. He elaborated, "I don't believe in having my family be rich. They don't need a lot of fancy cars to drive around. My goal is to make the foundation a billion and then after it's a billion, I might be old enough to think about passing on." This example illustrates the adage that wealth has its advantages—and its public responsibilities.

Colleges and universities in the United States are in essence *historic* institutions. This is readily apparent in our predilection for buildings that are old—or, perhaps, new buildings that are made to look old. Historic architecture is indicative of a crucial strand that runs deeper than the surface of bricks and mortar because the venerable buildings have been the sites of shared experiences and collective memory. This legacy is reinforced in the observations that historian Allan Nevins made in 1962 about how relatively young state universities had evolved over the preceding half century:

> One of the more difficult obligations of these new institutions has been the creation of an atmosphere, a tradition, a sense of the past which might play as important a part in the education of sensitive students as

any other influence. This requires time, sustained attention to cultural values, and the special beauties of landscape and architecture...This spiritual grace the state universities cannot quickly acquire, but they have been gaining it.[7]

The great state universities did, indeed, attract donors and acquire an ambience of great architecture and campus charm. The Hearst family, known for its fortune in newspaper publishing, took a special interest in the University of California campus at Berkeley by donating funds for the design and construction of numerous memorable buildings, ranging from the Hearst Mining Building to the Hearst Gymnasium for Women. At Indiana University the Lilly Family made certain that the state's flagship university had buildings for the library and performing arts that were comparable to any campus. By 1937 *Life* magazine's cover story on American colleges and universities described the emerging beautiful state universities as no less than the people's palaces, each with its grand columns and monumental buildings, thanks to generous donors.[8]

At best, philanthropy for higher education has been a mutually satisfying activity among donors and recipients that connects past and present and to provide for the future service and work of colleges and universities. Nowhere is this more evident than in the creative use of campus architecture combined with student memories the universities conveyed in their brochures and campaigns to inspire alumni and other potential donors. At Indiana University in 1993, the legendary President Emeritus and Chancellor, Herman B Wells, who had been a member of the Indiana University community for over seven decades, joined with the College of Education to sponsor "The Pathway Fund" whose motto was "paving the way to the twenty-first century." Donors were given the opportunity to have an actual brick inscribed in honor of an influential teacher or classmate. As the brochure noted, "Everyone enjoys searching the pathway for the names of fellow graduates and faculty from whom they learned so much...Come and see the hundreds of bricks already installed and watch as people stop to read the variety of wonderful inscriptions."

So, even though numerous commencement speakers have warned new graduates that "a college is more than bricks and mortar," projects such as Indiana University's "Education pathway" showed that the concrete and abstract could be joined, as inscribed bricks were the artifact that paid tribute to the heart and soul of the educational enterprise. The buildings themselves, however, are not the main draw. The magnetism is the collective experiences and shared memories that have animated the campus bricks and mortar.

The legacy of such fund-raising initiatives is the serious claim that belief and loyalty are crucial to making the American campus both endearing and enduring.[9] Without this historical and emotional character, US colleges and universities would be little more than lifeless props comparable to a deserted theme park. These strong convictions need not mask crises and controversies. Higher education in the United States is not without its problems—but these often are associated with its admirable and generous aspirations which are a works in progress and, hence, continually subject to reevaluation and healthy self-criticism. No nation has worked so hard and achieved so much in attempting to fulfill the dual goal of making a college education characterized by the challenging question, "Can we be equal and excellent?" Furthermore, the philanthropy associated with higher education has been the model and pacesetter for voluntary donations to a range of educational, artistic, scientific, social, and cultural giving at the local, state, and national levels.

The long tradition and large scale of philanthropy associated with American colleges and universities also signals that it is big business and serious business. This manifests itself in the increasing intersection of charitable giving (and receiving) with tax codes, court cases, legislation, and public policies. We attempt to include critical analysis of these dimensions, especially in our chapters dealing with foundations and with sources of conflict and competition among various higher education constituencies. Chapter 5, for example, includes discussion of colleges and universities within the larger topic of government relations and public policies for the nonprofit sector.

Philanthropy and higher education are themes that connect our past and present in a seamless web. The aim of this book is to provide higher education professionals, leaders, and scholars with a thoughtful, comprehensive introduction to the scope and development of philanthropy and fund-raising as part of the essential life and work of colleges and universities in the United States. Critical discussions about philanthropy and higher education ultimately raise questions about purpose and propriety—what are the missions of colleges and universities? What should be the purposes of higher education? Following from this with a shift to emphasis on purposes and aims of philanthropy, this book continually prompts readers to ask and critically discuss such fundamental questions as, "What are the aims and motives for giving?" and "What are the intended and unexpected consequences of giving for the donor, recipients, and other groups?"

To carry out this exploration we set forth in chapter 1 an historical survey of major themes, events, and developments that have shaped philanthropy and higher education since the seventeenth century. Then, in subsequent chapters we revisit many of the issues and topics introduced in chapter 1 to provide detailed consideration, always with an eye toward connecting past and present to consider—and reconsider—essential principles and controversies that have surfaced, whether in 1614 or 2014—and dates in between. So, for example, in our opening historical survey in chapter 1 we mention deliberately and specifically the emergence of great foundations between 1890 and 1920. Later, in chapter 3—titled "Philanthropists and Their Foundations"—we devote an explicit, distinct analysis to exploring the role of these legally incorporated charitable institutions. A comparable approach characterizes our treatment of endowments as a defining element in philanthropy and higher education, as chapter 4—titled "Endowments: Colleges and the Stewardship of Good Fortune"—resurrects and analyzes in detail information we first present concisely in the survey provided in chapter 1.

The interplay of numerous organizations and groups involved in philanthropy and higher education is complex. To bring a measure of clarity and distinction to this mix, our book is organized around two distinct categories. *Vertical Institutions* refer to colleges and universities, with the presumption that the campus is the primary source of teaching, research, and service as the essential missions of higher education. This is distinguished from *Horizontal Institutions*—foundations, government agencies, associations, accrediting bodies, advisory groups, consortia, and other entities which cut *across* the higher education landscape and whose fundamental purposes are to provide resources, regulations, and other supplemental services that interact with colleges and universities in carrying out the aims of philanthropy.[10]

Our focus is applied, interesting scholarship. We try to present informed, thoughtful data and analyses that will be interesting to colleagues and constituencies who are working—and continually learning and rethinking—about how support of higher education can be genuine and effective—and to try to fulfill numerous honorable goals. Our ultimate goal is for good research and discussion to lead to thoughtful reconsideration of the broad philosophy of voluntary giving to higher education. The audience and readership to which we direct this book include the following constituencies:

- Graduate students in higher education programs who are in a career path in college and university fund-raising and development;
- Graduate students in a variety of higher education specialties such as student affairs, academic deans, provosts, presidents, or other specialists who anticipate having fund-raising and development as part of their responsibilities;
- Incumbent presidents, provosts, academic deans, and vice presidents for development and institutional relations who wish to gain grounding and perspective on the day-to-day duties they have inherited, either by accident or design;
- Board members and trustees who, as part of their appointive roles, must quickly gain a grounding in the essentials of college and university fund-raising;
- Foundation leaders and boards of trustees;
- Donors—and potential donors—to higher education who wish to be informed and effective in their commitment and support;
- Federal and state legislators and, especially, their staff, who provide briefings on legislation;
- Members of CASE (Council for Advancement and Support of Education) along with present and future professionals at foundations and other philanthropic organizations who either give or receive donations to colleges and universities—and/or to such higher education thematic priorities as access, aid, or priority to specific fields;
- Members of ASHE (Association for the Study of Higher Education) who are primarily and predominantly professors of higher education whose graduate courses and seminars increasingly call for concise yet comprehensive attention to philanthropy as an important profession and field.

Our analyses are based on a combination of historical, philosophical, economic, and legal perspectives. Each chapter is presented as a self-contained essay and analysis. Throughout the work our aim is to distill significant scholarly works so as to be pertinent to the present and future planning for sound institutional activities and directions. And, in addition to the analytic perspective of information and data analysis, this book reflects and is animated by our underlying *belief* that support of higher education through philanthropy is a "good thing." It is central to the historic and future character of colleges and universities. In short, it is no less than a labor of love for institutions and their students, alumni, faculty, trustees, presidents, and friends we hold dear and whose values and contributions to American life are invaluable.

I

Connecting Past and Present: Historical Background on Philanthropy and American Higher Education

Philanthropy as part of American higher education has a distinctive character and strong presence.[1] At the institutional level, this was best illustrated in 2012 by Stanford University's successful completion of its five-year campaign to raise $6.2 billion.[2] A year later, on September 21, 2013, Harvard University announced a fund-raising campaign with a goal of $6.5 billion—the largest fundraising drive ever in higher education. This was no idle effort, as more than ninety thousand donors had already contributed $2.8 billion during the campaign's "quiet phase."[3]

Widespread media coverage understandably gravitates to these highly systematic, large scale initiatives by such internationally prominent universities as Stanford and Harvard. They are, however, not the whole story. One is hard pressed to name an established college or university—whether public or private—that does not have in place a sophisticated development office. But the practices and arrangements that are familiar to us at colleges and universities today have been neither inevitable nor predictable. Their evolution is a fascinating story of individuals, institutions, and episodes characterized by a mix of thoughtful decisions and unexpected events.

This chapter presents what has been the continuity and change in the development of US contemporary policies and practices for philanthropy in higher education. It provides higher education professionals with a fluid narrative whose essential question is, "What were the pivotal events that shaped familiar practices—or, caused us to veer in a new direction?" The themes and significant items introduced in this historical chapter will then be revisited and discussed in detail in pertinent subsequent chapters.

Soon after Harvard College had been granted its charter in 1636 by the Massachusetts Bay Colony college officials set to work drafting and publishing the first fund-raising prospectus—a pamphlet called "New England's First Fruits."

> After God had carried us safe to New England, and we had built our houses, provided necessaries for our livelihood, reared convenient places for God's worship, and led the civil government, one of the next things we longed for and looked after was to advance learning and perpetuate it to posterity; dreading to leave an illiterate ministry to the churches, when our present ministers shall lie in the dust. And as we were thinking and consulting how to effect this great work, it pleased God to stir up the heart of one Mr. Harvard (a godly gentleman and a lover of learning, there living among us) to give the one-half of his estate (it being in all about £700) toward the founding of a college, and all his library. After him, another gave £300; others after them cast in more; and the public hand of the state added the rest. The college was, by common consent, appointed to be at Cambridge (a place very pleasant and accommodate) and is called (according to the name of the first founder) Harvard College. The edifice is very fair and comely within and without, having in it a spacious hall where they daily meet at commons, lectures, and exercises; and a large library with some books to it, the gifts of diverse of our friends, their chambers and studies also fitted for and possessed by the students, and all other rooms of office necessary and convenient with all needful offices thereto belonging. And by the side of the college, a fair grammar school, for the training up of young scholars and fitting of them for academical learning, that still as they are judged ripe they may be received into the college of this school.[4]

Rudimentary by today's standards and technology, in its day "First Fruits" was a state-of-the-art publication and part of a sophisticated, effective initiative to promote philanthropy for higher education. Harvard delegates journeyed to England to enlist financial support by means of subscriptions for the important cause of creating and maintaining a college in the New World. All the elements of effective fund-raising were in place—mission, motive, commitment, purpose, and a plan. And, it worked! The pamphlet also reveals some other practices that characterize the American approach to supporting education. First, private giving often was in cooperation with public support, as it expressly notes that John Harvard's generous gifts led to other donors and, finally, "the public hand of the state added the rest." Also implicit in the concise text was the notion of *accountability* in which institutions and their delegates made certain to explain to donors how gifts were used in terms of educational purpose as well as the more concrete accomplishments, such as construction of appropriate buildings. The essence of these arrangements was *reciprocity*—in that each participating group had reasonable, fair expectations of the roles played by others.

To gain a sense of the serious commitment that the American colonies made to their newly founded colleges, it is useful to read carefully the terms and conditions set forth in the formal charters. Consider the following excerpt from the 1764 charter for the College of Rhode Island and Providence Plantations (later renamed as "Brown University" in honor of the generosity of the Brown family's donations):

> And furthermore for the greater Encouragement of this Seminary of Learning and that the same may be amply endow'd and enfranchised with the same priveleges Dignities and Immunities, enjoy'd by the American Colleges and European Universities, we do grant enact Ordain and Declare and it is hereby granted Enacted Ordained and Declared that the College Estate, the Estates Persons and Families of the President and Professors for the Time being lying and being within the Colony with the Persons of the Tutors and Students during their Residence at the College shall be freed and exempted from all Taxes, serving on Juries and Menial Services, and that the Persons aforesaid shall be exempted from bearing Arms Impresses and Military Services except in Case of an Invasion.[5]

These privileges and protections that the colonial government built into the academic charter included a mutual agreement of cooperation, as the charter terms required that the institution and its trustees adhere to strict educational purpose:

> Whereas Institutions for liberal Education are highly beneficial to Society, by forming the rising Generation to Virtue Knowledge & useful Literature & thus preserving in the Community a Succession of Men duly qualify'd for discharging the Offices of Life with usefulness & reputation they have therefore justly merited & received the attention & Encouragement of every wise and well regulated State, and whereas a Public School or Seminary erected for that purpose within this Colony, to which the Youth may freely resort for Education in the Vernacular & Learned Languages & in the liberal Arts and Sciences, would be for the general Advantage & Honor of the Government.

A further condition was that colleges themselves were expected to be community minded and philanthropic by seeking out talented youth and providing financial aid in the form of scholarships and fellowships. Again, the principle of good faith (literally, *bona fide*) was intertwined with *reciprocity* among the constituents. Otherwise, the investment in education would either dissolve or go awry as indulgent ventures without benefit to the commonwealth.

Illustrative of this compact was that colonial colleges reflected their standing as one of the most formal and privileged organizations of their time and place by keeping detailed records of annual revenues and expenses. It was no less than a requirement of fiduciary responsibility for trustees of the academic corporation. Since colleges enjoyed tax exemptions on real property and income, governors and the public from time to time expected accounting for the commonwealth. The problem for researchers today is that many ledgers were lost in fires and floods. Surviving financial documents are often fragmentary. Hence, we are indebted to the original and exhaustive reconstruction of financial records from several colonial colleges that Jesse Brundage Sears undertook. His detailed profiles of trends and practices were published in his 1922 book, *Philanthropy in the History of American Higher Education.*[6] In addition to summarizing financial trends Sears also provided annotations about terms and customs of the seventeenth and eighteenth centuries that help to make the collegiate records comprehensible for scholars in the twenty-first century.[7]

The dominant characteristics of colleges and philanthropy in the colonial era were as follows: first, many donations were made "in kind" or what sometimes was called "country pay"—goods and services—simply because there was a lack of hard currency or what we consider "real money." A College's records dutifully noted receipt of five sheep, bolts of cotton cloth, even a sugar dish. At first glance this practice seems quaint, even archaic, today in an era of credit cards, online payments, and electronic transfers. On close inspection, however, one finds that "donations in kind" as a substitute for cash gifts have been tenacious and attractive both to donors and recipients. To put this into more modern perspective, it is useful to recall the episode in Harper Lee's *To Kill a Mockingbird*, her classic novel about small town life in the South during the Great Depression of the 1930s: a farmer paid Attorney Atticus Finch for "legal work" by leaving a bag of hickory nuts on the lawyer's back porch. Finch explained to his young, inquisitive daughter that country folks didn't have much money on hand—a situation that instantly bonded the seventeenth-century colonists with twentieth-century farmers. Even today in the twenty-first century university athletic directors are pleased to accept donations of prime livestock from prosperous ranchers who join with coaches and all fans in wanting to make certain that the football team will be well fed before the big game!

Colleges in the colonial era relied on a practice known as "subscriptions" in which individuals along with such organizations as towns, churches or "associations" made pledges—that is, "subscriptions"—of gifts earmarked for future college support. As noted earlier with the example of Harvard's "First Fruits" pamphlet and campaign, this approach was especially successful as colleges in the American colonies sent delegates to England—with returns ranging from subscriptions of £1,000 to £10,000.

Another defining characteristic of philanthropy in the American colonies was that colleges received numerous gifts from a diverse range of donors. This was a sign of widespread and generous support. Most of these gifts were small. Yet this established an important, enduring precedent by which we still assess the effectiveness of fundraising for colleges today. For example, a development office takes justifiable pride in having a large percentage of alumni as donors—regardless of the amount or size of the donation. Once again, cash coexisted with "gifts in kind." Given that local monetary currencies were uneven and often suspect and that sterling silver from England was rare, colleges often preferred gifts in kind. Books were an especially prized bequest for several reasons. First, they were essential for the reading associated with collegiate scholarship. Second, there were few established publishers or presses in the New World so that even if a college had cash it was still difficult, if not impossible, to buy notable books.

Third, books in the seventeenth and eighteenth centuries had a real and symbolic value beyond the information conveyed by the printed word. A book was inherently valuable as a work of art, including such components as the quality of the leather binding, the typesetting, the type of vellum used for the pages, and the durability of the stitching. Furthermore, establishing a printing industry was an expensive venture. Little wonder, then, that John Harvard's gift of his cherished library was good news for the struggling new college in Massachusetts Bay Colony. This practice may seem quaint to us today—but, in fact, those books published in the colonial period have proven to be worth more than their weight in gold. On November 27, 2013 Boston's Old

South Church announced that it had sold its 1640 edition of the *Bay Psalm Book* for $14,165,000 at auction. According to the *New York Times* coverage, the small volume "already held a record as the first book printed in English in North America. Now it holds two: It is also the most expensive book ever sold at auction."[8]

One way to think about the founding of a college in the American colonies is that it was comparable to a young family literally creating a home from scratch. This often included acquiring the unspectacular but necessary durable goods such as lumber or a cask of nails to be used to construct the first college building. Inventories from the eighteenth-century colleges indicate detailed ledgers noting donations of table clothes, candle sticks, silverware, cutlery, glassware, desks, chairs, and other furnishings that were essential and often expensive when fitting the college building's dining commons or the president's house.

The most impressive gifts in terms of both generosity and educational vision were those for endowing professorships. In 1721 Thomas Hollis established a professorship of divinity at Harvard. In his "orders" he asks "that the interest of the funds be used, £10 annually for help to a needy student for the ministry—as many of these as the funds will bear." He reserved the right to sanction all appointments during his lifetime, then leaves it to the "President and Fellows of Harvard College," and asks "that none be refused on account of his belief and practice of adult baptism." The conditions which he places upon this, the first professorship established in America by private donation, are of interest. These are his words: "I order and appoint a Professor of Divinity, to read lectures in the Hall of the College unto the students; the said Professor to be nominated and appointed from time to time by the President and Fellows of Harvard College, and that the Treasurer pay to him forty pounds per annum for his service, and that when choice is made of a fitting person, to be recommended to me for my approbation, if I be yet living."

After the initial celebration of such generosity, a college president was left to ponder the sobering fact that the endowed professorship came with strings attached. Hollis's conditions included his right to approve appointments to the endowed professorship. He also had included stipulations about religious doctrine. What college boards and presidents learned over time was that such donor conditions could be at least confining. At worst, they pre-empted institutional prerogative and academic self-determination. The overriding legacy is that wise college officials eventually added statutes and regulations that curbed or even prohibited certain kinds of extreme donor control once a program was in place.

Hollis showed unprecedented generosity with a gift of £5,000 to endow a professorship of mathematics and natural philosophy. To gain estimate of this relative purchasing power, it is useful to note that among the more prosperous colleges a typical annual budget in the eighteenth century ranged from about £1,000 to £2,000—with student tuition payments accounting for about 70 percent of college annual revenues.

Although Hollis's terms for his endowed professorships have attracted the attention of historians and lawyers, it was exceptional. Many of the early large gifts were noteworthy in their lack of restrictions or conditions the donors placed on the recipient college. Yet in some instances even a well-intentioned gift saddled a college with responsibilities that were daunting. Foremost was a penchant for donors in England to provide funding for the education and salvation of Native Americans, who ostensibly would enroll for a special course of study at a college. Notable examples were programs at Dartmouth, Harvard, and The College of William & Mary.[9] The latter institution was beneficiary of a large gift from the estate of the famous English scientist Sir Robert Boyle. Boyle the chemist was more concerned about souls than science. He embraced the prospect of the royal college educating young Native Americans in Christianity. The scholarship program turned out to be ineffective and disastrous, as the young braves suffered illness along with social exclusion and marginalization at the College. In sum, they were never allowed to be accepted into the Anglo world of the college and colony. College officials were resourceful and eventually were able to gain permission to shift the Boyle funding to be used for the education of college students who might be preparing to educate Native Americans.

Most colleges in the colonial era had small enrollments, usually far less than a total of 100 students—with a few showing enrollments of about 200 in any given academic term. Small size meant that expenses were relatively low. College presidents were paid well in salary and also received generous perks such as grazing rights for their livestock and a house with no rental charge. Otherwise, there were few if any expenses for infrastructure or bureaucracy. The high esteem in which colonies held a college was demonstrated by the impressive architecture of the main or only college building—whether it be the Wren Building at The College of William & Mary, Nassau Hall at The College of New Jersey, or University Hall at The College of Rhode Island. Most instructors were transient, designated as "tutors." However, in some important cases, such as Thomas Hollis's large gifts to Harvard to create endowed professorships, some faculty were paid very well.

Colleges often were beneficiaries of gifts of land—one commodity that was relatively plentiful in the New World. At the same time, real estate was a fickle gift from the point of view of college officials, dependent on its location and potential uses. It was no less than our current distinction between beach front property versus swamp land. The *caveat* was that a college could be "land poor."

Philanthropy became increasingly important after the colonial and revolutionary period because new political allegiances signaled an end to customary government support from England. Under the auspices of the new United States, colleges forfeited the annual subsidies that earlier they might have received from either the English monarchy or from colonial governments. State governments had legal power to grant charters in the new nation—but were under no obligation to provide state funding that would be adequate to operate a college. In the twenty-first century today we may grumble about declining state appropriations for public higher education—but such disappointments are predicated on the expectation that states do have an obligation to use tax revenues as a source of regular biennial support for colleges and universities. No such obligation existed in 1800. A state legislator might opt one year to give a favored college the proceeds from a state lottery as a sporadic gesture—with no subsidy in future years.

What one does find in the first half of the nineteenth century is a groundswell of widespread private voluntary donations, as Americans came to be known as a nation of joiners—and, also, a nation of givers. Colleges gained from these practices of private giving—as did a spate of new public institutions, such as hospitals, orphanages, libraries, asylums, schools for the blind, and related services. The prototypical college of the mid-nineteenth century had a lean administrative structure—often confined to a president and to a hybrid officer called "the college agent" whose dual role was to travel the countryside in search of donors and/or prospective students who could afford to pay tuition.[10]

While each college had to rely on various sources to acquire revenues, one source of assistance came from associations and other formal organizations whose aim was to provide scholarship funds to attract students to certain professions. Most notable was the New England-based American Education Society—a Congregationalist-based charity that raised monies which then were offered as full scholarships to students who agreed to pursue a bachelor of arts degree at an approved college and then to study to be ordained as a Congregationalist minister. The important condition was that the scholarship recipient then agreed to serve as a missionary to an assigned, underserved locale—such as Hawaii. During the period 1815 to about 1840 the AES flourished and provided scholarships for about 15 percent of the college students enrolled in New England and the Mid-Atlantic regions.[11]

In the mid-nineteenth century philanthropists were persistent and pervasive in trying to be persuasive about serious curriculum reform. Foremost was the aim of successful entrepreneurs to convince colleges (often their own alma mater) to add courses and programs that were well-suited to the American economy. Engineering, surveying, applied sciences were typically advanced as appropriate and sorely needed antidotes to the hegemony of the classical curriculum.

Initiatives for curricular innovation tended to attract inordinate attention. Meanwhile, the staple of philanthropy and higher education was the persistent efforts of civic leaders and citizens to make certain that their home town had its own college. Historian Daniel J. Boorstin described this American tradition as commitment to founding "the booster college." It was especially prevalent in newly settled regions and states, spreading from East to West. These institutions truly were "community colleges" in that their students, alumni, and donors truly were part of the immediate town and adjacent country side.[12]

The Civil War usually is not hailed as a period of college building and fund-raising. In fact, its implications for philanthropy in the United States were substantial. The main legacy was the emergence of a highly organized, nationwide network of voluntary services—such as The Red Cross and the United States Sanitary Commission. Such organizations demonstrated how private giving and an independently chartered leadership and staff could mobilize supplies and services to respond to large-scale crises, including the ravages associated with war and battlefields. Historian John Whitehead has made the compelling argument that these privately founded and funded organizations created the "private" or nonprofit sector.[13] Their lack of graft and corruption, combined with effectiveness in treating casualties and providing a range of medical treatments and supplies stood out in bold relief to the clumsiness and corruption associated with war time relief programs sponsored by the federal government. A crucial connection to higher education was that several college and university presidents served on the boards and committees of the new private relief agencies—and eventually transplanted their organizational and work ethos to their own campuses. Colleges and universities also were integral to the Civil War in that many campuses in the South and border states served as hospitals for wounded soldiers from both sides.

The Civil War also was consequential for the funding and support of higher education in that secession leading to creation of the Confederate States of America created a window of opportunity for passage of the Morrill Land Grant Act in 1862. This massive legislation that included a formula for sale of Western lands to be allocated to create funding sources for higher education among participating states represented new, substantial involvement of the federal government in college and university curricula. It also pioneered the collaboration of public agencies and private institutions, as many of the federal-state revenue allotments were first distributed to such historic colleges as Dartmouth, Yale, and Transylvania and to such new institutions as Cornell University and the Massachusetts Institute of Technology to create new courses of study.

Private philanthropy was instrumental in expanding access in higher education for heretofore underserved constituencies—including African Americans, women, and numerous ethnic immigrant groups. The abolition of slavery and subsequent creation of the federal government's Freedman's Bureau led to some forays into building schools and colleges for African Americans. This was enhanced significantly by philanthropy from individual donors, private foundations such as the Slater Fund, and from church-related missionaries.[14] The results and later developments—including controversies—associated with the General Education Board and, later, creation of the United Negro College Fund, will be discussed in chapter 3, "Philanthropists and Their Foundations."

Women had gained some access to higher education in the first half of the nineteenth century with the founding of Mount Holyoke Female Seminary in Massachusetts, along with such pioneering ventures as teacher training colleges and seminaries in Miami, Ohio, and coeducation at Oberlin College. Between 1870 and 1920 these scattered initiatives were joined with large scale philanthropy that led to the founding—and sustaining support—of such colleges as Vassar, Wellesley, Smith, Bryn Mawr, Mills, and Goucher.[15]

A common thread in these various initiatives is that in the United States each group usually had the right to found a college and to obtain a charter from its host state. Philanthropy and private fund-raising were crucial because each group was left to its own efforts to cobble together adequate resources to operate a newly chartered college. The net result was a crazy quilt of special interest colleges. Church affiliation certainly designated a religious sponsorship. At the same time, it often was a surrogate or proxy for an ethnic group's efforts to create its own college.[16] A Lutheran college, for example, most likely enrolled a large number of students who were German or Scandinavian in descent. Migration throughout the continental United States combined with immigration from overseas was accompanied by extension of an existing trend: special interest groups continued to raise money to create colleges for their own constituencies. Religion—and denominational church affiliation was an important source of cohesion. This included the founding of numerous Catholic colleges, many of which were located in large cities in order to be accessible to families.

Following the Civil War philanthropy for higher education was transformed in part by the emergence of new, unprecedented industrial fortunes that coexisted with traditional patterns of small gifts by individuals, churches, and local organizations. Steel, oil refining, railroads, breweries, shipping lines, mining, land development, and banking were the sources of great wealth for a small number of individuals and their families. It was an era in which numerous civic and public institutions and organizations were objects of generous donors—museums, art collections, libraries, parks, academies, special research institutes, literary societies, symphony orchestras, and other performing arts.

One partial explanation for the escalation of large gifts was the emergence of a new professional role—fund raisers whose specialty was to cultivate donors. An interesting artifact of this development is the 1890 "Memorandum on Rules of Procedure" by Frederick T. Gates that provided a code of conduct along with strategies to those whose work was to "canvass" for charitable gifts. Gates' advice pamphlet became the manifesto of the so-called Honorable Beggars, the new "Middlemen of American philanthropy." In language that was forthright and pragmatic, Gates warned fund raisers about paying attention to details of grooming and dress along with a guide to signs and cues in talking to potential donors—all with the intent of closing the deal on an optimal pledge.[17]

Within this group of institutions that were beneficiaries of philanthropic generosity, colleges and universities were particular favorites of the major donors in the late nineteenth century. Higher education's good fortune was that many of the new capitalists opted to build magnificent campus architecture and even to endow namesake colleges, such as Vanderbilt, Johns Hopkins, Cornell, Carnegie, Clark, Tulane, Mellon, Tufts, Stanford, Tulane, and Rice that flourished as new universities. The new University of Chicago, which opened in 1893, enjoyed the large-scale philanthropy of John D. Rockefeller— but, alas, with no family name affiliation. Some established colleges such as Yale and Princeton gained from a new generation of wealthy donors as well as from prosperous alumni.

How large were these gifts? How much did they alter the scope and scale of higher education? Can we make any informed estimates as to their comparable worth today? In the late nineteenth century the largest gifts included $20 million from Leland and Jane Stanford in 1885, $3.5 million from Johns Hopkins in 1873, $34.7 million that John D. Rockefeller gave to the University of Chicago, the Sterling bequest to Yale for $15 million in 1918, and Henry C. Frick's bequest of $15 million to Princeton in 1919.[18] Using the United States Department of Labor's inflation adjustment calculator, a cautious estimate is that a gift made in 1913 has increased approximately 24-fold. By this standard, the previously mentioned gifts would be worth as follows in 2013 in dollars: Stanford University $480 million, Johns Hopkins University $84 million, Rockefeller's bequest to the University of Chicago would be worth $832 million, the Sterling gift to Yale was the equivalent of $360 million, and the Frick bequest to Princeton has an equivalent value today of about $360 million.

These actual dollar amounts along with contemporary equivalents adjusted for inflation reinforce the claim that the gifts were large. The liability of largesse was that the gifts were often windfalls—one time occurrences—whose stewardship was not always characterized by systematic planning or careful spending. As a result, some of these universities that enjoyed large gifts faced abrupt disappointments. Clark University in Worcester, Massachusetts exhausted its major gift by spending on campus construction—a priority that caused it to lose many of its top professors who left to accept faculty appointments at the young, thriving University of Chicago. By 1904 Stanford University was on shaky ground literally, figuratively, and financially. The stability of its physical plant was jeopardized by the tremors of the great San Francisco earthquake that destroyed several of its magnificent campus buildings. To compound its problems, the revenues and resources for current and future operation of the university were at risk due to a lack of a careful investment and spending plan. The financial situation was sufficiently dire that Jane Stanford, widow of Leland Stanford, wrote checks from her personal bank account to help the university meet monthly payments on salaries and bills. Rice Institute along with Stanford University also was interesting in that at the onset neither charged tuition. The Johns Hopkins University, hailed as the exemplary strong academic university of the late nineteenth century, faced a troubled situation by 1910. One indicator of spendthrift organizational behavior at Stanford and elsewhere was the relatively low (and annually declining) endowments the major universities reported in 1910.

From today's perspectives, the generous gifts by a new breed of donors may seem to have created an idyllic era for higher education. At the time, however, the giving and receiving were characterized by uncertainties and tensions along with heroic expansion. Commodore Vanderbilt deflected bothersome money seekers by giving them free one way tickets to Central America—booked for passage on Vanderbilt's own ships, of course. Ironically, Vanderbilt the transportation mogul never did visit the Methodist University in Nashville that bore his name. Andrew Carnegie had serious doubts about the ability of universities to undertake advanced research when they also were committed to teaching undergraduates. This led him to create an organizational model apart from a campus—the new Carnegie Institution for Science in Washington, D.C.

Unbridled ambition was combined with unchecked spending at many of the new great universities. For example, the ambitious young president of the new University of Chicago, William Rainey Harper, continually raised the eyebrows and blood pressure of benefactor John D. Rockefeller by overspending and taking on new, unapproved construction projects. The complications of large bequests was shown by the curious case of the Rice Institute—now known as Rice University. William Marsh Rice, whose Texas fortune had been made in real estate, cotton trading, and timber, drafted a will in 1891 that gave a large sum for the founding of a distinctive small university in Houston. Although Rice died in 1900, construction and opening of the university was delayed by more than a decade.[19] The complication was that the will was held up in probate because of the allegation that Rice's personal attorney had forged a version of the will that shifted the proceeds of the estate with the Attorney as the prime beneficiary. To seal the deal he then enlisted the butler to murder the sleeping Rice, using chloroform. This type of scandal featured in tabloids was not good news for academe.

An important exception to the general rule of undisciplined spending was Harvard University—which strangely enough did *not* receive a transformational gift from a single donor during the boom in philanthropy between 1880 and 1910. Indeed, its most conspicuous architectural addition was Harvard Stadium, a classic revival design facility that seated about 50,000 fans and opened in 1904. Rather than building an entirely new campus, Harvard's president, Charles Eliot, staked out a distinctive institutional strategy of building funds for university investment (funds that would became known as "endowment") from numerous sources, including alumni solicitations. In contrast to the "boom and bust" characteristics of single large gifts at new universities such as Stanford and Johns Hopkins, Harvard took a long view that emphasized publicizing the names and amounts from donors and adhering to a principle of seeking unrestricted gifts all the while weaning the university away from dependence on tuition payments for operating and building the institution. Historian Bruce Kimball has brought attention to this policy of "free money." What one sees from President Eliot's practices and his own writings on the topic was an institutionalization of the conviction that informed donors would be interested and generous, often with repeating gifts.[20]

Harvard under Eliot's direction introduced some precepts that became part of strategy. For example, Eliot believed that a good practice was for the university to avoid showing a surplus at the end of each fiscal year. His rationale was that a modest shortfall created a sense of need that attracted concerned donors. Eliot also discouraged using existing investment funds to pay for construction, arguing that new donors probably could be attracted readily with the prospect of naming rights for a new building—which, hence, would be paid by new money. The net result was a self-perpetuating loop of giving that fulfilled institutional needs followed by the surfacing of new needs and new donors, always with unfinished good business waiting in the wings.

Essential to these fund-raising principles was a new definition of the role of a college or university president: to be a financial builder whose legacy was to leave the institution with increasing wealth, especially in the form of an ever-expanding endowment. This was in the American collegiate tradition of service that, of course, required presidential commitment to asking donors and alumni for money. The difference was that by 1910 the Harvard model was to build and grow for the long run. It was a distinctive, perhaps unique, designation because elsewhere university presidents tended to emphasize that their fund-raising efforts were to be directed to such emphases as campus construction, academic planning, or curricular innovation. In many cases fund-raising was urgent and expedient as a means to balance the annual budget. In contrast, the Harvard plan nurtured by President Eliot also signaled a new discipline in presidential fund-raising, as a college had to unlearn the custom of accepting indiscriminately virtually any gift even if its conditions were confining and sand-bagged a college to fund projects that really were not germane to institutional mission or were insufficient to meet project expenses. The landscape of American higher education was littered by bell towers and quadrangles whose maintenance expenses persisted long after the building donors' gifts had been spent.

The large gifts to prominent institutions are understandably the feature story of energized, expanded philanthropy in the late nineteenth and early twentieth centuries. They were not, however, the whole story. It is important to keep in mind the breadth of giving and its impact on institutional innovation. Sociologist Burton R. Clark has documented this in his study of the creation of what he calls "The Distinctive College."[21] Notable in this category were the founding of Reed College in Portland, Oregon and the energetic transformation of existing colleges, such as Swarthmore College with its Honors program and Antioch College of Ohio that fused liberal education with work study. In addition to Clark's case studies, two significant examples illustrate this phenomenon of private college diversity and innovation in the early twentieth century—Berea College in the mountains of eastern Kentucky and Deep Springs College in the California desert, close to the Nevada border.

Berea College's president had initiated a new emphasis for the college's mission and constituency—namely, to provide affordable liberal education combined with a work-study program for sons and daughters of mountaineers. The term at times was "Highlanders"—and, later, referred to the Appalachian regional culture. Important for philanthropy was the president's sustained, successful fund-raising forays in the Northeast—with numerous donors from New York City. Berea's endowment grew from $150 million in 1985 to $1.1 billion in 2007, enabling the college to provide its distinctively affordable education.

Another distinctive college that was founded in the early twentieth century was Deep Springs College, located in the desert on the border of California and Nevada. Its founder and leader was industrialist

L. L. Nunn. At the heart of the campus that opened in 1917 was a working ranch which was combined with a rigorous liberal arts curriculum. The all-male student body remained small, with fewer than 30 students enrolled per year. Although the college's students had high SAT scores and outstanding high school transcripts, the college did not confer the bachelor's degree. The custom was for its students to transfer to four-year colleges after completing two years of classical studies and mathematics at Deep Springs. On balance it was a testimony to the diversity and innovation marbled throughout American higher education, yet provided neither a model nor sufficiently large critical mass of alumni that would make its presence obviously consequential beyond its limited charge and special mission.

One peculiarity of colleges and universities in the United States was that they invoked a tradition of and commitment to the residential campus experience—as distinguished from the urban universities of Europe. On close inspection, however, one finds that most colleges could not afford to build dormitories to accommodate most of their undergraduates. Hence, it was newsworthy when a major gift actually enabled a college to construct on-campus housing that aligned collegiate image and collegiate reality. Such was the rare case between 1928 and 1930 when Yale alumnus Edward S. Harkness gave a total of about $30 million to Harvard and to Yale for their respective construction of the "Harvard House Plan" and the "Yale Residential Colleges."[22] The crucial codicil is that such a large gift for the bricks and mortar of "the collegiate way" was unusual both in the purpose and generosity of the Harkness bequest.

By 1920 with the tapering of the huge individual gifts combined with the imposition of federal income taxes starting in 1917 that may have discouraged some donations, a number of prestigious and seemingly wealthy colleges and universities faced financial problems. As a result by the 1920s a new generation of presidents started to pay attention to—and implement—the investment emphases pioneered by Eliot at Harvard. Illustrative of the late, last great private gifts for creating a new university came about in the early 1930s with the opening of Duke University in Durham, North Carolina. In fact, the "new" Duke University was a legacy of a transformed Trinity College. The popular image was that the Duke bequest came primarily from its tobacco fortunes. On closer inspection, one finds that the central source was from Duke Energy and other utilities stocks and bonds. The impressive Neo-Gothic campus was monumental, continuing the tradition of heroic architecture that donors such as Rockefeller, Vanderbilt, and Rice had started decades earlier. Duke University also continued a tradition in which preoccupation with grand buildings and public appearance encountered problems. The $40 million endowment was large, but evidently, still not adequate to provide funding for all the landscaping and monuments originally planned. Preoccupation with heroic architectural exteriors sometimes meant that attention to educational details were overlooked. At the grand opening of the campus, professors in the economics department were surprised to find that despite a magnificent interior, in several instances three professors had to share a single office.[23]

More important than such miscues was that an era of large scale construction of an entire campus was winding down. At the same time the popularity of large gifts to a single campus came to an end because major donors increasingly shifted toward organized philanthropy. In short, this meant the incorporation of trusts and foundations—often committed to an agenda of broad goals, as distinguished from funding and building a single magnificent campus. The new line up of philanthropy and higher education included the Carnegie Foundation for the Advancement of Teaching, the Carnegie Institute, the Rockefeller Foundation, the Rosenwald Fund, and the General Education Board—as we shall discuss in chapter 3: "Philanthropists and Their Foundations." How and why was this change important? Illustrative of the difference in focus was that instead of building a brand new campus, by 1930 the Rockefeller Foundation was using its resources to fund extensive research and development into such national projects as the Social Science Research Council, with attention to providing pilot studies and prototypes for kinds of social and economic data federal agencies ought to consider collecting and analyzing.[24]

In place of windfall philanthropy from major donors, colleges and universities started to build their own ongoing infrastructure for philanthropy. One enduring innovation from the early 1900s was the appearance of Alumni Associations. These would use affiliation with Alma Mater as a base for socializing at campus events along with annual fund-raising campaigns. They provided a readily available listing of prospective donors and their addresses. These entities also posed new questions and sometimes problems for campus governance. To whom was an alumni association responsible? If it had its own executive directory and board, how did its accrued funds and decisions mesh with, for example, the directives of the college or university president and trustees?

During the 1920s when colleges and universities did attempt fund-raising campaigns, they often fell far short of their goals. These early in-house initiatives often lacked adequate coordination, organization, accurate mailing lists, and the attention to deadlines and details that were crucial for success. As a result several colleges looked to new organizations such as the firm of John Price Jones to handle their fund-raising campaigns.[25] If one considers philanthropy for higher education in the broad scope of *all* charitable fund-raising immediately following World War I, the initiatives (and fund-raising achievements) of colleges and universities paled in comparison to the national campaigns for community services, including the precursor to United Way, the "community chests." Voluntary associations of Americans also showed unprecedented commitment and skill in responding to international catastrophes and crises. An influential, effective leader was Herbert Hoover whose organizational abilities, engineering background, and dedication made food relief for Belgium a model of large scale philanthropy both in its success at acquiring donations and then providing lifesaving delivery of food to a starving population.[26] Hoover's legacy as a philanthropist and administrator often has been obscured by criticism of his record as president of the United States at the onset of the Great Depression. In the 1940s Hoover's intelligence and planning skills carried over to his service to his alma mater—as a trustee and major donor to Stanford University during the years in which Stanford transformed itself from a comfortable campus into a dynamo as the prototype for the modern research university of the Cold War era.[27]

If one were to travel to campuses nationwide around 1925 one would find with remarkable frequency the appearance of a new "Memorial Stadium"—large football arenas seating between 30,000 and 60,000 and named in honor of alumni and state citizens who had lost their lives serving in World War I. This was especially important at state universities because it showed that these public institutions were "coming of age" as a source of statewide cohesion marked both by increasingly regular state tax subsidies plus private donations. It also confirmed and extended the primacy of intercollegiate football as a shared experience for alumni and donors as fans. Once in a while enthusiasm and expectations for stadium construction surpassed realistic goals and actual fund-raising results. At Southern Methodist University, a fund-raising shortfall for a new football stadium prompted the president and board to garnish faculty and staff wages to cover construction bills.

On a more selective scale than the statewide or broad alumni-based campaigns for stadium fund-raising, some astute state university presidents relied on prestige and affiliation to bring together select groups of alumni donors. One finds at the University of California the charismatic president, Robert G. Sproul, mobilized a small group of influential alumni known as "The Order of the Golden Bear" which would become tantamount to a "kitchen cabinet" and sounding board—and source of large gifts—for the university's president's consideration and use. The University of Wisconsin was innovative with its new WARF—acronym for the Wisconsin Alumni Research Foundation—created in 1925 to provide a formal home for university patents and royalties. At Indiana University, transformation of private fund-raising took the form of creating the "IU Foundation." The net result was that such initiatives provided universities with discretionary monies that could be used to fund special projects and to help achieve a margin of excellence beyond customary obligations.

Between 1930 and 1950 one sees the spread of an interesting strategy for special purpose fund-raising: the creation of separate corporations affiliated with a university structure. Namely, at state universities, especially in the South, shortfalls in tax revenues and state subsidies drained state university operating budgets. At the same time intercollegiate football, which had a late start in the South, gained momentum as a source of popular entertainment for the general public as well as for students, alumni, and campus constituencies. The problem that surfaced, especially during the Great Depression, was how to provide ample funding for football, regardless of the tax support shortfalls for the educational budget. A solution pioneered by the University of Georgia athletic department was to create a private corporation, usually with a name such as "State University Athletic Association (SUAA)," that was both a part and apart from the host public university.[28] The SUAA had its own board of directors and staff, often with the director of athletics and the university president as ex-officio board members. This became the potent vehicle by which the intercollegiate athletics department could raise money quite apart from other university programs and departments.

This type of structural innovation and strategy worked well to circumvent standard procedures of funding and salaries. For example, at the University of Kentucky immediately following World War II the newly founded University of Kentucky Athletic Association (known as the UKAA) provided an additional tool for recruiting high profile head coaches. For the Commonwealth of Kentucky the state law was that no state employee could receive more than $5,000 salary per year. Furthermore, all state university employees were classified as state employees. To circumvent this salary cap the UKAA did two things: first, it raised money from private donors; second, it hired the new coach—Paul "Bear" Bryant—as an employee of the UKAA, not the university.[29] This arrangement made life better for coaches and athletics directors, but at the same time complicated traditional definitions and practices for hiring and paying within a campus community. It also meant that fund-raising was lopsided toward some university units while the academic, non-athletic side of the institution languished. Such imbalances were ignored by presidents and state university boards. Later, university boards of trustees would create comparable units—for example, a "university foundation"—for supplementing state university presidents' salaries beyond caps set by governors and state legislatures.

Another important innovation that surfaced between World War I and World War II was the starting around 1936 of an important addition to the philanthropy of higher education—the sustained, systematic contributions from business corporations.[30] This was especially beneficial to independent colleges and universities, although eventually *all* institutions gained, whether "private" or "public." The details of this development are discussed at length in chapter 5: "Government Relations and the Nonprofit Sector," dealing with legislation and policies.

When famous foundations were inclined to provide funding to higher education after World War II it tended to follow the example of the Rockefeller Foundation's strategy in the 1930s in supporting the Social Science Research Council. The successors to such initiatives included the Ford Foundation's project in which five universities were selected to be models of change in the curriculum and faculty for the Master's of Business Administration degree. The hope was that these exemplary new programs would be influential and then be imitated elsewhere. In a similar vein, the Ford Foundation contributed multimillion dollar grants to eight universities—including Yale, Duke, and the University of Michigan—to shore up and rethink graduate programs in public policy.[31]

The general problem of the lack of student financial aid rather than donations to a single campus characterized large philanthropy efforts after World War II. The Council for Financial Aid to Education was incorporated in 1952 "with funds supplied by the General Education Board, the Alfred P. Sloan Foundation, the Carnegie Corporation,

and the Ford Foundation's Fund for the Advancement of Education."
Similarly, in 1957 business and academic leaders formed the Informal
Committee for Corporate Aid to American Universities. Illustrative
of the public relations efforts by the Council were the following in
the 1960s:

Give To the College of Your Choice. Now.
  Sixty Years Ago You Didn't Need a College Education.
  In fact, you didn't need much of anything except a willingness to
work 16 hours a day. For 8 cents an hour. Under brutal conditions.
  But times have changed drastically.
  Life for the working man is more challenging. Safer. More stimulat-
ing. And far more rewarding.
  Why?
  Many things have helped. Especially an endless flow of technologi-
cal improvements and discoveries. Many of which came from college
campuses, and from college-trained men and women.
  We must sustain this flow of ideas. Only in this way, can we
increase the productivity that will maintain and increase our standard
of living.
  America's colleges need your help. They are in deep financial trouble.

A few years later a Council poster proclaimed, "Make America
Smarter! Give MORE to the college of your choice!"
  The Council for Financial Aid to Education reported in 1962
more than $42 million in corporate contributions. The Council was
significant for two reasons: first, it provided hundreds of colleges a
connection with a collective, nationwide fund-raising medium—one
in which the general aim was to persuade and remind the American
public that "going to college" was central to the American Way—and
needed continual support for student financial aid. Second, this latter
emphasis on student scholarships helped remedy a long-time shortfall among most colleges—namely, few colleges had the resources ear
marked for scholarship funds to assist academically able yet financially needy applicants. Even at older, wealthier institutions such as
Yale, Harvard, and Princeton, deans of admissions offered little in
the way of grants. Most institutional aid was limited to prizes, work
study programs, and loans. Thanks to the initiative and example of
the Council for Financial Aid to Education, followed by the appearance of new federal student financial aid programs starting in 1972,
student financial aid ascended in terms of institutional priority and
available resources.

Large gifts for university endowments and campus building still surfaced periodically. A good example was Emory University in Atlanta, which had over time enjoyed the support of families associated with the locally based Coca-Cola Corporation. This included a 1979 gift from Robert and George Woodruff of $105 million in Coca-Cola stock. Generations of appreciative Emory students celebrated this legacy (and their friendly rivalry with crosstown Georgia Institute of Technology) with the following campus jingle:

Emory, Emory, Thy future we foretell
We were raised on Coca-Cola, so no wonder we raise hell
When'er we meet Tech's engineers
We drink them off their stool
So fill your cup, here's to the luck
Of the Coca-Cola school![32]

By 1980 articles about higher education, whether in the popular press or professional journals, broadcast a message of bad news. Colleges, along with hospitals, social service agencies, museums, performing arts centers, and other charitable organizations were depicted as "an endangered sector," mired in "the crisis of the nonprofits."[33] Illustrative of the archaic practices that were financially draining institutions was the following account of Boston University's business office by Lewis Mayhew in 1980 that, "As late as 1967, its financial records seemed to be maintained in pen and ink in schoolboy notebooks. The cautious thrift of the place was well revealed by its maintaining balances of several million dollars in non-interest gathering checking accounts, with the business manager pleased that the bank did not charge for checks written."[34] Elsewhere, fund-raising and development practices often were timid and tepid. The University of Virginia, for example, had never undertaken an organized capital campaign.

These incidents were symptomatic of what Berkeley economist Earl F. Cheit described as "higher education's new depression," whose clouds had been sighted on the horizon as early as 1973, and threatened to be an extended monsoon season that lasted over a decade.[35] The financial condition of higher education was sufficiently weak that the Carnegie Commission on the Future of Higher Education estimated that somewhere between one-fourth and one-third of American colleges were at risk of having to shut down.[36]

Contrary to the grim predictions, almost all colleges and universities did survive the turbulent 1980s. The explanation is that they heeded the messages for institutional reform in matters of data collection as part of decision-making for development and fund-raising became increasingly professionalized, along with comparable innovations for their counterparts in admissions, financial aid, and business affairs. Contrary to the stereotype of colleges and universities as slow to change, these various units undertook no less than a "managerial revolution" to put the academic house in order. Furthermore, at many colleges and universities, presidents, boards, and administrative leaders accepted the challenge to implement an entrepreneurial evolution characterized by proactive decisions based on systematic data analysis. Nowhere was this more evident than in their changes in development and fund-raising that went from being peripheral and casual activities to central and dynamic features of campus initiatives.[37]

A sign of recovery starting around 1985 was that a handful of independent colleges and universities set themselves apart in their commitment to "Buying the Best."[38] Over the next quarter century state universities, including the prestigious flagship institutions, tended to lag behind their independent counter parts. A partial explanation for this lag was that a tradition and commitment to systematic and large-scale fund-raising was still uneven among state universities. Also, some foundations restricted grant applications to independent colleges and universities. After 1980, however, the sharp contrasts between "private" and "public" institutions in development activities tended to blur. Indicative of the changing atmosphere was that in 1991 the University of Virginia undertook its first capital campaign. A staple line that state university presidents delivered in after-dinner remarks to alumni and friends was, "We used to be state supported. Then we were state assisted. Now we are state located." Concerned about the growing problems that state universities faced in competing for faculty talent, in 2007 the William and Flora Hewlett Foundation made a gift of $113 million as a challenge grant to the University of California, Berkeley to create 100 endowed faculty chairs.

The last decade of the twentieth century was characterized by the spread of increasingly large fund-raising campaigns across all institutional categories. In 1999 Harvard University announced that it had met its goal of $2.1 billion that it had set in 1992. Prosperous alumni and a booming economy led the vice president of Middlebury College to call these years the "Golden Age of Philanthropy."[39] Successive gains in both fund-raising success and high returns on endowment investments were tempered in 2008 with an abrupt, prolonged fall of the stock market. Despite such setbacks, private fund-raising remained—and surged—as a central strategy for college and university financing throughout the first decade of the twenty-first century.

Academic leaders also had to consider the sobering reports that although private foundations still contributed substantially for projects undertaken at colleges and universities, these gifts had tapered, as a host of topics and fields outside the campus increasingly competed for foundation funds.[40] Another significant legacy of the latter part of the twentieth century was that the entry of the federal government into sponsored research with creation of the National Institutes of Health, the National Science Foundation, and the National Endowment for the Humanities changed the landscape and balance of private and public support for university-based research and development. What this meant was that those university professors who were in demand, whether by foundations or federal agencies, to undertake large-scale sponsored research projects acquired great prestige and power within their institution and nationwide within their professional and academic specialties.[41] No doubt their host universities benefitted in terms of grant dollars and prestige for these enterprising professors—but not to the extent or in the same way as when foundations gave money to the institution rather than to the individual professor. It was another variation on the theme of external influences on the internal life of the American campus. A comparable new deal for student financial aid emerged after 1972 when the federal government's programs in student financial aid programs ranging from Pell Grants to Guaranteed Student Loans, reconfigured the dynamics and proportions of external support to higher education.[42]

By 2000 the funding model for higher education at colleges and universities in the United States worked best when these multiple funding streams—tuition dollars, private donations, foundation gifts, state subsidies, and federal research grant dollars—were opened to full throttle. As economist Ronald G. Ehrenberg of Cornell University documented in his book *Tuition Rising: Why College Costs So Much* there was little incentive to rein in the escalation of college costs.[43] Rather, the all-American strategy in higher education was to pursue prestige by pressing hard—and then, harder—to raise money that constituted the requisite resources for bigger and better programs. When this approach worked well for an institution, it was exhilarating and energetic, as certainly was the case around 1994–2000. It was, however, a funding approach that was not well suited to handling adversity or pessimism, a lesson that ambitious colleges and universities relearned periodically. This was especially true when the national economy went into a prolonged recession between 2008 and 2014. Increased emphasis on development and private fund-raising frequently was the favorite solution invoked by presidents and boards of trustees in such situations where colleges sought to balance budgets, tend to shortfalls, and provide for future growth. The paradox of fund-raising success was that even a university that succeeded in raising a billion dollars in 1994 was quick to tell reporters that this good fortune still left the university with a tight budget—further evidence that the inclination was for colleges to spend all that they raised.[44]

At the same time this impulse to rely on fund-raising seldom closed the gap for malnourished institutions. To the contrary, it frequently accentuated the difference between colleges with large endowments and those without.[45] Philanthropy for higher education also changed dramatically at this time with the emergence of such new entities as The Bill and Melinda Gates Foundation and the Lumina Foundation as influential players in the higher education agenda, both at the level of institutional priorities and national public policies.[46]

2

Giving and Receiving: Major Philosophical Concepts and Theoretical Issues in Philanthropy

Although the practice of philanthropy is ancient, its study as a distinct field of inquiry, or as a subject worthy of the sustained attention of established scholars in other disciplines, is relatively recent. In the past four decades, however, a great deal of attention has been devoted to the study of philanthropy, resulting in an ever-increasing flow of articles and books on the subject. Consequently, the field is quite dynamic and robust, if also still unsettled in terms of some of its theoretical constructs.

The fact that philanthropy is only now the focus of significant scholarly attention is somewhat odd since people in the United States have long claimed philanthropy as their top civic virtue. This is done with considerable justification; according to respected sources, nine out of ten people in the United States donate time or money to at least one charitable cause every year.[1] Giving and volunteering are a consistent thread in the fabric of American culture. Perhaps an even stronger thread than participating in key aspects of the democratic process since more people in the United States give than vote.[2] The amount given also is noteworthy. Giving in the United States exceeded $316 billion in 2012, roughly 2 percent of Gross Domestic Product (GDP) according to *Giving USA 2013*,[3] an annual publication that has tracked charitable giving in this country on an annual basis since the mid-1950s.

In higher education, we have long known that a college or university's ability to attract philanthropic resources is a strategic asset. In our competitive system, an institution's ability to raise funds is a primary determinant of its quality and prestige and, oftentimes in the private college sector, a determinant of survival. Furthermore, philanthropy gave birth to and continues to nurture a whole sector of public life in America, the nonprofit sector, that has become one of the defining characteristics of the nation. The other two sectors, the commercial (for-profit) sector and government, are widely studied and have been for many years. The difference is that the nonprofit sector lacked an identity until the last quarter of the twentieth century. Growing awareness of and appreciation for the importance of the nonprofit sector to American democracy played a major role in stimulating interest in the study of philanthropy.

Perhaps no other subject lends itself so well to "why" questions, which typically are attempts to get at issues of meaning, as does philanthropy. Why this project? Why this cause or organization? Why this amount? Why now? And the biggest "why" of all: Why give of one's resources for the benefit of others, many of whom are unknown to the donor? Some of philanthropy's growing body of literature addresses these questions. "Why" questions are notoriously difficult to answer, however, as evidenced in the literature, which reflects a variety of perspectives and a lack of settled opinion. This lack of consensus stems, in part, from the fact that most scholars who are doing research and writing about philanthropy examine it under the lens of another, more firmly established field of study (e.g., economics, history, philosophy, religion, sociology, sociobiology). That being said, the cross-disciplinary and interdisciplinary nature of philanthropy, in combination with the giving habits of the American public, make it accessible to and of interest to many people.

Of course, not all the articles and books about philanthropy address its "why" questions. Many of them focus on the "how to" questions concerned with increasing philanthropic giving to colleges and universities and other charitable organizations—that is, fund-raising. Although this chapter is concerned with the "why" questions, the authors understand philanthropy and fund-raising as two sides of the same coin and will discuss fund-raising and the role of the development office in higher education in chapter 6.

In the meantime, any starting point for addressing the "why" questions requires a definition of the term "philanthropy" and thus a distinction between charity and philanthropy, which often are used interchangeably but have different meanings. In its literal sense, philanthropy means "love of mankind," the word having been formed by a combination of Greek terms, *philo* meaning "love" and *anthropos* meaning "man" or humankind. Charity, the English translation of the Latin *caritas*, is also most often translated as "love," but as we shall see, it has religious connotations that give it a more narrow and specific meaning than philanthropy in contemporary usage. There are other words—altruism, beneficence, and generosity—that also are used interchangeably, or in place of, philanthropy. The relevance of research by evolutionary biologists and sociobiologists into altruism among other species, economists' focus on the concept of "impure altruism," and a philosophical and social movement known as Effective Altruism prompt us to give particular attention to altruism, as well as charity and philanthropy, in this chapter.

Defining Philanthropy

In a 1958 *American Quarterly* article, Merle Curti reported that philanthropy first appeared as an English word in 1628 and meant "love of man, charity, benevolence, humanitarianism, social reform."[4] Because the social reform aspect of philanthropy suggested the application of reason to the solution of social ills and needs, the term found favor with Enlightenment thinkers. In widely accepted modern usage, philanthropy, which can be either secular or religious, is less concerned with aiding individuals than it is with reforming society. Charity, by contrast, is often understood as a religious duty to relieve the pain and suffering and to address the basic human needs of others, especially the less fortunate members of society. Charity is rooted in the tradition of almsgiving and engages individuals in direct acts of compassion and service to others.

This is consistent with the view of noted historian of American philanthropy Robert Bremner that philanthropy is a more expansive concept than charity. According to Bremner, "The aim of philanthropy in its broadest sense is improvement in the quality of human life."[5] While charity is concrete and individual, and philanthropy is abstract and institutional, the two need not be at odds. In fact, Robert Gross has suggested that "as dual impulses, they are the equivalent of the two commitments taken by physicians in the Hippocratic Oath: One vow is to relieve pain and suffering, the other is to cure disease."[6]

Another way of highlighting the distinction, as well as the compatibility, between charity and philanthropy utilizes the familiar saying of Lao-Tse: "Give a man a fish, you feed him for a day. Teach him to fish, and you feed him for a lifetime."[7] Although the two actions are juxtaposed as opposites, clearly there are occasions when it is appropriate to give a hungry man a fish (charity). However, if one wishes to help that man become self-reliant and free from hunger, then the appropriate action is to teach him to fish (philanthropy). In contemporary usage, charity is generally considered to be among the expressions of philanthropy, a subset of the whole.

One of the chief advocates for establishing philanthropy as a field of scholarly pursuit was Robert Payton, former head of the Exxon Foundation who was instrumental in the founding of the Indiana University Center on Philanthropy (now the Indiana University Lilly Family School of Philanthropy). In a 1988 book, *Philanthropy*, Payton offered a brief working definition of philanthropy that, because it embodies key concepts, has stood the test of time and remains viable after a quarter century of use. Moreover, it is consistent with and reflective of Bremner's contention that philanthropy's aim is improvement in the quality of human life. For Payton, philanthropy is "voluntary action for the public good," the sub-title of his book.[8]

This definition raises its own set of questions, of course. What does "voluntary action" mean? And who gets to decide what constitutes the public good? At its core, a voluntary action is an action willingly undertaken, it is uncoerced. Although there is no absolute and universal agreement on this point, there is a general consensus that coerced behaviors are by definition not philanthropic. A coerced action is one that is forced or required, such as the paying of taxes. Being pressured by a friend, business associate, or former classmate to make a gift does not in this sense constitute coercion; even if there are unpleasant consequences, one can refuse the entreaties of friends and associates. In contrast, failure to pay taxes may result in fines, the confiscation of assets, and even imprisonment of the guilty party.

Although Payton's brief definition has withstood the passage of time and a substantial degree of scholarly criticism, one should not imagine that it or Bremner's definition stand as the sole or exclusive definition of philanthropy. This point is illustrated in the position taken by Lawrence Friedman and Mark McGarvie, who are contributors to, as well as coeditors of, *Charity, Philanthropy, and Civility in American History* (2003). Their work is an intentional counterpoint to Bremner, whose post–World War II consensus interpretation of American history they find to be lacking in the degree of critical analysis expected of twenty-first century scholars. Whereas Bremner had defined philanthropy in terms of its overall impact, that is, improvement in the quality of human life, Friedman and McGarvie focus on the intentions of philanthropists. "In our view," they write, "the giver's intent becomes the acid test to distinguish who is and who is not a philanthropist."[9] According to their model, what philanthropists intend is to impose their visions, ideals, or conceptions of truth upon society, doing so with missionary zeal. While the philanthropic ventures of these individuals are oftentimes attentive to the concerns of recipients, in some instances they are not.

Surely Friedman and McGarvie are right to insist that philanthropists act on their vision of a good society. What is debatable is whether or not all philanthropists (i.e., people who engage in philanthropy) intend to impose their visions on society or simply act to bring about that which they believe to be good. No doubt some philanthropists have sought to use their wealth to push their visions, ideals, or conceptions of truth. But to suggest that all philanthropists are intent upon imposing their views on society seems arbitrary, even if there is only a hairsbreadth's difference between "imposing" and "bringing about."

In order to make a difference for good, one must bring about some change in an existing status quo. Vision is important to philanthropy because it gives direction to the desire to create change that will enhance the quality of life (i.e., the public good). Philanthropy is all about the good and visions of the good society. Of classical philosophy's three motivations—the search for truth, the search for beauty, and the search for good—philanthropy is an expression of the search for good. For this reason, philanthropy is sometimes referred to as moral action; its study is an inquiry into the social history of the moral imagination.

These observations notwithstanding, it is far more useful to define philanthropy—the activity of philanthropists—in terms of its outcomes instead of the intentions of its practitioners. It is useful to do so because public policy decisions cannot be based on something as individualistic and open to interpretation as donor intent. And encouraging philanthropy has long been an important matter of public policy in this country.

From the perspective of public policy, philanthropy in the United States is the sum of all gifts with monetary value made annually to those organizations qualifying under Section 501(c)(3) of the Internal Revenue Code to receive tax-deductible contributions. Whether or not those gifts are actually deducted from the income tax returns of the donors who made them is immaterial. The nonprofit organizations that are eligible to receive tax-deductible contributions are exempt from federal income taxes, and in many localities, they also are exempt from property taxes. These privileges that provide incentives for giving to such organizations have been features of United States public policy since the earliest days of the nation's income tax system. The policy remains intact because the charitable, religious, and educational organizations classified as 501(c)(3) organizations are deemed to serve public purposes. In this instance, policy reflects and attests to the nature of philanthropy as a public good.

However, the monetary approach to defining philanthropy fails to take into account the value of volunteering as an action for the public good. Periodic efforts are made to assess and value the volunteering of time and talent that occurs annually and routinely in this country, and the numbers—both the hours served and their value—are huge. But information about the giving of assets with monetary value (cash, securities, real estate, art) to organizations that are qualified to receive tax-deductible gifts is much more readily available through tax returns and the informational filings required of nonprofit organizations. Gifts of blood and tissue (e.g., organ and bone marrow transplants) also fall outside the usual tabulations; while the action is philanthropic, society has been reluctant to attach a monetary value to such gifts.

Although Section 501(c)(3) of the Internal Revenue Code was not created until 1954, the definition of the public good that it embodies traces its roots to Elizabethan England and the adoption in 1601 of the Statute of Charitable Uses. While there are differences between the purposes that are delineated in Section 501(c)(3) and the Statute of Charitable Uses, there is also a remarkable similarity between the two.[10] This similarity reveals a long-standing consensus on both sides of the Atlantic about the activities, and those organizations whose purpose it is to perform them, that constitute a benefit to the public interest. Continued use of the word charitable as the legal "term of art" is a vestige of this heritage; while in 1601, philanthropy was not yet an English word, even if it had been, the influence of religion in society was so pervasive that charity would likely have been the term of choice.

When Jesse Brundage Sears was doing research for what would become *Philanthropy in the History of American Higher Education* late in the second decade of the twentieth century, the 501(c)(3) classification system had not yet been developed. Nonetheless, his working definition of philanthropy as it relates to higher education institutions holds true today. Sears said that in his study "philanthropy" is used to include "all gifts except those from State."[11]

The practice of private giving for public purposes has been a mainstay of American society since the earliest days of the nation.

Moreover, it is a practice that continues to grow. The voluntary giving that totaled $203.45 billion in 2000—the first time that it broke through the $200 billion barrier—had grown to $260.28 billion in 2005 and $316.23 billion by 2012.[12] Because the practice of philanthropy is deeply ingrained in the American psyche, Payton says that over time, he came to realize that it is not just a practice, but "a tradition, with some coherence, sense of direction, and abiding values."[13] The fact that American philanthropy is a tradition helps explain its self-perpetuating, ever-increasing nature. The tradition itself recruits newcomers to the practice and helps ensure the continued growth of the amount given.

Indeed, Ellen Condliffe Lagemann has written that American philanthropy represents "a long tradition of…efforts to establish the values, shape the beliefs, and define the behaviors that would join people to one another."[14] Lynn and Wisely also report that there have been three distinctive philanthropic traditions in the United States's relatively brief history: relief, improvement, and reform. While charity is associated with the tradition of relief, giving in support of higher education is an expression of improvement.

Given these many definitions and perspectives, is there an essential fact about philanthropy? And, if so, what is it? We think the essential fact about philanthropy is its duality as a private form of expression and a public form of action. Because philanthropic gifts are voluntarily made, they are a form of private expression. People express their personal values through giving and volunteering. In the process, they align themselves with the causes and organizations that reflect their interests. Because donors are intrinsically motivated to satisfy their expressive and self-actualization needs, philanthropy is a vast reservoir for social improvement. Because it serves public purposes, philanthropy makes possible a pluralistic approach to solving society's problems, thereby enabling Americans to be less dependent on big government for solutions to society's problems. While Peter Frumkin (2006) first gave expression to the fact that philanthropy is at once both private expression and public action,[15] his finding is consistent with Robert Payton's definition of philanthropy as voluntary action for the public good.

The dual nature of philanthropy helps account for the divide between fund-raising and philanthropy as expressed in the interests of practitioners and scholars and in the literature. Fund-raising focuses on the private expression side of the coin, whereas scholarship on philanthropy mostly addresses the public action side of this single coin.

Altruism

Late in 2013, there was widespread public outrage over the ruling of a Texas judge who decided on a sentence of probation instead of prison for a 16-year-old who had killed four people while driving drunk. Soon after, Sanjay Gupta, MD, interviewed psychologist Wendy Walsh on his weekly CNN program. The teenager's defense attorney had argued that his client suffered from "affluenza," the effect of having been given too much and held accountable for too little by his wealthy parents. Gupta, a neurosurgeon and assistant professor at Emory University School of Medicine, sought insight from Walsh on whether or not parents could indeed do harm to their children by giving them too many material possessions. In her response, the psychologist said that research has shown that consumerism and materialism do not actually make people happy. She continued, noting that three things have been proven statistically to make people happy: exercise, altruism, and strong, healthy relationships. These three things, Walsh said, are the keys to happiness.[16]

In her brief elaboration, Walsh defined altruism as giving back or doing charity work. She did not use the word philanthropy, reflecting an inclination shared by many in the scientific community. Although altruism is not really synonymous with philanthropy, its currency in the literature as well as the popular media suggests that it merits special attention in this or any other overview of conceptual and theoretical issues in philanthropy. In fact, much of the energy that has gone into conceptualizing the process of giving and receiving in recent years has been devoted to the origins of prosocial behavior, altruism in particular. More specifically, evolutionary biologists and sociobiologists have sought to determine if the evolutionary process has programmed us to be altruistic and thereby naturally inclined toward philanthropy.

With that as background, let us begin this exploration of altruism with a look at its meaning. Generally speaking, dictionaries define altruism as "an unselfish regard for the welfare of others." Altruism's synonym is selflessness. It is the opposite of egoism and selfishness and all that is captured in the phrase "survival of the fittest." Its connection to philanthropy is evident even if the two are not synonymous.

However, altruism is also a problematic term when applied to philanthropy, as it may imply a superhuman form of pure selflessness. In that context, multiple motives for a philanthropic act, including some that are self-regarding (not absolutely selfless), yet far from selfish, become cause for cynicism. We will look at this again and consider a proposed solution in the section of this chapter on donor motivation. For now, two other contexts—science and ethics—in which altruism is frequently applied, will be examined.

Although popular among scholars, altruism's implied meaning seems to vary, depending on the discipline of the person using it. Noting the different meanings as assigned by psychologists and evolutionary biologists, Steven Pinker has cautioned that altruism is an ambiguous term. In its psychological sense, altruism is a motive to benefit another as an end in itself rather than as a means to some end. When used by evolutionary biologists, however, altruism is defined in terms of behavior: "biological altruism," according to Pinker, "consists of behavior that benefits another organism at a cost to oneself."[17] Pinker is quick to note that while these two uses are different, they are not incompatible. Nonetheless, the distinction is important because altruistic behavior is not exclusive to humans. In fact, in comparison to social insects, ants and bees in particular, humans are rank amateurs as altruists. Among social insects, most members of the colony or hive do not reproduce. They spend their lives performing a task assigned to them based on the group's division of labor; the queen alone reproduces. Moreover, some of these insects are ever ready to make the ultimate sacrifice, giving up their lives to protect or defend the colony or hive. In light of natural selection's preoccupation with survival and reproduction, it would appear, on the surface at least, that altruistic traits are bad for the individual and that altruism is incompatible with evolution. This issue was troubling to Charles Darwin, as it has been to generations of his scientific successors.

Among those successors, an interesting array of scientists has theorized that selection works on multiple levels ranging from the individual gene to the organism to the group. Two of the best known of these scientists are Richard Dawkins (*The Selfish Gene*, 1976) and Edward O. Wilson.[18] Their articles and books have contributed to the scientific understanding of how natural selection works, and they have popularized the study of evolutionary biology among a large segment of the public. (Another segment continues to deny or doubt the theory of evolution.) More important for our purposes, evolutionary biologists have shown that altruism contributes to, rather than detracts from, individual and group fitness.

One of the fundamentally important constructs to emerge from evolutionary biology is the idea that natural selection is responsible not only for our eyes, ears, nose, opposable thumbs, and upright stance but also for our basic mindsets and the motives that drive human behavior. Darwin's Theory of Evolution rests upon the notions that all of life as we know it evolved over many millennia and that all traits, behavioral as well as physical, exist because they contribute to the survival and reproduction of species. Does this mean we are wired (pre-programmed) to be philanthropic? Such would appear to be the position claimed by authors of two fairly recent books. Lee Alan Dugatkin's 2006 book, *The Altruism Equation*, has as its subtitle *Seven Scientists Search for the Origins of Goodness*. Oren Harman's 2010 volume, *The Price of Altruism*, is subtitled *George Price and the Search for the Origins of Kindness*.[19]

These suggestions notwithstanding, there are significant differences between humans and social insects. Among them is intentionality. Ants and bees respond to genetic forces, but humans will their actions. This is why psychologists' use of the word altruism takes on a different meaning (motive) from that assumed by evolutionary biologists (behavior) when they use the same word. Nonetheless, the evolutionary theory of altruism makes important contributions to our understanding of prosocial behaviors that are in our nature as humans and in the survival interests of our species. It does little, however, to explain the differences in the philanthropic habits and practices of people from different countries, cultures, and religious traditions.

The other use of altruism that has contributed to an increase in its usage in recent years is in regard to a philosophical and social movement known as Effective Altruism. Although prevailing attitudes in the United States and elsewhere during the past century have favored the expansive concept of philanthropy over the more narrow focus of charity, the Effective Altruism movement is challenging some of philanthropy's bedrock beliefs and practices emphasizing giving that more closely resembles charity, but without the religious overtones and motivations. One of the characteristics of American philanthropy is that it favors the able and aspiring. Progressive Era philanthropists led by Andrew Carnegie adopted the tenets of scientific philanthropy, and since then philanthropists in this country typically have made enhancing the quality of life the primary purpose of their giving. They have left to government the lion's share of responsibility for providing a social safety net. As a result, colleges and universities, research institutes, museums, and various cultural organizations have flourished. In contrast, the Effective Altruist movement believes it is morally wrong to put giving in support of educational and cultural institutions ahead of saving lives, feeding and clothing the poor, and relieving pain and suffering.

Additionally, effective altruism holds that because all lives are of equal value, giving should be directed to where it will do the most good—anywhere on the planet. Typically, the same amount of money will buy more good—that is, relieve more suffering and save more lives—in the developing world than in an industrialized and generally prosperous nation. In other words, effective altruism does not begin at home; it begins wherever it will be most effectively deployed to do good. Moreover, its advocates urge donors to support those organizations that are deemed to be most efficient, which generally means those organizations that use the smallest percentage of funds raised and received to meet administrative and personnel expenses.

To some extent, this movement can be seen as a natural consequence of living in an increasingly global community with 24-hour news organizations that bring news of the world into individual homes. It also reflects a feeling among many that developed countries are not doing enough to help underdeveloped countries. Additionally, it reflects a skepticism that developed among many donors after public revelations about high salaries paid to some nonprofit executives and abuses of the public trust by some organizations that appear to exist primarily to raise money, instead of delivering on their missions. More importantly, this emerging movement represents a definition of the good that places its highest value on preserving human life and, for some, animal life, and the meeting of basic survival needs. That priority takes precedence over enhancing the quality of human life, which was philanthropy as conceived in the past.

While the Effective Altruism movement has its critics, and the authors would count themselves among them, it also has powerful advocates. Moreover, we would give it high marks for taking seriously the idea that philanthropy is moral action and for encouraging donors to think seriously about the causes and organizations they support. Among effective altruism's most notable proponents is the Australian moral philosopher and Princeton University professor Peter Singer, who speaks and writes frequently about it.[20] We draw particular attention to it in the context of this chapter for several reasons: one is that we do not think it is a passing fad that will soon fade away. Another is that the movement focuses attention on some of the major issues of concern and debate about philanthropy and the way it is practiced in the United States.

One issue put in the spotlight by effective altruism is public debate over the deductibility of gifts on US income taxes. Do all gifts to 501(c)(3) organizations, generally known as charitable nonprofits, have equal value? Should a gift to the opera or an art museum be eligible for the same tax deduction (i.e., the same rate) as a gift to a food pantry or a homeless shelter? Should a gift made to an organization that will spend it overseas be as deductible from US income taxes as a gift that will be spent in this country? Is giving simply a good thing to do, or do we have a moral obligation to give? If it is the latter, are we also morally obligated to relieve the misery and suffering of others if it is in our power to do so?

With regard to the question of whether or not gifts to arts, educational, and cultural organizations should carry the same deduction as gifts to food pantries and homeless shelters, there are other issues attached to it. The overwhelming majority of gifts to arts, educational, and cultural organizations are made by educated people from the upper socioeconomic classes. A higher percentage of giving among working-class Americans goes to religion and to organizations that provide human services. Because higher income taxpayers are in higher tax brackets than lower income earners, the government effectively subsidizes their gifts at a higher level. Furthermore, only income earners who have a greater number and amount of deductions have an incentive to complete the longer version of the income tax filing form, which is required in order for one to deduct his or her charitable gifts from his income taxes in the first place. What this means is that in reality, only about a quarter of Americans complete the long form and take income tax deductions for their gifts. The other three quarters of the population file the short form and forgo taking specific deductions for their gifts. This fact has given credence to arguments that reducing or eliminating the charitable deduction would adversely impact giving in the United States. Others argue that the deductibility of gifts is a key to obtaining the major gifts that nonprofits, especially higher education institutions, depend upon to meet their funding needs.

This is not the place to delve into the ethical and philosophical issues that surround the debate over philanthropy versus charity; however, the authors wanted to acknowledge them in part simply to let readers know that there are significant issues in philanthropy that remain unsettled. Most importantly, some of these issues have significant public policy implications that could have a bearing on the future of philanthropy and higher education.

Theory of the Gift

While life scientists have looked to biology and evolution for the origins of altruism, a diverse group of thinkers, led by anthropologists and sociologists, has probed both ancient and modern practices involving giving and receiving in search of insights that will help us understand why philanthropy has existed across time and cultures. Philanthropy is giving writ large. It is the sum of millions of individual gifts. In this sense, the gift—the individual gift made for public purposes at least—is philanthropy's molecule. The base assumption in this line of reasoning is that if you want to know more about the whole that is philanthropy, the place to start is the individual component, which in this case is the gift, and practices of giving and receiving. Another assumption is that all gifts, whether for public purposes or not, share a commonality that causes us to refer to them as gifts. What is that commonality? And what do we mean when we use the word "gifted" to refer to the talent of an artist or musician?

Fortunately, Lewis Hyde wrestled with these questions in his 1983 book *The Gift: Imagination and the Erotic Life of Property* and has provided convincing answers. Hyde defines "gift" as something bestowed—not obtained by one's own efforts. In this sense an artist may be said to be gifted, and an object that in another context is an economic commodity becomes a gift when presented by one party to another. One of Hyde's most important findings is that "the giving of a gift tends to establish a relationship between the parties involved" and, thus, gifts are agents of social cohesion.[21]

In his exploration of the nature of gifts, Hyde finds that they are used to mark times of change and individual transformation, for example births, rites of passage, marriage (including that most peculiar, yet common gift, the bride given in marriage), housewarmings, and even death (bequests). Additionally, he observes that gifts themselves are often agents of change. The realization or development of a talent may well change one's life. More commonly, the influence of a great teacher's instruction, when viewed as a transformative gift to his or her students, is an agent of change. Not only do gifts serve as agents of change, but on occasion they are bearers of new life. Hyde illustrates this point by reminding his readers that new parents often regard the birth of their child as a gift. Moreover, religious leaders have long taught that all things, and especially all life, are gifts from God.[22] A gift in the form of donated blood, a kidney, or other vital organ is both a gift of life and a gift that is unquestionably an agent of change.

Hyde's *The Gift* draws heavily on the work of French anthropologist Marcel Mauss, whose *Essai sur le Don* was first published in 1925 and is widely regarded as the seminal work in this line of inquiry. *Essai sur le Don* was translated into English in 1954, four years after the author's death, as *The Gift: The Form and Reason for Exchange in Archaic Societies*. Mauss's ethnographic research focused on gift-exchange systems among the potlatch societies of Northwest Coast American Indians, the native people of Polynesia (especially the Maori), and the Trobriand Islanders of Melanesia.[23]

Among Mauss's key findings is that receiving a gift creates a sense of obligation for the recipient to reciprocate. This sense of obligation is crucial in the societies he studied since there would be no exchange, only one-way transfers of goods, without it. Given the vital importance of the obligation to reciprocate—as well as the obligations to give and receive gifts—it is perhaps only to be expected that the social system engaged not just the honor of the giver and the recipient of a gift but also the dominant institutions of society (i.e., its legal, economic, moral, religious, and aesthetic dimensions). To explain the comprehensiveness of the social norms that regulated and sustained the system of gift exchange in these societies, Mauss developed the concept of the total social fact. As the system of gift exchange illustrates, a total social fact defines social reality or the social as reality for members of the society.[24]

In her reading of Mauss, Mary Douglas was struck by the significance of his finding that gifts, even when they constitute the system of exchange, serve to draw those who give and those who receive them into relationship with one another. Because this is not the case for parties who engage one another in trade, Douglas concludes that "the theory of the gift is a theory of human solidarity."[25] Another of Mauss's conclusions is that "generosity is an obligation... This is the ancient morality of the gift, which has become a principle of justice."[26] Furthermore, Hyde observes from his reading of Mauss that in potlatch societies, "status and generosity were always associated: no man could become a man of position without giving away property."[27] According to Paul Veyne's 1992 classic, *Bread and Circuses*, this was no less true of status attainment among Greeks and Romans of classical antiquity.[28]

Following Mauss, some anthropologists adopted the evolutionary view that market practices and values gradually but inevitably replaced the many forms of archaic gift reciprocity, leaving only holiday gifts and those exchanged within the family. Historian Natalie Davis notes, however, that Mauss himself spoke of gift exchange as a permanent part of social life. Davis also notes that a new generation of anthropologists and historians, herself included, seek no such universal pattern of evolutionary stages, where a total gift economy dwindles to occasional presents. "Rather," according to Davis, "gift exchange persists as an essential relational mode, a repertoire of behavior, a register with its own rules, language, etiquette, and gestures."[29]

In her exploration of *The Gift in Sixteenth-Century France* (2000), Davis sought to determine what conviction or prescription kept gifts moving in that time and place, where commerce was the dominant mode of exchange. Davis found the presence of what she refers to as two age-old core beliefs. In the first, giving is a response to divine blessing. It affirms, as an article of faith, the notion that "everything we have is a gift of God, and what comes in as a gift has some claim to go out as a gift."[30] In this conception, there is a vertical cycling of gifts.

Perhaps the best visual image of this core belief is Giotto's early fourteenth-century depiction of *Caritas* in the Arena Chapel in Padua. Giotto's personification of charity implies both love of God and love of neighbor. In the fresco, *Caritas* lifts up her heart to God in her left hand while extending a bowl laden with fruit to her neighbor(s) in her right hand. "The accompanying inscription stresses her generosity to all and the worthlessness of earthly goods—which the fresco makes explicit in the bags of money on which she stands."[31]

In the second of the two core beliefs, giving is justified in this-worldly or secular terms. This belief maintains that people are held together by reciprocity, as Aristotle had pointed out centuries earlier in his *Nichomachean Ethics*. Reciprocity is created by gifts and benefits, as well as by production and trade.[32] According to Davis, the image of the Three Graces, from Graeco-Roman antiquity, was the favorite way for learned people in the sixteenth century to visualize the horizontal movement of gift reciprocity. The Three Graces are sisters, young women who form a circle holding hands while facing one another. In Seneca's much-quoted phrase about the three circling sisters: "One of them bestoweth the good turne, the other receiveth it, and the third requiteth it."[33]

The image of the Three Graces mirrors, of course, the obligation to give, to receive, and to reciprocate that Mauss found to dominate the system of exchange in archaic societies. According to Davis, the core belief depicted in the Three Graces rests on the assumption that gratitude is an essential factor in making society go round.

While these two core beliefs differ, they do not oppose one another. Davis writes that "These two core beliefs—one evoking the Lord and a vertical cycling of gifts, the other evoking social need and a horizontal movement of benefits among humans—were thought to complement each other in the sixteenth century."[34] The same is true in twenty-first-century America, where charity and philanthropy are complementary practices that spring from different motivations paralleling those embodied in the two core beliefs. Moreover, it is entirely possible that the same donor will be motivated to give on some occasions by one belief and on different occasions by the other.

In her examination of the roles played by gifts in sixteenth-century France, Davis observed that "Birth, marriage, and death were shaped by an intricate choreography of gifts."[35] Additionally, she found that gifts sustained relations and enabled people to create solidarity with each other, to mark and soften relations, to acknowledge services, and to seek protection, alliance, and advancement.

The idea that gift exchange creates relationships of an entirely different nature from those between parties to an economic transaction receives an especially exhaustive treatment in Richard Titmuss's classic *The Gift Relationship: From Human Blood to Social Policy* (1970; 1997). Titmuss examined differences between blood collection systems in which blood is donated and those in which blood is purchased. Among his findings is that people who have themselves been beneficiaries of donated blood are more likely to give blood and to do so more than once. He also found that blood freely given is much less likely to be contaminated with impurities (disease) and substances (drugs) that make it unusable. Typically, the motives of a person giving blood and a person selling blood are quite different. Titmuss found this difference in motives to be the salient factor in accounting for the differences in quality, which is striking, between the two blood supplies. In the one instance, the donor is seeking to promote the well-being of others; in the other, self-interest is the primary motive of the person who sells his or her blood.

Interestingly, Titmuss found in Mauss's work on *The Gift* the conceptual tools he needed for analyzing his data. Citing Mauss, Titmuss writes that in systems in which the exchange of goods and services is not an impersonal but a moral transaction, gifts bring about and maintain personal relationships between individuals and groups.

Titmuss's primary interest, however, was not in gift exchange among parties who knew one another, but in acts of benevolence (donating blood) toward people who were unknown to the donor. He referred to these as "stranger relationships," and even titled one of his chapters "Who Is My Stranger?"[36] Nonetheless, he found within the concept of the gift as moral action a conceptual basis for understanding the motives of blood donors. Although most blood donors do not give out of anticipation of a future need to receive a return gift, Titmuss concluded that these gifts could best be understood within the context of reciprocity and social solidarity.[37]

In Titmuss's conception, all members of society have both moral and social obligations to give and to repay the larger order of which they are a part. Society supports this sense of obligation with sanctions such as dishonor, shame, and guilt. "Gift relationships," according to Titmuss, "have to be seen in their totality and not just as moral elements in blood distribution systems; in modern societies, they signify the notation of 'fellowship,' (which is)...conceived of as a matter of right relationships which are institutionally based."[38] In other words, giving establishes and sustains relationships even when gifts are made to strangers because gifts promote solidarity, thereby serving as an antidote to alienation. These observations also illustrate why psychologists refer to giving as prosocial behavior.

Among classical philosophy's three great motivations—the search for truth (knowledge), the search for beauty (aesthetics), and the search for the good (ethics)—giving for the benefit of others (whether blood or money) falls within the search for the good. As Titmuss notes, human welfare is itself an ethical concept and an expression of the search for the good. With respect to blood donors, he wrote: "To the philosophers' question 'What kind of actions ought we to perform?' they replied, in effect, 'Those which will cause more good to exist in the universe than there would otherwise be if we did not so act.'"[39]

As an economist, Kenneth Boulding's interest in philanthropy 40 years ago made him something of an anomaly. The vast majority of his colleagues were either uninterested in or stymied by altruistic or other-regarding behavior that so clearly contradicted the dominant economic image of humans as rational (i.e., self-interested) benefit-maximizers. Boulding was not only interested in philanthropy, but he also made important contributions to the development of theory regarding motivations for philanthropic behavior.

Whereas Hyde has defined "gift" as something bestowed, Boulding defined the term as "a one-way transfer of exchangeables."[40] Such transfers may bring a sense of satisfaction (James Andreoni's "warm glow") but no material benefit to the person making the gift. Not all one-way transfers are philanthropic, of course, but as Robert Payton has said "all philanthropic transfers are one-way."[41]

A one-way transfer obviously differs from an exchange, and it is for this reason, according to Boulding, that it is extremely hard to explain charity or philanthropy using the conventional theory of exchange. But exchange is only one of the social organizers. A gift (or grant, which is the term Boulding prefers for philanthropic gifts) is an expression of benevolence that indicates an integrative relationship between the giver and recipient. In his use of "integrative," Boulding refers to that "set of social relations involving status, identity, community, legitimacy, loyalty, love, and trust."[42] Moreover, the usual objective of a one-way transfer is to redistribute resources in a direction the giver (donor, benefactor) finds desirable. That is, people tend to give to those organizations or causes with which they identify (typically because of shared values) and believe to be important.

Given the obligation to reciprocate in the archaic societies studied by Mauss, Levi-Strauss, and others, many observers have noted that in those societies at least, to give was to receive. If this is the case, what then is the difference between a gift system and an economic system of exchange? And how can it be said that a gift system is more integrative than an economic system? The difference, according to Boulding, is that a gift does not carry with it, as a formal condition, the obligation to reciprocate. Accordingly, when the recipient of a gift does reciprocate, even if the two events are separated in time, his or her action establishes an integrative relationship between the parties. In this sense, writes Boulding, "reciprocity has a function in building a sense of community and a more complex structure of personal relationships that exchange pure and simple is unable to perform."[43] An economic exchange has no such power to create community, identity, and commitment.

While these insights are important and useful, Boulding's greatest contribution to the study of philanthropy is the concept of serial reciprocity. It is this concept that enables students of philanthropy to link the findings and insights of anthropologists, historians, and other scholars about the role of the gift in human relations to motivations for philanthropic giving. In introducing this concept, Boulding writes:

A very interesting aspect of reciprocity is what might be called "serial reciprocity," in which a gift from A to B creates a generalized sense of obligation on the part of B. This obligation is satisfied by a gift from B, not to A, but to another party C, who in turn satisfies his sense of obligation to another party D, and so on.[44]

In elaborating on the concept of serial reciprocity, Boulding comments that the receipt of a gift frequently creates an almost unconscious sense of obligation to reciprocate. Michael Moody explains this unconscious sense of obligation in terms of equity theory, which assumes that people seek a balance of inputs and outputs in any relationship or interaction. From this perspective, a gift or benefit (good deed) creates an asymmetry or imbalance in a relationship. The recipient of the gift then feels the need to reestablish the balance through reciprocation, either directly to the donor or through serial reciprocation.[45] Boulding felt that serial reciprocity was an especially useful concept in understanding relations between generations. It also helps explain how gratitude works as a motivation for giving.

Thanks to Boulding, we now have a language for comprehending and explaining the sense of obligation that compels people to repay the benefits they have received by providing benefits to someone other than their benefactor. In its serial or indirect form, Moody tells us, reciprocity "loses some of its utilitarian edge and becomes more akin to values such as gratitude and stewardship."[46] Gratitude and stewardship, while not specifically religious terms, are basic tenets of the Judeo-Christian faith. In this sense, serial reciprocity provides justification and motivation for both religious and secular giving. Benjamin Franklin illustrates this point with regard to religious motivations for giving. Believing God to be the great benefactor, Franklin's religion "consisted in the belief that men should show their gratitude to God by the only means in their power, promoting the happiness of his other children."[47] Indeed, one of the teachings of Jesus was, "Freely ye have received, freely give" (Matthew 10:8).

Moody maintains that the tradition of "passing on" (which is sometimes expressed as "paying forward" and on other occasions as "paying back") is the most widely practiced and historically significant application of serial reciprocity.[48] Payton agrees, claiming that "*pass it on* is one of the philanthropic commonplaces of our culture."[49] Moody also maintains that "doing good for future generations is perhaps the most appropriate way to repay what we owe to past generations."[50] This sentiment appears to be shared by Joe Engle, a New York City resident and philanthropist who has provided $10 million to help needy students attend his alma mater, Ohio State University. Engle, an octogenarian at the time of his gift, was quoted in a *Wall Street Journal* article as saying: "There is no such thing as a self-made man. You are given certain talents, a good memory or ambition or perseverance, and it behooves you to pay it back."[51] This aspect of humanity is perhaps most beautifully captured in the words of developmental psychologist Joan Erikson. According to Erikson, "In the beginning we are what we are given. By midlife, when we have finally learned to stand on our own two feet, we learn that to complete our lives, we are called to give to others so that when we leave this world, we can be what we have given."[52]

In 1957, the noted sociologist Claude Levi-Strauss published an essay he titled "Reciprocity, the Essence of Social Life."[53] Reciprocity has enormous explanatory power to a degree reminiscent of gravity. Like gravity in the physical world, reciprocity is a force that propels movement in the social world. Reciprocity is the foundation on which the theory of the gift is built. It is the integrative force that animates a circular pattern of exchange relationships characterized by the obligations to give, to receive, and to reciprocate. In its serial form, it prompts individuals to make one-way transfers primarily for the benefit of others. These one-way transfers satisfy a sense that one has received gifts or benefits or blessings (whether from a divine or secular source) and is obligated to reciprocate in some fashion, even though it is not possible to reciprocate directly to one's benefactor.

Several of the themes reviewed in this section will reappear in the discussion of donor motivation.

In Search of a Philosophy of Philanthropy

What are the fundamental principles that undergird philanthropy, justify its existence, and guide its actions? Interestingly, this is not a question that has attracted much scholarly attention. Philanthropy is moral action, and as such, it is informed by ethics but not by the ethical principles of a particular school of philosophy. The late Robert Payton and his frequent writing partner, Michael Moody, sought to address this deficiency in their 2008 book, *Understanding Philanthropy*.

Payton and Moody took as their starting point the question, Why does philanthropy exist? Their answer has an appealing succinctness: because things often go wrong. They identify philanthropy as an appropriate, and often preferred, response to this reality. And even when things do not go wrong so badly as in the case of natural disasters (or economic disasters), it is almost always possible to make things better, to enhance the quality of life. This is true if for no other reason than that life chances vary. There is a profound unevenness in the opportunities afforded the world's people to have healthy, productive lives, and to fulfill their potential.

With these answers to their starting question in mind, Payton and Moody began their search for a philosophy of philanthropy, a philosophy that is sufficiently broad to encompass voluntary action aimed at relieving pain and suffering, righting wrongs and confronting injustice, providing educational opportunity, sponsoring scientific research, and promoting the arts. Clearly, it would need to be a practical philosophy that is ready to roll up its sleeves and go to work, yet one that allows its adherents to be inspired by hope and the belief that it is possible to change the world for the better. It would be necessary for this philosophy to accommodate the idea of progress—the belief that it is possible to make a difference for good. While shunning pessimism, it also would need to avoid embracing a naïve optimism. Payton and Moody found a philosophy that meets these tests in meliorism, a doctrine rooted in pragmatism.

The dictionary definition of "meliorism" is "the doctrine, intermediate between optimism and pessimism, that the world can be made better through rightly directed human effort."[54] The novelist George Eliot is credited with coining the word "meliorism" for the purpose of naming the mid-point between optimism and pessimism. In this sense, meliorism is similar to the virtues enumerated by Aristotle in the *Nichomachean Ethics*. Aristotle's virtues are cast as the mean between opposing extremes.

A meliorist, Payton and Moody tell us, is someone who believes that "social conditions can be modified to improve life chances and advance the public good."[55] Philanthropy is the means by which meliorists achieve these ends. Meliorism's tie to pragmatism is critical since philanthropy must be a practical activity if it is to make a difference. While hopeful, philanthropy must also be more realistic than either optimism or pessimism. Fortunately, there is ample evidence to support the claim that on the whole the human condition has been improved through purposeful (rightly directed) human effort and that "the human condition is better now than it was in the past largely because of human interventions."[56] Recent reports of the eradication of polio in most of the developing world, an initiative of Rotary International and the Bill and Melinda Gates Foundation, affirm this claim.

Change Theories

Although there remain pockets of resistance, gradually over the past two decades, both practitioners and scholars have come to believe that at its heart, philanthropy is about change. To make a difference for good is to bring about a change in some existing status quo. To the extent that there is one at this point, the debate is over the actual agent of change. Is it the gift, the donor, or the idea that causes the change?

Anna Faith Jones has argued that while philanthropy is essential as a means for fostering change, "it is not the change agent itself."[57] She goes on to say that consumed as we are with money, it is people—and only people—who have the power to bring about social change. Likewise, E. Bruce Heilman, chancellor and former president of the University of Richmond, said in an interview with one of the authors that "No gift, regardless of size, ever changed a college or university. Vision changes organizations. Large gifts make possible the change that transformational leaders envision."[58]

In addition to the school of thought which maintains that it is leaders who cause change, there is another which asserts that ideas drive history. In their study of the role of philanthropy in shaping the American system of higher education, Curti and Nash recognized the role of leaders and ideas, as well as philanthropic gifts, as agents of change. "Too often ideas alone are given credit as the moving force in history without recognition of the crucial role of material resources in transforming abstractions into reality. Of course, ideas are indispensable, and so is leadership, but without money the necessary impetus for innovation is often lacking."[59] In their conception, it is the combination of idea, leader, and gift dollar that brings about change in response to changing conditions.

Another school of thought credits government and its interventions with driving history, while yet another gives more weight to social movements. Recent work by Prewitt suggests that a promising approach to developing a taxonomy for classifying the thousands of private foundations now in existence in this country is to categorize them on the basis of the change strategies implicit in the types of grants they award. For example, those that believe ideas drive history invest in research and intellectual efforts, whereas those that believe government interventions drive history invest in policy analysis and advocacy.[60] From this perspective, both the gifts of individual donors and foundation grants are understood to be agents of change.

A strong advocate for understanding philanthropy in terms of change, Peter Frumkin has written that "using private charitable dollars to pursue public purposes is by its very nature an act that implies the status quo must change in some way."[61] Similarly, Goldmark has noted that "Philanthropy is generally harnessed to one of two great purposes: conservation of something of value, such as a forest or a collection of works of art, or constructive change in some human condition, behavior, or system."[62] Likewise, historians Friedman and McGarvie describe the philanthropist as someone who has "energetically and deeply cared about the needs of others and the broader society and has sought passionately to render decisive change."[63] The sine qua non for being labeled a philanthropist is giving some portion of one's money or material resources away, usually a generous sum, for public purposes—that is, deploying money to bring about change.

In a line of reasoning similar to that of Prewitt, Frumkin argues that philanthropy is, in fact, animated by theories of change. In his 2006 book on strategic giving, Frumkin encourages donors to think strategically about their giving and to adopt strategies that reflect both the values they wish to express and their beliefs about the forces that bring about positive change. He identifies five theories of change that influence donors, either consciously or subconsciously, to support particular causes and institutions with their gifts. The first of these is the cultivation of outstanding individuals; this individual-level approach to change is based on the premise that leaders are the primary driving force in history and the belief that gifts that enable people to help themselves are more likely to have a lasting effect than those that offer only a short-term intervention. The second is institution building, which reflects a belief that the best way to change a field, or society at large, is to create and support strong organizations. The third is similar to the second, but its focus is on creating or supporting networks and collaborations among organizations; it embraces the concept of the power of many being greater than the power of one. The fourth is politics, which appeals to donors who believe that the best way to change society for the better is through the political process, prompting them to direct their gifts to public awareness, civic engagement, and public policy initiatives. The fifth of Frumkin's theories of change is based on the premise that ideas are the driving forces of history, prompting donors to invest their philanthropic resources in the production of new ideas and paradigms that may reorient entire fields and lead to important breakthroughs in basic knowledge.[64]

A change strategy that Frumkin does not identify, but Prewitt mentions, is empowerment or social justice. Although Prewitt warns that social empowerment comes dangerously close to being charity instead of philanthropy, there is ample evidence to suggest that this change strategy has been at the heart of many gifts made in the past (e.g., the founding of colleges for women and for African Americans of both sexes) and in contemporary philanthropy. In many—if not most—instances, gifts and grants made by individuals and foundations represent a blending of two or more of the change theories or strategies enumerated by Prewitt and Frumkin.

Donor Motivation

Donor motivation is the topic that grapples head-on with the biggest "why" question of all: Why do people give of their private resources for the benefit of others? While the question is simple, the answer is not. Just as there is no single answer to the question, "What is the purpose of all giving?," there is no single answer to the question, "Why do people give?" In fact, it is not only possible but likely that multiple motives are involved in the gift-making process. Furthermore, it is entirely possible that different motives are at work in producing the same action by different people.

So convinced is he that multiple influences—interacting with and overlapping one another—play a role in producing philanthropic gifts that Boston College sociologist and philanthropy scholar Paul Schervish has coined the phrase "mobilizing factors" as a replacement for "donor motivation."[65] Although the phrase is an apt one, most existing literature refer to theories of donor motivation; so we will continue to use that term. Five broad categories of donor motivation will be presented and the distinguishing features of each briefly discussed. They are religion, altruism, exchange, psychosocial, and teleological.

Although wealthy donors are sometimes accused of making gifts just for the tax benefits, the people making those statements rarely are aware that tax deductions do not reduce the cost of making a gift to zero. The deductibility of gifts means that the government shares in the cost of making them, which provides an important public policy incentive for philanthropy. The justification for this incentive is based on the fact that philanthropic gifts serve public purposes. Nonetheless, in numerous studies and surveys, the incentive has been found to be a weak motivation for giving. The difference the incentive makes is in the size of gifts and, thereby, the total amount given.

The fact that the tax deductibility of gifts is a weak motivation for giving is consistent with what psychologists have come to understand about motivation in recent decades. Daniel Pink, whose 2009 book *Drive* popularized new ways of thinking about motivation, identifies three categories of motivations or drives: biological, extrinsic, and intrinsic. Biological motivations compel us to satisfy urges (to eat, drink, and have sex). Extrinsic motivations might well be thought of as rewards and punishments. For generations only these two types of motivations were recognized, but thanks to the work of Harry Harlow and Edward Deci in the second half of the twentieth century, the existence of intrinsic motivation is now widely accepted.[66] Intrinsic motivations are associated with self-actualization. They compel behavior that leads to satisfaction and gives purpose to life. In fact, Pink proclaims that instead of being the extrinsically motivated profit-maximizers of classical economic theory, we are intrinsically motivated purpose-maximizers who strive to find or create purpose and meaning in our lives.[67]

To the extent that the tax deductibility of gifts is a motivation, it is an extrinsic motivation and a fairly weak one at that since the reward it offers is not as great as the cost of the gift. The concept of intrinsic motivation provides helpful context for understanding the motives that compel individuals to voluntarily give away that which is theirs for the benefit of others who are unrelated and, in most cases, unknown to them. Motivation would not be an issue, of course, if giving were not voluntary. The fact that it is both voluntary and widely practiced in this country makes it a subject of particular interest not only to fund-raisers and students of higher education but also to financial and legal advisers, policy makers, and to philanthropists (at all levels) themselves.

Religion—Although religion has long been credited with being "the mother of all philanthropy," it is also widely acknowledged that religion is the least studied of the motivations for giving.[68] Concern about correlation not being causation aside, many people see a strong connection between the fact that the United States is one of the world's most religious countries and is its most philanthropic. We know from Max Weber's 1956 classic, *The Protestant Ethic and the Spirit of Capitalism*, that religion has played a major role in shaping the culture of the United States.[69] We also know from the work of a great many scholars that religion conveys a type of moral authority that motivates human behavior.

One of Cascione's most interesting findings in his research on donor motivation is that even those donors "who are not religious often use religious language and concepts to frame their generosity."[70] In his elaboration on this finding, Cascione cites the work of Wood and

Houghland (1990) who found that religion provides a language for moral discourse that allows "individuals to think and talk about their actions in selfless terms."[71] These findings support the idea that religion has played a major role in shaping the American tradition of philanthropy. Moreover, even as church attendance in the United States declines, religion's influence on American culture remains strong.

Judaism, Christianity, and Islam are the three dominant religions of the Western world. The three have in common two commandments that believers and followers of each regard as fundamental: "love thy God with thy whole heart and thy whole mind" and "love thy neighbor as thyself."[72] These commandments are at the heart of religious motivations for giving and the tradition of charity or almsgiving found among believers of all three faiths.

Whether or not they actually tithe, many believers give in response to injunctions concerning generosity found in sacred texts. In essence, they give because they believe God expects it of them. For others, giving is in response to the feeling that they have been befriended by a loving God.[73] For these believers, a sense of personal blessing leads to feelings of gratitude that lead to generosity. In both cases, giving that is motivated by religion is done primarily in order to bring the giver into closer relationship with God.[74]

The commandments to love God above all else and to love one's neighbor as oneself are at the heart of a Thomas Aquinas teaching that Schervish has made the centerpiece of his identification model of caritas. As Schervish reminds us, Aquinas taught that these two commandments represent the convergence of love of neighbor, love of self, and love of God. This teaching provides moral and religious justification for Schervish's conclusion that it is not the absence of self (altruism) that motivates one to give but the presence of self through identification with the needs of others. In this model, which will appear again in the section on psychosocial motivations, the giver satisfies her or his needs by meeting the needs of others. According to Schervish, the civic version of this model of donor motivation was given expression in Tocqueville's concept of self-interest properly understood.[75]

Altruism—the persistence of altruism, defined as the unselfish desire to live for others, as a theory of donor motivation is a bit of a mystery. Nonetheless, the prevalence of altruism as a presumed motivation for giving justifies another brief look at it here.

Although it is evident that people frequently act for the benefit of others, there is no compelling reason to believe that their motives are or need to be entirely selfless as "pure altruism" would require.

In fact, there is evidence that multiple motives or motivating factors are present in most instances of giving. Moreover, as we have seen in Schervish's self-identification model, the religious teachings that most influence Western culture establish the self (or oneself) as the appropriate point of reference in deciding how one is to act toward others (i.e., in moral decision-making). Empathy is also embedded in the Golden Rule: the way I would want to be treated is the standard for determining how I should treat others. Yet it seems that for some people, a good deed must be selfless in order to count.

Finding that many people derive a sense of satisfaction from giving, which he found to be incompatible with the supposed selflessness of altruism, the economist James Andreoni coined the phrase "warm-glow giving." He used it to describe a form of impure altruism that he found to have greater predictive power than pure altruism.[76] What is less certain is why Andreoni decided that altruism was the motivation that compelled people to make philanthropic gifts. Nonetheless, the tendency to believe so persists and, as we have seen, the term has a great deal of currency in discourse about philanthropy.

While Andreoni's initial assumption that altruism was the dominant motivation for giving was questionable, his conclusion was correct. Outside the realm of the social insects, there is no pure altruism. Accordingly, while the term may be useful to evolutionary biologists, it tells us little or nothing about donor motivation. Perhaps, as Batson has suggested, if the term could be re-defined to include any motivation whose ultimate goal is the benefit of another or others, it would be more useful. There is reason to believe this is, in fact, the word's intended meaning in common usage.

Exchange—Andreoni's 'warm-glow' theory represents a form of exchange: donors make gifts in exchange for a feel-good feeling or warm glow. Social approval is another frequently mentioned motivation that represents a form of exchange. Reciprocity, which was discussed at some length in the section of this chapter on the theory of the gift, is also based on the idea of social exchange. This means that 'giving back' and 'paying forward,' giving that is motivated at least in part by gratitude, also belong to this category. Although it is not always acknowledged, social exchange theory is the understanding of donor motivation at the core of most courses and training programs for fund-raisers. Accordingly, familiarity with it is of particular importance to our purposes here.

By definition, exchange is always two-way. Exchange theory assumes that the benefits of philanthropy are both public and private.

It assumes further that people make voluntary contributions in order to receive some private benefit.[77] This private benefit does not negate or diminish the public benefit of the gift since it may only be the satisfaction that comes from expressing one's values or furthering an interest one has in common with the recipient organization. An exchange of values is different, of course, from an exchange of valuables, and IRS regulations prohibit donors from receiving benefits that have any significant monetary value.

Interdependent relationships such as those that exist between alumni donors and Alma Mater are readily understood in terms of social exchange theory. The key to effecting exchanges that lead to fund-raising success is aligning the interests of individuals with the interests and needs of charitable organizations. And while social exchange is not unique to the interdependent relationships that exist between higher education institutions and their constituencies, the natural alignment of interests and values between colleges and their former students are evident in a society where institutional affiliations are valued and deemed part of one's identity.

As we will discuss more thoroughly in chapter 6, an important function of the advancement or development office is to market the institution's funding needs as opportunities for giving that will allow donors to express or affirm their interests and values. Simply presenting needs is rarely sufficient to stimulate giving. Otherwise, the neediest causes, including the neediest colleges and universities, would receive the most money in the form of charitable gifts.

Psychosocial—The distinction between exchange and psychosocial motivations is subtle and nuanced. Nonetheless, the distinction is important. Donor self-expression, or self-actualization, is the primary goal of psychosocial motivations. Exchange motives may still be present as motivating factors since neither precludes the other, but meeting the psychic and social needs of donors is primary when psychosocial motivations compel individuals to give.

Frumkin has observed that an essential purpose philanthropy performs is that of allowing individuals to find meaning and purpose in their lives.[78] Psychosocial motivations are closely associated with the individual's search for meaning, which has long been recognized as a powerful motivation. In Schervish's identification model of caritas, people link their destiny to the destiny of others and fulfill their own needs by meeting the needs of others. Whether it enables one to find meaning in life or to fulfill one's destiny, philanthropy can—and often does—have a powerful impact on the donor. This is vitally important as Frumkin notes, "because philanthropy depends on the goodwill and motivation of donors."[79]

One's values are shaped by a host of biographical, psychological, and cultural influences. These values are expressed in the decisions we make and the actions we take. Among those actions are voluntary transactions of both an economic and, for most Americans, philanthropic nature. In both cases, our actions are statements about who we are, what we value, the life we aspire to, and the world in which we want to live. When the desire to express these values is at the forefront of our gift-making, psychosocial motivations prevail.

Teleological—Donor motivations that belong to the teleological category recognize the recipient organization (the aim or target of the gift) as the key factor in the decision to give. In other words, the distinguishing characteristics of the organization, especially its mission, motivate individuals to give to it. In this view, Americans are generous, at least in part, because there are so many attractive reasons to give. The 1.1 million charitable nonprofit organizations in the United States[80] have characteristics and missions that compel giving to them.

Observing that while Americans are generous, they do not give indiscriminately, Kelly insists that "decisions to make a gift are dependent on the intended recipient."[81] This claim is supported by the wide variety of charitable causes and organizations that depend on philanthropy for some portion of their income. Some individuals have a passion for art museums, others for history or science museums. Some people support the opera while others give to medical or scientific research. Some donors give to alleviate poverty or to combat homelessness or domestic abuse. Many give to Alma Mater or to the schools where their children were educated.

"Be True to Your School," the 1963 pop music hit by the Beach Boys, speaks of the importance of institutional affiliations, especially loyalty to Alma Mater, in American society. But do colleges and universities, or other charitable organizations, have characteristics that motivate people to give? Kelly not only answers that question in the affirmative, but she also criticizes philanthropy scholars who "study giving in isolation of the donor's relationship to specific organizations, whereas organizational relationships are fundamental to the study of fund raising."[82]

What are the characteristics of colleges and universities that might compel giving? Cascione's answer to this question is that they embody the dreams and aspirations of American society.[83] Higher education provides individuals with the tools they need to support themselves and their families while also making a contribution to society. The oft-repeated statement that the American Dream begins in the classroom reflects people's faith in learning as a catalyst for both individual and national progress.

For alumni in particular, affiliation with Alma Mater often becomes important to one's identity. Job resumes, wedding announcements, and obituaries frequently list the names of educational institutions attended, and people wear clothing proclaiming their institutional affiliations. Identity and association, which Schervish refers to as communities of participation,[84] are key factors in donor motivation. Based on her research into the giving habits and motivations of the wealthy, Ostrower concluded that "a deep sense of involvement with particular organizations is the very motivation, and even precondition, for larger donations."[85]

Given the role of identity in teleological motivations, one might reasonably question why Schervish's self-identification model was discussed in the psychosocial category and not here. The quick answer is that Schervish's model focuses more on the biographical, psychological, and cultural influences that shape the donor's identity than on the characteristics and missions of the organizations one supports. The longer, more complex response is the reminder that mixed motives—interdependent and overlapping—are the rule. There is no reason why motivations associated with religion, altruism, exchange, psychosocial, and the teleological categories cannot all influence the decision to make a gift.

The Nonprofit Sector

Organizations that in the United States are known as nonprofits are typically known in other parts of the world as NGOs, or nongovernmental organizations. In both cases, the name given to these organizations refers to what they are not, rather than what they are. Although no alternative has taken hold, several have been suggested, most notably independent sector. In fact, Independent Sector (IS) was the name chosen in 1980 by John W. Gardner and other leaders for a membership organization that advocates, mostly at the federal level, for nonprofit organizations (and NGOs). No sooner was that name chosen, however, than critics pointed out that far from being independent, the sector is very much dependent on both the government and commercial (for-profit) sectors for its existence and ongoing operations. Other names that have been suggested include voluntary sector, civil sector, and third sector.

Just as the nonprofit sector suffers from a naming problem, it has yet to generate a distinct theory that explains its existence and symbiotic relationships with the other two sectors, commerce and government, of American public life. The most notable theories that have been put forth have the dubious distinction of being known as "failure theories." On the one hand, the nonprofit sector exists because of market failure; on the other, it exists because of government failure.

The marketplace provides goods and services when there is a profit to be made from doing so. If there is no profit to be made for the owner or owners (stockholders) of a business, then the commercial or for-profit sector has no reason to enter the space. Thus, market-failure theory highlights a defining characteristic of nonprofit organizations: they do not distribute profits. Nonprofit organizations may well generate operating surpluses (excess revenues over expenses) as fiscally healthy ones usually do, but the nondistribution constraint prohibits them from distributing those surpluses (profits) to directors, trustees, or other stakeholders.[86] This nondistribution constraint may become a crucial factor for transactions when trust is a major concern. If crucial information is unavailable to a consumer, she may choose a provider who has no incentive to make a profit from the transaction, especially for services such as health care and elder care. In other instances, if there is no profit to be made, there will be no commercial provider of the good or service.

The voluntary associations that so impressed the young French nobleman Alexis de Tocqueville[87] when he visited the United States in the early 1830s are important elements of US cultural heritage. Tocqueville was impressed that when a need relating to the common good emerged, Americans came together in voluntary associations to meet it. One consequence of this heritage is the reluctance to look to big government as the solution to problems or even to allow government to decide what the best solutions are. Maintaining pluralism in American society and allowing for multiple approaches to solving society's problems is one of the most frequently cited arguments in support of sustaining America's tradition of philanthropy.

As a result of the phenomenon Tocqueville witnessed, many voluntary approaches to meeting social needs preceded government services in this country. In other instances, because government in a democracy responds to the preferences of the median voter, services that many people—but not a majority—desire are not provided by the government. In response to this government failure, nonprofit organizations, with the support of those who value the service, often step forward to fill that space.[88]

It is not just markets and governments, of course, that fail to solve problems and meet society's needs. Sometimes the nonprofit sector lacks the resources to meet the demand for services. In these instances, philanthropic failure occurs. This pattern can be seen in the history of American higher education. Early in the nineteenth century, rapidly growing demand for higher education caused states to begin opening colleges and universities. In more recent years, demand for greater flexibility in scheduling and in approaches to learning has created opportunities for for-profit providers.

The failure theories provide context for Kelly's claim that "giving allows people to go beyond majority rule (government) and consumer demand (business) to join others who think and believe as they do."[89] Philanthropy gave birth to the nonprofit sector and continues to nourish it. Private giving for public purposes remains a mainstay in American life because it allows people to make possible what they, individually, believe is important.

The fact that much of the theory of the nonprofit sector, as well as methodologies for the study of it and of philanthropy, are still evolving makes this a dynamic and exciting time for both scholars and practitioners. There also is a growing level of interest in the field as suggested by recently reported data. An article in the winter 2014 edition of *Stanford Social Innovation Review* reports that 295 US colleges and universities are now offering instruction in nonprofit management or philanthropic studies or both. This number represents a nearly 16-fold increase since 1990 (Mendel, 2014, 61–62).[90]

3

Philanthropists and Their Foundations

Foundations represent the institutionalization of philanthropy. They are the formal, legal structures that allow an individual or group to gather resources and then carry out deliberate policies and programs. Philanthropic foundations occupy a prominent place in the development of higher education—and in US public policies, based in part on antecedents from England followed by distinctively American modifications over four centuries.[1] In the mid-nineteenth century the Slater Fund and the Peabody Fund were foremost examples of foundation activity—but they were literally "exceptional," which meant they remained isolated and limited in their influence. This marginal character for philanthropic foundations, however, would soon change dramatically and permanently.[2] Analysis of a chronological succession of selected, significant case studies over the past century in this chapter is intended to illustrate the continuity and change in the role of foundations in shaping American higher education into the twenty-first century.[3]

Starting around 1900 foundations in the United States were transformed into prominence with the creation of the great Trusts based on industrial wealth—such as the Carnegie Foundation for the Advancement of Teaching, the Carnegie Corporation, the Rockefeller Foundation, the Rosenwald Fund, the General Education Board, and the Russell Sage Foundation.[4] These fall into the category of "private foundations," as distinguished in the tax code from public or community charitable foundations. The private foundations represented unprecedented philanthropic support as suggested by Andrew Carnegie's gift of $480 million to the various Carnegie philanthropies, followed closely by John D. Rockefeller's providing $445 million for the assorted Rockefeller initiatives.[5] To put these two bequests from a century ago into context, each would be worth more than $10 billion in 2013.

Later, between 1934 and 1970 the Ford Foundation, the Rockefeller Brothers Foundation, the Lilly Endowment, the Sloan Foundation, the Mellon Foundation, the Pew Charitable Trusts, the Howard Hughes Medical Research Institute, the Guggenheim Foundation, the Packard Foundation, and the Hewlett Foundation represented a new generation of organized large-scale philanthropy whose major initiatives often have included support of various aspects of higher education. These also reflected a parade of new, changing sources of economic development in the United States, as the foundations' endowments were based on fortunes made in pharmaceuticals (Lilly Endowment), copper mining (Guggenheim), banking (Mellon), automobiles (Ford and Sloan), Hollywood movies and aeronautics (Hughes Medical Research Institute), and computers (Packard and Hewlett). In the early twenty-first century preeminent foundations that have commanded public attention for their focus on higher education include the Lumina Foundation and the Bill and Melinda Gates Foundation, with the latter foundation drawing from commercial success in computer software.

The large private foundations understandably attract the most attention, both today and a century ago. One part of their legacy is that they provided a model for creation of hundreds and, now, tens of thousands of new foundations that represent a diverse range of resources and purposes. Many of the newer, smaller foundations represent a family's commitment to serious estate planning. A convenient guide to the extent of this foundation phenomenon is provided in the annual editions of *Giving USA* and *The Foundation Directory*. Whereas a major foundation may have its own office building or even a campus, most have a modest physical presence either as a rented office suite or, in the case of small foundations, sometimes nothing more than a computer file or a manila folder in an attorney's office cabinet. Despite these differences in scope and size, the assorted private foundations share common ground in their legal moorings, tax exemption status, and in their attractiveness to donors and recipients.

What the wealthy industrialists discovered around 1900 was that giving money away was not easy. For many of them, it was more difficult and perplexing than making their fortunes in such endeavors as oil refining, steel manufacturing, banking, or building railroad lines. A major contribution of a foundation was to bring coherence out of chaos. It represented what was then known as "scientific philanthropy" in which systematic giving replaced haphazard and perhaps frivolous donations. This transformation was no less than part of a larger movement in American society—what historian Robert Wiebe called a "search for order."[6] A price to pay for this incorporation was that the great donor—such as an Andrew Carnegie—forfeited individual control of the fortune. Systematic philanthropy entailed the creation of an organization that included a charter, a board of trustees, an executive director, and an administrative staff replete with internal procedures, priorities, program reviews, balance sheets, field notes, and various forms of record keeping. This formal arrangement also created an opportunity for the emergence of a new, influential figure in American public life—foundation officers such as Frederick T. Gates, Henry Pritchett, Beardsley Ruml, Abraham Flexner, Simon Flexner, and McGeorge Bundy—all of whom exercised control over those who sought access to foundations and funding—and who helped set a foundation's agenda amidst myriad possibilities.

According to historians Barry Karl and Stanley Katz the creation of the great philanthropic foundations between 1900 and 1930 was significant for public policies in the United States because they provided a distinctive compromise that allowed truly "national" endeavors directed at societal problem-solving without an overwhelming presence of the federal government and its regulatory agencies.[7] This theme will receive detailed attention in chapter 5: "Government Relations and the Nonprofit Sector: Legislation and Policies in Philanthropy and Higher Education." For this chapter it suffices to note that most charitable and philanthropic activities were limited and local in scope prior to the creation of major foundations after 1900.

The lack of a strong federal involvement in education and other social programs and services early in the twentieth century gave the great foundations two benefits that enhanced their influence. First, it meant that foundation initiatives in reforming public schools or higher education faced little comparison or competition with federally funded programs. Second, the absence of federal regulations provided an unrestricted, open field for foundation executives and boards to pursue the kinds of initiatives they selected without nuisances of compliance or restrictions. The primary headache energetic large foundations faced in staking out nationwide or regional reforms would be if their widespread initiatives violated state and local laws or customs—a situation that surfaced where state law mandated racially segregated educational, health, and social service systems in the South.[8]

The emergence of major philanthropic foundations changed the ecology and energy of American higher education, both directly and indirectly, in shapes and substance still prevalent today. Colleges and universities could not assume that they were the main or exclusive object of foundation support. They had to compete in a diverse arena for projects and priorities. Furthermore, the great foundations eschewed the fancy of major donors in the late-nineteenth century to indulge in building a complete new campus as a memorial. After 1900 a college or university president would be less likely to have personal access to a "captain of industry" as a sole or major benefactor. Foundation executives leaned toward a new agenda characterized by such generic challenges as improving medical research, solving problems of public health, finding a cure for a particular disease, increasing agricultural production and food distribution, harnessing scholarly expertise to inform public policies and debates, extending schooling opportunities for American youth, or changing the structural and cultural domain of race relations or social class.

A good example of this transition is the Rockefeller Institute and the related founding of Rockefeller University. At first glance this may appear to be a continuation of the preference for founding new universities. In fact, one finds that it demonstrated a markedly different approach grounded in a new specialization since Rockefeller University was not a typical university campus, but rather, an advanced institution for research on particular topics in medicine carried out without the trappings of undergraduate education, intercollegiate sports, fraternities and sororities, or a landscaped campus. It was one example of philanthropy which signaled that henceforth educational institutions, including established colleges and universities, had to mix and mingle with such other topical interests as committing to advanced research or to the cultivation of fine arts collections or sponsorship of the performing arts in order to be a priority for foundation dollars.

The United States stood in stark contrast to the highly centralized national systems of educational administration that had been established in European nations and in Great Britain. This distinctive vacuum meant that on balance, two foundations—the Carnegie Foundation for the Advancement of Teaching and, later, the General Education Board funded by John D. Rockefeller, assumed the role of a de facto national ministry of education. The result was a uniquely American scenario marked by the convergence and coexistence of *vertical* and *horizontal* institutions in which colleges and universities, both public and private, were chronically cash strapped and, hence, forced into a position where their continual pursuit of external resources meant that they inherited the burden of proof to persuade the affluent foundations that *their* particular academic programs were worthy of foundation funding.

The case of the Carnegie Foundation for the Advancement of Teaching (CFAT) provides significant insights into the purposes and phases of the new great foundations as transformational agents in American higher education.[9] Its president, Henry Pritchett, had been president of the Massachusetts Institute of Technology, and brought to philanthropy a sustained commitment to inculcating American higher education with "standards" and "standardization." The watchword of the CFAT was that it stood for "private power for the public good." These lofty goals were operationalized to include creating a pension fund for college professors while at the same time influencing colleges to increase the size and academic quality of their entering classes. This was a carrot-and-stick strategy in which the CFAT would provide funding for faculty pensions on the condition that the cooperating college would agree to specified changes in admissions requirements and degree. It also was an example of where a major foundation underestimated the expense of its program when the CFAT officials came to the sobering realization around 1917 that they did not have enough money to continue any longer the original intent of providing eligible colleges with all the funds for their campus pension plan. The revised strategy was for creation of the TIAA-CREF pension plan whose funding came from contributions by colleges and their professors.

Between 1910 and 1930 the CFAT gave high priority to analyzing and exposing the serious shortfalls in American higher education. This included Abraham Flexner's 1910 landmark study of deficiencies in medical education in the United States and Canada, and, later, his comparable report on legal education that made allegations about the weaknesses of evening law schools.[10] Perhaps the most publicized report sponsored by the CFAT was Howard J. Savage's 1929 nationwide study of abuses in college sports programs. It was both comprehensive and controversial, as it received front-page headline coverage in most newspapers across the United States. Numerous presidents and coaches at prominent colleges and universities fumed and blustered in their disavowals of the CFAT report. The primary author, Howard Savage, stood his ground and countered with convincing documentation to stand by his allegations. The residual message was that an external perspective provided by a foundation study was more likely than a campus's internal audit to prompt institutional reforms. There was little doubt that the CFAT had undertaken systematic analysis of pressing problems. Yet the relation of research and reform remained unclear and uneven. Flexner's 1910 critical report on medical schools was followed by massive closings of free-standing, proprietary medical schools whose admission standards and academic work was suspect. The enduring question was whether the CFAT report had fomented closures and reforms or, perhaps, the shake out among marginal medical colleges was due to market forces created by a proliferation and overexpansion of medical schools with little cause-effect from Flexner's CFAT report. If Abraham Flexner's 1910 report on medical education at least showed some signs of shaping reform, his subsequent study of law schools floundered, generating little change. Beyond these specific episodes, the larger question facing foundations was the extent to which analysis and exposure of educational deficiencies necessarily led to reform.

After 1930 the CFAT was accepting commissions tantamount to consulting fees from various national and state authorities to undertake surveys and studies of particular programs, ranging from curricular reform to public pension systems. The residual point is that these various activities were part of an overarching commitment to bringing "standards and standardization" to American education. It certainly included higher education—and by extension reached to include public high schools. If one were to raise and make more consistent admissions standards for college entrance, then one had to include reshaping the structure and content of high school studies and transcripts.

One legacy of this initiative was the so-called Carnegie Unit to provide a short-hand designation of a secondary school course that was adequate in academic content and calendar to pass muster for college admission. At the other end, trying to bring coherence to the bachelor of arts degree conferred nationwide by hundreds of colleges in the United States stretched up the educational pyramid since it was a strategic move to demonstrate to academic officials in Europe and England that American students could, indeed, be qualified to undertake study for the master's and PhD at established universities on the continent and at Oxford and Cambridge. A good example of a work that consolidated the CFAT criticisms of American higher education was Abraham Flexner's 1930 book *Universities: American, English, German* which was based on a series of lectures Flexner had been invited to give at Oxford University in 1929.

The CFAT decision to undertake such projects as the reform of high school curricula, college admissions requirements, to document the shortfalls in medical schools, and to analyze the excesses of inter-collegiate athletics provides a crucial insight into foundations' roles. The major foundations had the resources and inclination to tackle problems that an individual college or university was either unable or unwilling to resolve. It meant that a foundation could prompt educational institutions to go beyond "business as usual." It epitomized the concept of horizontal influence that attempted to make changes *across* the higher education landscape. By this criterion meaningful assessments of CFAT projects are difficult to measure. For example, prior to World War II its support of Swedish sociologist Gunnar Myrdal's report on race relations in the United States, published as *An American Dilemma,* had little if any direct economic impact nor did it produce a cure for a disease.[11] It was, however, over the long run influential in shaping numerous civil rights ideas and initiatives, including eventually the 1954 Supreme Court case involving *Brown* v. *Board of Education.* How does one calculate a precise cost-benefit report for the CFAT investment in this research project?

The General Education Board (GEB) was established in 1903 by John D. Rockefeller. Its broad charter was to sponsor and support aid to education in the United States "without distinction of race, sex or creed." According to the archivist of the Rockefeller Related Organizations, its original program included an array of institutional and programmatic funding—including college and university endowment grants; fellowships; assistance to developing state public school systems; and, contributions to colleges and universities for annual operating expenses. The influential figure in the creation and scope of the GEB was Frederick T. Gates, long-time philanthropic advisor to John D. Rockefeller.[12] Although the formal charter and mandate were broad and at one time or another included assistance to educational programs in each and every state, the initial emphasis of the GEB was to work to improve education in the South. Furthermore, this often included focus on enhanced public education for Blacks in those states characterized by dual school systems defined by race and prescribed by state law.[13]

Foremost among its early initiatives was to promote the establishment of public high schools in Southern states. It did so by means of direct grants and also by assembling teams of experts in planning and development so as to create within these states public and legislative support for extending public schooling to include high school as part of a permanent system funded by regular taxation. After 1920 the GEB extended its projects to numerous economic and social issues in the South which were supplements and complements to its original emphasis on public education. It included matters of health (e.g., the eradication of hookworm), regional diet, and regional agriculture. Later, medicine—including international medical care and health systems—became integral to GEB priorities.

Initial and influential leadership for the GEB was provided by Wallace Buttrick. One of the interesting innovations Buttrick championed was grass roots-field work. GEB representatives devoted a great deal of time to canvassing the regions and sites where they were initiating new projects. This connection and diplomacy were especially important as Northerners undertaking educational reforms in the South.[14] At the highest level of the foundation, Frederick T. Gates brought to the GEB some influential, innovative principles and practices. He emphasized systematic planning and evaluation in assessing the effectiveness and worth of philanthropic projects. Under his leadership the GEB represented what was then called "scientific philanthropy," an approach that institutionalized professionalism and planning in large-scale gifts and projects. The case of the GEB is pertinent to the study of philanthropic endowment spending patterns for two reasons. First, in 1920 John D. Rockefeller loosened the GEB's constraints on limited annual spending with the explicit intent of having its board and officers devote substantial endowment resources to significant problems immediately. Second, the GEB was guided by a planned phase out and spend down. In 1940 all projects except for selected ones dealing with the education of Blacks in the South were brought to closure. These remaining programs were scheduled to end in 1960, at which time the GEB would be dissolved. The GEB appropriated slightly more than $321 million for its sponsored projects from its founding in 1902 and its dissolution in 1960.

Frederick T. Gates warrants particular biographical mention even though he was not a donor. He was one of the foremost pioneers in American philanthropy, both as a fund-raiser and, later, as a gatekeeper for John D. Rockefeller's varied, large projects. In reviewing Gates' early professional life one finds that he "wrote the book" for an audience of serious fund-raisers. He set forth in no uncertain terms standards of conduct and effective strategy, much of which remains vital a century later. And, if one considers the adage, "It takes one to know one," Gates was well-suited to sift and screen the myriad supplicants who besieged such wealthy figures as John D. Rockefeller and Andrew Carnegie. Gates, the son of a Baptist minister, acquired experience in raising money for churches and church-related schools.

In 1888 he was appointed secretary of the newly formed American Baptist Education Society. His work there included his plans and advocacy for creating a great Baptist university. In 1889 Gates met John D. Rockefeller, himself a Baptist. Gates's university vision impressed Rockefeller—and was integral to the founding of the new University of Chicago. In addition to this specific achievement, Gates's great contribution in the formative years of large-scale philanthropy was to combine religion with his genius for organizing and implementing complex programs that led to solution of significant problems. He was a pioneer in the development of professional expertise in foundations and philanthropy. Gates dissolved the stereotypical schism between commerce and education, as he was one of Rockefeller's principal advisors at Standard Oil. Eventually this led to Rockefeller's reliance on Gates for investments and philanthropic ventures. He was the principal architect in mapping out the vision and mission of the General Education Board. And, later, Gates would serve as president of the GEB. It also gave momentum to the increasing trend of having board members from industrial corporations also serve on boards of colleges and foundations.[15]

The General Education Board, one of the historically famous undertakings in the twentieth century, is a paradox in American philanthropy. Some reasons for this observation are as follow: First, it had strong "brand recognition." The official name of the General Education Board was nationwide recognized and for a long time as GEB. Yet its identity was often blurred or confused—with no recognition of the Rockefeller funding in the name; or, to another extreme, when it was associated with the Rockefeller philanthropy, it often was mistakenly assumed to be a program under the auspices of the Rockefeller Foundation (which it was not). Indeed, John D. Rockefeller Sr. provided funding for the establishment of the GEB prior to the founding and chartering of the more famous, more recognized, and enduring Rockefeller Foundation.

Second, the GEB relied from start to finish on substantial investment in evaluation, field work, assessment, and review. This included its own sponsored studies, its periodic reports, and its evaluations of the work and progress of those foundations and institutions to which it made substantial grants. This was in marked contrast to the Rosenwald Fund, as noted in the preceding case study. The GEB often attempted to minimize devoting its resources to its own infrastructure—relying often on providing grants to other, existing foundations and educational programs. The GEB was a pioneer in large-scale educational philanthropy. In its 58 years of existence it awarded over $324 million for varied and diverse educational programs. Its emphasis was on policies, programs, and people—with little concern about actual bricks and mortar construction of schools or other facilities. In education, for example, one of its initial and foremost aims was to promote the idea of state and local governments committing to the systematic creation of the public high school. Similarly, in its substantial support of agricultural programs, the aim was to increase agricultural productivity in the South so as to reduce poverty.

One recurrent allegation about John D. Rockefeller Sr.'s impact on the nation's economy was that his industrial empire based on the Standard Oil Corporation showed what was called the "curse of bigness."[16] In contrast, the experience of Rockefeller's support and choice of leaders for the General Education Board illustrated a "blessing of bigness." The abundance of resources Rockefeller provided for the GEB enabled it to take on and persist with addressing significant issues and reforms in American education. What stands out as remarkable about the GEB was its long-term combination of thoughtful, informed ground work provided by experts then followed by perceptive and resilient decision-making as it monitored the progress and problems of its forays into education, agriculture, and medicine. In lesser hands, the huge endowment might have been squandered. Evidently, John D. Rockefeller Sr. did not meddle into GEB affairs, as he had selected carefully and wisely Gates and Buttrick, as the ones who steered the course of several large, inter-related programs. When his son, John D. Rockefeller Jr. became active in working with GEB officers, his intervention often was in thoughtful, helpful ways to assure that sponsored programs did receive ample funding in a timely manner. According to Raymond B. Fosdick in his 1962 book about the GEB, *Adventure in Giving*, between 1932 and 1952 the GEB initiated a succession of measures intended to increase the fluidity and liberalization of endowment grants.

Most charters and mission statements for nonprofit organizations and foundations are simultaneously inspiring and vague. One obvious explanation for this tendency is that it provides foundation boards with latitude in selecting programs to sponsor. And, it also suggests genuine aspiration to do good works. In the case of the GEB, the mission statements were not gratuitous. The GEB over six decades had the combination of funding, expertise, and commitment to make substantial headway in working "to extend, if they could, the boundaries of education here in America, without distinction of race, sex, or creed."

The GEB helped extend the notion of schooling beyond "business as usual" by exploring broadly influences on educational attainment. For example, one of it most influential contributions to enhancing the quality of life in American was its systematic study of hookworms and the lack of adequate toilets and sewage disposal in the South. It is no exaggeration to say that the improvement of the schoolhouse was closely related to the GEB-informed analysis of the outhouse. Furthermore, its example of studying education in broad context helped explain and dispel the regional stereotype of the archetypal "lazy Southerner." Continuing from this, among the numerous initiatives and accomplishments of the GEB, one that stands out exemplary in its magnitude, difficulty, and eventual success was the commitment to nurturing the comprehensive public high school as an integral, widespread institution in American society. Most of the GEB work in this line focused on public school systems in the Southern states—including both all-White and all-Black public high schools. It did also have implications in all states nationwide. To suggest the glaring void the GEB set out to fill was that in 1909 there was a grand total of *seven* public high schools in the entire state of Georgia.

By the post-World War II period and certainly with the winding down of the GEB in 1960, public high schools in Georgia and other previously underbuilt states had become expected institutions in virtually all counties and communities. The GEB hardly can claim—nor seek to claim—that it was entirely responsible for this institutional innovation and extension. The GEB was, however, involved and integral in concert with a variety of private local groups, other foundations, and state governments on this venture precisely during the decades in which public high schools in the United States came of age.

The GEB's original focus was on public schooling for Blacks in the South.[17] This topic remained during the entire lifespan of the GEB. However, as historians Eric Morse and Alfred Moss noted in *Dangerous Donations*, their 1999 study of Northern philanthropy and Southern Black education from 1902 to 1930, the GEB leaders faced a crucial dilemma. The issue was whether resentment by Southern governors and legislators to GEB's attention exclusively to schooling for Blacks would derail GEB work. The GEB directorate was sufficiently resilient and pragmatic to heed this warning and make a crucial change in their projects—namely, the inclusion of the shortfalls and problems of all public education in the South—both for Black and White students.

Along with institution building, the GEB invested wisely and generously in long-term research that would both analyze their contemporary initiatives and also provide critical planning guides for the future. An excellent example of this investment was the GEB's support of the work of sociologist Howard Odum at the University of North Carolina in the comprehensive study of regional culture and race relations in the American South. Not only did Odum's projects illuminate systematically and deeply ingrained social patterns in the South, they had the positive secondary effect of bringing sponsored research and advanced scholarship to a high level that endured—and brought national respect to social science research conducted by faculty and graduate students at universities in the South.[18] In sum, the GEB's six decades of attention to regional change and extension of public schooling were imperfect, yet remarkable in their scope and endurance. It was an excellent example of private philanthropy stimulating work for the public good that most likely would not have taken place otherwise.

Although the CFAT and the GEB were the most influential and enduring sources for educational reform in the first half of the twentieth century, the Rosenwald Fund warrants mention for its lessons and legacies during the same era. It was established in 1917 with a charter granted by the state of Illinois establishing it as "a corporation not for profit" that was authorized "to receive and disburse funds for philanthropic causes." Its formal purpose was commitment to "the well being of mankind." Its endowment was made possible by the donations of its namesake, Julius Rosenwald, who was president and a major stockholder of Sears, Roebuck and Company in Chicago. Rosenwald's initial experiences in philanthropy were his acts of private-giving as an individual. This included an interest in and commitment to race relations, with particular emphasis on support of educational programs to assist Blacks in the segregated South. Most influential in this socialization into large scale philanthropy was his acquaintance and then friendship with Booker T. Washington. Central to this initiation and interest were Rosenwald's site visits to Tuskegee Institute in Alabama, where he was hosted by Booker T. Washington. Rosenwald also gave generous support to Jane Addams's Hull House and numerous other progressive social projects in Chicago.

In 1915 Rosenwald explored possibilities to transform his individual giving into a formal institutional setting, which culminated in the creation of the Julius Rosenwald Fund. It was distinctive among the emerging, major foundations of the era in that it was housed in Chicago—whereas most, such as the Rockefeller Foundation, the General Education Board, and the Carnegie Foundation for the Advancement of Teaching, had their headquarters in New York City. The Julius Rosenwald Fund also was distinctive, perhaps unique, in its design to be a limited-life foundation that would exist for only one generation. According to the final reports published in 1949, between 1917 and 1948 the Julius Rosenwald Fund made appropriations of $22,249,624 to educational and charitable programs.

During its 31-year life, 1917 to 1948, the Julius Rosenwald Fund sponsored projects in education, health and medical services, race relations, and various other areas for a total amount of slightly more than $22 million. Annual expenditures were remarkably stable and consistent, almost always close to the mean of about $700,000 per year. The signature program of the Fund was the school-building project in which over $5 million was devoted to stimulating matching grants at the grass roots level for construction of 5,000 sound, safe, attractive public school buildings for African-American children in those states whose educational systems were by law racially segregated. Indeed, the so-called "Rosenwald School" would become the well-known icon and symbol of Julius Rosenwald's individual and corporate philanthropy. The school buildings were the hub and heart from which numerous related initiatives in social and educational change would emanate. This hallmark program provided the most visible, tangible, and enduring sign of the Fund's fidelity to Julius Rosenwald's principle of the efficacy of a finite lifetime for a philanthropic foundation. As such, the Rosenwald Fund has justifiably endured as a pioneer and an example of "best practices" in limited-life philanthropy in the twentieth century.

In reading secondary sources on the biography of Julius Rosenwald, along with periodic and annual reports for the Julius Rosenwald Fund compiled by Edwin R. Embree, a key point is that 1932 was a watershed year due to three crucial intertwined events: first, in accordance with decisions made by the Fund board and president, it was the end of the famous school-building program.[19] Second, 1932 was the year of an unexpected reduction of the Rosenwald Fund endowment due to its investments in Sears Roebuck stocks that had plummeted from a high value of $190 per share in 1929 to $33 dollar per share; and, third, the death of Julius Rosenwald himself in 1932 indelibly altered the cast and script of the Rosenwald Fund. In one fell swoop, the acclaimed initiative had lost its visionary founder, major donor, the bulk of its assets, and signature project.[20]

The official summary of the termination of the Rosenwald School program in 1932 shows a glowing report card, as mentioned earlier: namely, funding of over $4 million that led to construction and operation of more than 5,000 new school houses in the rural South. That net report suffices, however, only if one relies on counting buildings as the result or end product. Even Rosenwald and Fund officials such as Edwin R. Embree noted that their actual goal always was to be more—and more significant—than just bricks and mortar. The overarching purpose was to promote better race relations among Whites and Blacks in the South throughout 15 Southern States. Unfortunately, it is difficult to test out claims one way or the other because Rosenwald Fund directors and staff devoted little attention to program evaluation, in marked contrast to the GEB's extended initiatives dealing with public education and health in the South during the same era.

Among the great industrial fortunes made early in the twentieth century, automobile manufacturer Henry Ford was a late comer to large-scale philanthropy. Although Ford was legendary for his success in bringing the assembly line to mass production of the Ford Model T in Detroit, his business acumen also faced some large-scale embarrassments. He had his plants wired for direct current when the coming mandate was for alternating current. In the 1930s he lost millions of dollars in bizarre ventures in South America where his vision was to create in the Brazilian Amazon a model village that would be simultaneously a new, inexpensive source of rubber for his automobile tire manufacturing and a model of a company town that included codes of conduct for workers ranging from prohibition of alcohol to requiring a diet of brown rice and brown bread—all of which led to absenteeism, desertion, and finally, outright worker revolt and violence.[21] Immodestly named "Fordlandia," it was a venture that demonstrated how even the richest man in the world could woefully misjudge and mismanage an expensive enterprise. Furthermore, sales of Ford automobiles unexpectedly plummeted in the early 1930s. He and his son, Edsel Ford, had the Ford Foundation created in 1936 as a convenient, legal site to place family and corporate wealth as a strategy to avoid or, at least delay, taxes. It remained inactive for over a decade, with its grant-making planning operations first starting in 1947.

The Ford Foundation stands out as one of the interesting, ironic cases both for higher education in particular and foundations in general that probably would have surprised—and perhaps angered—founder Henry Ford. His favored projects had included conservative nostalgia, such as building and maintaining a museum at Dearborn and nearby historic Greenfield Village. The unexpected innovations and experimental projects that would characterize the Ford Foundation after World War II—and after the death of Henry Ford—have been documented in a refreshingly lively account of the internal life of a major foundation, written by Dwight McDonald in 1956.[22] McDonald, for example, cites early Ford Foundation leaders for providing the models of "philanthropoids" whose press releases and public speeches were presented in the distinctive language of "foundationese."

The Ford Foundation was prominent as the largest, wealthiest foundation in the United States. In 2013, for example, its endowment was slightly over $10 billion. This is formidable and places it in the top five foundations today. Yet this contemporary profile pales in comparison to its worth in the first two decades following World War II. For example, around 1960 the Ford Foundation's assets peaked at $12 billion—worth approximately $95 billion in 2013, which is almost three times greater than the assets of the wealthiest foundation—the Bill and Melinda Gates Foundation— today. The original Ford Foundation leadership team of businessman Paul Hoffman and former University of Chicago President Robert Maynard Hutchens did not rush into business, as they devoted three years to drafting a massive Study Report between 1947 and 1950.

Despite a slow, delayed start, once the Ford Foundation started making grants it did so in a conspicuous way, awarding an average of $45 million to $50 million per year between 1951 and 1954. Hoffman and Hutchens were neither hesitant nor modest in making large grants in their high-priority initiatives. Also newsworthy was that their policies and programs soon became associated with controversial projects associated with a leaning politically to the left with an emphasis on international studies—testimony to the imprint of Robert Maynard Hutchens. According to Dwight McDonald's 1956 book, *The Ford Foundation: The Men and the Millions*, in 1954 the Ford Foundation spent four times as much as the Rockefeller Foundation and ten times as much as the Carnegie Corporation—giving it a public presence that was unprecedented. By 1953 both Hoffman and Hutchens had been relieved of their duties, with a San Francisco attorney, H. Rowland Gaither appointed as the new foundation president. Interesting to note is that in its first years the Ford Foundation made an explicit decision to avoid funding for projects involving the natural and physical sciences, the arts, and medicine. Eventually, however, foundation leaders would reverse their initial avoidance of health and medical programs.

An important development in support of independent higher education came about in 1951 when the Ford Foundation created the Fund for the Advancement of Education. Emphasizing innovation beyond "business as usual," this helped a variety of colleges and universities explore new curricula. And, in 1955 the Ford Foundation made an award of $210 million that was allocated among 630 private liberal arts colleges. Its emphasis was on encouraging institutions to raise faculty salaries among a large, diverse group of independent colleges. Since eligibility for foundation awards required an institution to have regional accreditation, a number of colleges were prompted to shore up both curricular and financial structures in compliance with accreditation standards. A few years later, the Ford Foundation identified a smaller group of 126 institutions that would share in an award of $50 million—once again, with emphasis on raising faculty salaries. Many of the programs included conditions of matching grants in which participating colleges were obliged to raise fresh, new dollars synchronized with the foundation monies.

The short-term result was external support for independent liberal arts colleges in a time of financial crisis. The long-term benefit was strengthening of the tradition of large-scale philanthropic support for higher education. Viewed in tandem, the two strands of different emphases constituted an effective support strategy. Philanthropy that limited itself to underwriting bold, innovative programs provided incentives for exploration and cutting-edge features at the colleges. In contrast, emphases on direct support for raising faculty salaries certainly contributed to helping colleges maintain "business as usual." Yet, in fact, even this seemingly cautious, conservative approach had a strong multiplier effect that invigorated the liberal arts colleges. It meant that they now could compete with other kinds of institutions both to retain established faculty and, above all, to be able to compete for new PhDs from strong universities. Liberal arts colleges, thanks to the foundation support, were increasingly able to attract a new generation of committed scholars to their teaching ranks. The challenge for a president or provost was to identify those graduate students at major universities who combined both skills in advanced research with the essential passion for teaching and undergraduate education. All colleges and universities gained from the Ford Foundation officer Sidney Tickton's sustained commitment to developing institutional research data collection and analysis that would become part of the fabric of campus planning and decision-making. This contribution once again emphasized the role of a foundation in prompting colleges to go beyond "business as usual." In a comparable spirit, the Ford Foundation set out to raise academic standards and promote interdisciplinary teaching and research in selected fields, such as business administration. To do so it provided funding for Masters of Business Administration programs at a few selected universities such as Stanford, Harvard, Columbia, Cornell, and the University of Chicago.[23] The strategy was that over time other universities would observe and then follow the innovative examples of these respected institutions. By the mid-1960s the Ford Foundation encountered severe financial and political problems. Foundation assets plummeted to $2 billion due to dependency on Ford Motor Company stock. The political controversies surfaced with allegations that the Foundation had knowingly been complicit with the United States' Central Intelligence Agency operations.

A foundation, however, is not necessarily consistent or homogenous among its programs. In marked contrast to allegations of CIA involvement under leadership of McGeorge Bundy from 1966 to 1979 was, later, its 1993-appointment of Allison Bernstein to head up the Ford Foundation's Education and Culture Program and its $58 million biennial grants budget with an emphasis on improving opportunities for women, minority students, and underfunded urban public schools. Bernstein noted that her role was to help make the Ford Foundation a "catalyst for change," and to ensure that "we're not in the business of building buildings or contributing to endowments." The Ford Foundation's philanthropy "is directed toward helping to construct models that can point the way that things can be improved. That kind of demonstration is very important in a society that has gotten very cynical about what works."[24]

Foundations and institutes funded by John D. Rockefeller had been among the pioneering efforts to connect health and higher education. An interesting sequel in this tradition of support for medical research is provided by the Markey Foundation whose planning was started around 1975. Lucille P. Markey, grande dame of Kentucky's famed Calumet Farm, had the Lucille P. Markey Charitable Trust operate for only 15 years, beginning in 1983 and ending in 1997. During its decade and a half of operation, the Markey Trust distributed over $500 million in support of biomedical research.

Lucille Parker Markey was the widow of Warren Wright, whose father had founded the Calumet Baking Powder Company. The younger Wright, who had become president of the company, sold it in the late 1920s to the firm that would become General Foods for a sum of $32 million. Following her husband's death in 1950, Lucille took over management of Calumet Farms and also remarried. Much of Lucille Markey's wealth came from oil and gas interests she also inherited from her late husband's family. Lucille's charitable interests turned increasingly to human health with gifts she made to Rockefeller University to further arthritis research and to the University of Kentucky, where her second husband was treated for colon cancer, to establish the Lucille P. Markey Cancer Center.

The Lucille P. Markey Charitable Trust began operations in 1983, a year after Lucille Markey's death. The assets were of sufficient magnitude to have made it one of the nation's largest foundations. Lucille Markey viewed perpetual foundations as memorials to the donors who founded them which held no attraction to her. She wanted her money applied to grants and put to work, administered by people she trusted to honor her intentions. For these reasons, she limited the life of the Markey Trust to 15 years and the number of trustees to 5.[25]

The Markey Trust opened its headquarters in Miami in 1984. In addition to having a streamlined governance structure, an early decision by the trustees to make fewer but larger grants meant a smaller staff, which was supplemented by extensive use of consultants. Realizing that other institutions were addressing the clinical aspects of health care, Mrs. Markey had decided that her estate should be dedicated to basic, as opposed to targeted, biomedical research. One of the first activities of the Trust in 1984 was to hold a series of three "think tank" meetings with distinguished biomedical researchers in California, New York, and London. These conversations were the genesis of what would become the Trust's best-known program. The Markey Scholars and Fellows Awards in Biomedical Sciences program, which was announced in late 1984, provided long-term financial support for postdoctoral fellows and young faculty members. The program was soon expanded to include funding for outstanding young researchers from the United Kingdom and Australia, who were named visiting fellows and supported for two years as postdoctoral fellows at US research institutions. The trustees would ultimately allocate a total of $63,093,900 to funding the Markey Scholars and Fellows Awards, the first of its three major program categories.

In 1985 the Trust launched the Research Program Grants initiative. The largest of the three major grants programs, the Research Program Grants were designed to enable established investigators with proven records of excellence to address important issues in the biomedical sciences. These grants were made to institutions. In addition to supporting the work of established scientists, they assisted in the establishment, reorganization, or expansion of significant biomedical research centers or programs. During the life of the Trust, these grants accounted for $325,338,175 of its total funding (National Research Council, 2004).

The General Organization Grants program, the third of the Markey Trust's three broad categories of funding, began in 1988. It was designed to address the gap that had developed between fundamental biological research and clinical research. The problem, referred to as the "bed-bench gap," stemmed from the fact that an insufficient number of clinical researchers was being produced to translate the discoveries of biomedical science into practical medical practice. The solution was to encourage more students to pursue translational research. The Trust awarded a total of $62,121,700 to improve education and training of PhDs and MDs who were planning careers in biomedical research to better prepare them for basic clinical research and research in molecular medicine. The purpose of bridging the gap between biomedical research and its clinical application involved bringing about organizational change within recipient institutions, thus the name General Organization Grants.

The Markey Trust officially closed its doors in June 1997. Between 1983 and 1997, the Trust gave a total of $507,151,000 to basic medical research and research training. The total value of the Trust was $545,520,000, which included $149,565,000 in investment income. Its administrative and operational costs amounted to $29,087,000, or approximately 5 percent of the total trust. Additional expenses included $10,529,000 in investment and mineral depletion costs (National Research Council, 2004).

In 1997 when the Markey Trust was nearing its planned end, the trustees asked the National Research Council (NRC) of the National Academies to evaluate the Trust's approach to supporting programs in basic biomedical science. A primary objective of the evaluation was to determine if the Markey Trust might serve as a model of philanthropy. Agreeing to undertake this study, the National Academies established the Committee on the Evaluation of the Lucille P. Markey Charitable Trust Programs in Biomedical Sciences. The committee's report, *Bridging the Bed-Bench Gap: Contributions of the Markey Trust*, was published by the National Academy of Sciences in 2004.[26] Lucille P. Markey's decision to limit the life of her eponymous foundation (charitable trust) to 15 years yielded several beneficial outcomes. Administrative and operational costs were kept low, allowing more of the Trust's total value to be directed to its mission. Distributing all of the Trust's funds over a limited period of time meant that more funds could be distributed in a given year. And, by awarding larger grants, the Trust was able to produce a greater impact on institutional behavior, to facilitate organizational change, and to enable training programs to be established. Moreover, the relatively short lifespan of the Trust meant that the trustees started with the end in mind and never lost focus or their enthusiasm for fulfilling the donor's intent to focus on medical research issues that were ripe for solution.[27]

The case of the Markey Trust underscored an observation made in 1963 by Clark Kerr, the influential president of the University of California: namely, that medical and health sciences would become the source of focus and energy of the modern, multipurpose American university. In the same short book based on his Godkin Lectures at Harvard, Kerr noted that in the second half of the twentieth century, the nation's industrial economy characterized by steel manufacturing and railroads was being replaced by the "knowledge industry."[28] Nowhere was this prediction more fulfilled than in the transformations and wealth associated by the new enterprises of software and computer applications. Foremost in this new wealth and philanthropy was the William and Flora Hewlett Foundation, drawn from the Hewlett Packard enterprises emanating from Stanford University in the 1930s, eventually fostering the innovative enterprises of Silicon Valley, and leading to creation of the foundation in 1966. In 2013 the Hewlett Foundation reported an endowment of $7 billion and typically awarded over $200 million annually in grants for education, social reform, and for community development programs in the San Francisco Bay Area.

If the Hewlett Foundation symbolized a first wave of computer fortunes as a base for philanthropy and higher education starting in the 1960s, then its successors by the 1990s included Steve Jobs of Apple and Bill Gates of Windows and Microsoft. For Bill Gates, corporate wealth was a prelude to transformational philanthropy with his creation and funding of the Bill and Melinda Gates Foundation, whose assets of about $38 billion are the largest among foundations in the United States. Founded in 1994 the Gates Foundation quickly gained the attention and applause of the scientific research community. For example, *Science Magazine* gave prominent notice in 1999 to the Gates Foundation for its contribution in leading foundations to return to science funding, as its $230 million commitment to research focused on vaccines, reproductive medicine, and public health placed it second only to the Wellcome Trusts in total dollar commitment to science research and development—ahead of such older, established foundations as the Howard Hughes Medical Research Trust, the Packard Foundation, the Keck Foundation, and the Rockefeller Foundation.[29]

In the period 1999 to 2013 the Bill and Melinda Gates Foundation's stewardship of this substantial wealth was its clear focus on selected, significant topics—namely, global health, global development, and—in the United States—school-college relations. The net result is that the Gates Foundation tends to avoid thoughtless sprawl that can fritter away even a large endowment. In the area of American education, the Gates Foundation is ironic in that Bill Gates was a college dropout whose decision to leave Harvard College without completing a degree evidently did not seem to impair his achievements as an inventor and entrepreneur. The foundation's focus on college preparedness has helped shift attention from the 3 Rs to the 3 Is—initiatives, image, and influence. And, these have been the catalyst for a fourth new "I"—intrigue. Some recent articles have raised questions and eyebrows about whether the Gates Foundation has ventured into *political* advocacy for education reform. The Gates Foundation commitments are significant and inspiring. Their promotionals on National Public Radio invoke goals of health and opportunity for all, noting that "every life has equal value." These bring to mind benevolent corporations such as General Electric's advertisements in the 1950s that told the American public, "Progress is our most important product." In its "College Ready" and "Postsecondary Education" areas, the Gates Foundation takes on problems that individual schools, colleges or universities are unlikely to tackle on their own. One good contribution of the foundation to education is that its numerous grants have provided encouragement and seed money to many innovative education organizations—along with grants to familiar, established agencies and associations.[30]

The Gates Foundation website is impressive in its forthright note to constituencies and grant recipients that they subject all projects to rigorous evaluation and metrics. This internal scrutiny of components, however, does not tell how (or who) assesses the overall effectiveness of the College Ready program or the Gates Foundation itself. Solving big problems often has been cast in metaphors of war—such as the War on Poverty, the War on Drugs, or the War on Crime. So, if the College Ready initiative is cast as a "war on college attrition," it brings to mind World War I—long, dreary episodes involving high-powered technology and a lot of investment and effort. Much of it had fought back and forth over the same terrain—with little net gain. One question that follows from these investments and initiatives is that of how and how much have the traditional advantages of family and wealth changed in the sweepstakes of going to college—and graduating from college?[31]

When educational initiatives overlap with legislation, the analogy of World War I campaigns is especially apt. For example, in the June 7, 2013 issue of *The New York Times* a headline states, "House Republican Introduces Education Bill." The article elaborates that Congressman John Kline of Minnesota introduced legislation to replace the decade-old "No Child Left Behind" federal education law—intended to reduce "the federal footprint" in the nation's schools. One is left to ask, "How—if at all—does this mesh with the Gates Foundation's general goals and specific grants?" "Does this reinforce or resist the Gates Foundation initiatives?" Does the Gates Foundation care—or have involvement one way or the other? Whereas a battle such as Argonne in 1918 was dense with smoke from artillery and mustard gas, the education campaigns are hard to follow due to the smoke and mirrors of proclamations and public relations among a complex cast of allies and adversaries in Washington, D.C.

The College Ready initiative made awards in 2013 to 44 grantees—with the largest award of $12,630,000 going to Educause. Large grants included the Aspen Institute and Ednovo—each of about $3,615,000. Most grants, however, were modest—between $100,000 and $500,000. The running total is 1,543 grants since the Foundation started this initiative prior to 2009. In recent years the Gates Foundation typically offers between 163 and 245 grants per year. Most newspaper articles understandably go to announcements of large grants. But one also ought to consider that another source of public curiosity and press coverage includes the other extreme: namely, its small grant awards. When, for example, the Gates Foundation lists a grant of $387 to the New York City Department of Education—it strikes an outside observer as a puzzling partnership between a large foundation and a large school district.

The Gates Foundation clearly is a leader in the amount of fresh private money devoted to education reform. Their awards make a difference in operating budgets of some educational centers. Furthermore, some other major foundations tend to look to the Gates Foundation to set the agenda and path for where their respective foundation grants will go, creating a multiplier effect. But for a university or a state department of education, the Gates Foundation grants are a small percentage of a university or other major organization's research budget. Another way to gauge the relative financial presence of the Gates Foundation is to compare its grants to those of federal agencies. The Gates Foundation has given between $2.2 billion and $4 billion per year in all areas, not just education. The National Science Foundation research budget was $7 billion per year. The National Institutes of Health was $31 billion. Hence, the Gates Foundation may have some potential to make a difference on the margins. Yet given the much larger annual grant budgets of the major federal agencies, its resources probably will not be sufficient to fulfill the foundation's aim to increase substantially educational opportunities and achievement.

If even relatively well-endowed philanthropic groups such as the Gates Foundation do not have sufficient resources to fund direct solutions to national problems of college going, what is the aftermath? Both critics and advocates for foundations agree that one fall back strategy is to press toward influencing public policies. The problem with such an approach is that it comes dangerously close to violating the legal and customary compacts for tax-exempt private foundations to avoid overt lobbying. Educating the public and various constituencies on issues is allowable. Full force lobbying of Congress or federal and state agencies, however, is less certain as legitimate conduct for foundations.[32]

The relation between colleges and universities and philanthropic foundations is imperfect, but it is compatible and has elements of cross-fertilization. The flow of talent and leadership from universities to foundations in such roles as executives and as researchers has been persistent and strong. This includes the president of the University of Chicago, Robert Maynard Hutchens at the Ford Foundation after World War II, and McGeorge Bundy, academic dean at Harvard, at the Ford Foundation from 1966 to 1979. The foremost recent example is that of former Princeton President William Bowen serving as president of the Mellon Foundation where for two decades he led a strong commitment to such varied projects as digitalizing scholarly publications as well as undertaking systematic studies of higher-education problems and issues. At best such appointments have been a source of both creative continuity and tension as one shifts from a college presidency to head a foundation. At worst, it leans toward insularity and in-breeding. On balance, it seems to have been a healthy synergy.

Private foundations are formidable in American society with annual charitable contributions of about $45 billion per year. Their aggregate assets of $628 billion are spread across more than 84,000 foundations filing annual reports with the Internal Revenue Service. They are diverse in size and wealth. Two-thirds of these have assets less than one million dollars each and fewer than 7 percent of foundations have endowments of more than $10 million. As reported in preceding case studies, the wealthiest include the Gates Foundation with $38 billion, with several of the designated foundations having assets of about $3 billion to $10 billion. It means that higher education has been a beneficiary of some of the wealthiest foundations along with generous support from the diverse range of all private foundations.

Given this profile, a closing question is "How does one make sense of the balance sheet and net contributions of philanthropic foundations' contributions to higher education in the United States between 1900 and 2014?" Fortunately we have access to recent thoughtful, systematic commentaries. Foremost is the appraisal by long-time foundation leader and analyst Waldemar Nielsen in 1985, followed by the anthology edited by Ellen Condliffe Lagemann in 1999.[33] The various contributing analysts tend to agree that the philanthropic foundations have been essential to the success and stature of American colleges and universities by having provided generous funding combined with directives for recipients to engage in innovative, socially progressive programs. This has included curricular additions that have been characterized by high academic standards, extended to new fields and applications. In other words, higher education in the United States between 1900 and today probably would have been far more complacent and limited in its scope and vitality without the prodding and incentives of the foundations.

A major tipping point, however, has been the relative influence and financial clout of private foundations in the past 60 years during which the federal government awakened from its timidity and slumber to assert influence (and funding) in selected, crucial areas of postsecondary education—namely, in sponsored research and development following World War II, and, later, with the introduction of massive federal programs of student financial aid starting in 1972. Recall that in the early twentieth century there were few federal programs geared toward colleges and universities, either for research or for student aid. The conventional wisdom has been that in this new era of federal funding that developed in the half century following World War II, philanthropic foundations had to readjust to a political and fiscal environment in which their resources paled in comparison to the relatively new federal government presence. Furthermore, spending on education has persisted as one of the largest categories of state government spending nationwide. At best, some have argued that the major foundations became comparable to a "distant early warning system" in which their innovation and resilience allowed them to provide pilot studies and maps, which federal agencies would then follow with much larger funding than the foundations could provide. This interpretation has not met with unanimous agreement, as some expert analysts have expressed reasonable doubt that the philanthropic foundations have been as creative and innovative as has been proclaimed.

Another enduring question is that of accountability for foundations that purport to represent voluntary action and private institutions for the public good. The dilemma is that such claims are difficult to test, especially since many foundation initiatives' primary goals have been accompanied by secondary, unexpected consequences. Foremost in this contemporary reconsideration is the imbalance in accountability. A foundation most likely has built in demanding tests of compliance with those organizations or researchers who receive their grants. However, in stark contrast to this internal scrutiny, one is hard pressed to find overriding evaluation of the foundations themselves. The autonomy afforded to philanthropic foundations is generous. Their boards and officers have great latitude in the projects they choose to pursue and the recipients they select for grant funding. In short, the Trusts enjoy trust from the public and from federal and state governments.

In sum, the foundations are generous and set out to do good works—and their records of efficiency and effectiveness remain more a matter of public trust than demonstrated achievement. Some of this stems from foundations' tendency to state their missions in broad, altruistic goals. So, they receive high marks for intent. However, if a foundation makes a claim such as "achieving access to higher education" or "improving the quality of life," such lofty goals probably provide a temporary reprieve from critical analysis. Who could be opposed to such ventures? Eventually, though, the corollary question surfaces, "Who could accomplish this—and how would we know?" They are both difficult to measure and difficult to achieve. Where does one find external scrutiny and peer review of foundation decisions comparable to the evaluation which foundation officials demand of their grant recipients? Are such essential concepts of "efficiency" and "effectiveness" applied to the overall work of a foundation, not just its component programs? Has any foundation truly achieved a stated goal such as widespread improvement of the quality of life? In trying to do so, how *efficient* are foundations in their use of dollars? A related but distinct question is how *effective* are they in achieving such goals, regardless of expense? Annual reports are a step in the right direction—but these often succumb to the superficial level of glossy brochures and public relations. Annual Internal Revenue Service reports now available on such internet resources as *Guidestar* have increased public accountability, yet even such reports are cursory and raise more questions than they answer about the operation of a foundation.

Foundation officials often bristle at any concerted demand for them to explain thoroughly their decisions and priorities. And, in the main, they have been allowed this relative autonomy and public trust. Apart from outright fraud, embezzlement, or mismanagement of funds, most foundations are free to operate so long as they answer satisfactorily to their boards of trustees and file accurate, annual IRS reports. It also is difficult for external analysts from such disciplines as sociology or history to gain access and full disclosure of foundation records and operations that would tell the story of both the achievements and dysfunctions of various foundation program strategies. And, even if such organizational research were possible, one has to ask, "To what end?" To push hard on external accountability probably would be mistaken as it would jeopardize the overall good works and contributions the legal and customary arrangements for philanthropic foundations have contributed to the quality and access of American higher education.

The net result of this external deference to foundations' actions and operations, whether in 1814 or 2014, is an American Dilemma. The United States persists as a nation that is optimistic, generous, and supportive—yet continually pays a price of disappointment or uncertainty as to whether its trust and support of philanthropy has led to accomplishing admirable goals of social justice and the difficult balance of equity and access in higher education combined with improving academic standards. In the twenty-first century we still struggle with the challenges raised by John W. Gardner who drew from his experience as a foundation president, a member of the presidential cabinet as secretary of Health, Education and Welfare, and also as a co-founder of the national organization, *Independent Sector*. For Gardner, the primary question for American higher education and philanthropy was the question of excellence—namely, "Can we be equal and excellent too?[34]

Gardner's question persists as an appropriate challenge. A corollary is that one surprising revelation by foundation officials and academic leaders is that some problems are more predisposed to solutions—and, also, the solutions are more demonstrable than others. Medical research is attractive because funding the research and development to find the cure to a disease is both inherently important and it is explainable to the American public. One can announce, for example, the discovery of a vaccine that prevents polio. And, in terms of impact, one can administer and then count vaccinations, followed by monitoring declines in the occurrence of a disease. Health programs involving research and development may be expensive yet they have a reasonable chance of being ultimately possible—and then provable or at least amenable to compilations. In contrast, the ambiguities of a societal goal such as changing attitudes, beliefs, and cultural norms about schooling and going to college are deceptively elusive and subject to unexpected consequences. They provide the reminder that the allegedly "soft" social sciences deal with "hard" problems to ascertain and then to solve. As such, in the United States colleges and universities persist in partnership with philanthropic foundations in these admirable albeit complex, elusive quests.

4

Endowments: Colleges and the Stewardship of Good Fortune

Perpetual endowments are the hallmark and lifeblood of colleges and universities in the United States.[1] In a survey of more than 800 institutions for the 2012 fiscal year, 231 reported an endowment surpassing $250 million. At the high end this included Harvard University at $30.4 billion, Yale $19.3 billion, the University of Texas System $18.2 billion, Stanford $17 billion, and Princeton $16.9 billion. There was a severe drop-off to the next cluster that rounded out the top ten in rankings: Massachusetts Institute of Technology, $10.1 billion; University of Michigan $7.7 billion, Columbia University $7.6 billion, Texas A&M System $7.6 billion, and Northwestern $7.1 billion.[2]

One caveat is that a focus on gross endowment may tend unwittingly to give an advantage to institutions with large enrollments. So, a good companion litmus is to provide a snapshot of those colleges and universities with highest endowments per student. By this measure, one finds some reshuffling in rankings among the top independent colleges and universities—yet all remain within the top tier. State university systems with large endowments and large enrollments tend to fall out of the top tier of per capita rankings. Conversely, a significant lens is that the per capita measure brings into focus some small coeducational liberal arts colleges and some women's colleges as members of the top 10 to 15 institutions. Princeton's per capita student endowment of $2,233,000 places it first by a substantial measure. It is followed by Yale at $1,649,000 per student, Harvard at $1,449,000 per student, Stanford $1,073,000, MIT $932,000, Swarthmore $918,000, Amherst $903,000, Williams $854,000, Grinnell $817,000, Wellesley $656,000, and Washington and Lee

at $568,000. Perhaps the most significant implication of the endow-
ment rankings, whether by gross or per capita reports, is the missing
institutions as one proceeds down the list. The drop-off in per capita
endowment is swift and steep even among academically prestigious
institutions that are able to charge high tuition. Institutional development and fund-raising offices stand out dramatically due to their
potential to provide a college with a margin of difference in the ability
to plan and support educational initiatives. The constructs generated
by endowment data reinforce the financial fact of life that colleges
and universities with modest or low endowments rely disproportion-
ately on year-by-year revenues from student tuition and fees. Hence,
they tend to forfeit the discretionary resources that provide enduring
sources of institutional confidence and innovation.

Today the customary definition of "sound practice" in manag-
ing an academic endowment is that to spend more than the annual
accrued interest is to be a poor steward of resources since, after all,
universities are intended to educate and exist forever. And most often,
this has been operationalized to mean limiting annual draws from
endowment to less than 5 percent even when interest rates surpassed
that figure. But this conventional wisdom and standard practice are
not the whole story. As John D. Rockefeller—one of the legendary
donors to higher education a century ago—told his advisors why he
was reluctant to set up a perpetual endowment for an educational
project, "Forever is a long, long time."[3]

And, due to the visibility of congressional hearings over the past
four years in which university leaders were questioned about their
policies of relatively little spending from endowments that had enjoyed
several years of double digit percentage growth, one now finds serious consideration of proposed legislation intended to alter this customary behavior of academic institutions' endowment management.[4]
For example, in 2006 universities with an endowment of more than
one billion dollars had reported a one-year percentage return of
15 percent and a ten-year return of more than 11 percent.[5] The gist
of the congressional discussions was to draft legislation that would
require colleges and universities to spend substantially at an accelerated rate from endowments, rather than think only in terms of a minimal annual payout. This realignment leads to a distinct yet related
reconsideration of the assumption that perpetuity of endowments was
universally both desirable and obligatory.

This theme in the Congressional panel discussions brings to the surface a potential change that prompts reconsideration of the historical

customs and statutes of charitable trusts and academic endowments that have been dominant for over four centuries in American higher education. The foremost public policy question for this chapter is, "What would be the multiple consequences—pros and cons—of a state or national policy which made colleges and universities required to spend down their endowment at a fixed spending rate that was more than a minimal annual rate commensurate with the annual interest income? And, second, a policy which would require endowments to be spent down in a fixed period of time?" Finally, the related concern is, "Are there good reasons for donors to colleges and universities to opt *voluntarily* to increase spending and place time limits on gifts?"

Our approach is to review recent events that introduce questions of policy reconsiderations. This includes grounding our research in economics by reference to an influential theory on higher-education spending—namely, Howard Bowen's "revenue theory of costs."[6] Second, this study will explore endowment policies by drawing at the start from a detailed case study of an important institution—Harvard University. Harvard University, of course, is not a typical college or university. It is the largest, oldest and wealthiest academic institution in the nation. As such, it is significant because it is prestigious, powerful, and by extension, an influential model that other institutions often attempt to emulate—and is one that attracts public and legislative attention. The magnetism of historic, wealthy institutions as a base from which to start the study of endowments as a significant case has precedent, as suggested by Henry Hansmann's 1990 article on the general topic, "Why Do Universities Have Endowments?," whose detailed financial analyses were drawn largely from detailed records of Yale University—an institution comparable to Harvard in that it is old, prestigious, and wealthy.[7] Furthermore, a half century ago sociologist David Riesman's *Constraint and Variety in American Education* used the example of Harvard to depict the academic procession with the metaphor of the head of a snake, whose actions and decisions are eventually albeit belatedly followed by the tail of other ambitious institutions.[8] Most recently this phenomenon of imitating the universities that are rich and famous has been presented in sociologist Gaye Tuchman's analysis of the corporate character of the American campus, *Wanna Be U.*[9]

Large endowments are, for example, not the exclusive domain of independent (private) academic institutions. In 2006, for example, three state universities—namely, the University of Texas, the University of California, and Texas A&M—were listed as having endowments that place them in the top ten of all colleges and universities. Indeed, fund-raising with an eye toward building an endowment has become a widespread goal if not achievement across the landscape of American higher education, as 230 institutions had an endowment of more than $200 million in 2006. Within this group, 62 colleges and universities had an endowment of more than one billion dollars.[10] And, as noted in the summary of college endowments in 2012 presented at the start of this chapter, the imperative for all colleges to raise private money and to try to build a strong endowment has increased, despite disastrous years for the stock market, philanthropy, and fund-raising between 2008 and 2010.

A third feature of this exploration is to analyze the recent debates by exhuming and examining the influential works and policies associated with the French economist of the late eighteenth century, A. J. Turgot, with deliberate attention to those writers, donors, reformers, and government officials in the United States who were influential in shaping the essential policies and practices of endowments. Our analysis draws from events within the period circa 1900 to 1930: namely, during the formative period of the great foundations, what were the deliberations in terms of federal tax law? How did incentives or deterrents for endowments fit into the essential discussions? Were concerns raised about perpetual endowments—even if they did not prevail in ultimate decisions? Have they resurfaced periodically at crucial junctures when, for example, there were congressional reforms of the tax code with implications for philanthropy?[11]

How American Colleges and Universities Behave: An Economic Theory

Any discussion of endowments is closely tied to the patterns of getting and spending exhibited by a college or university. One of the most influential explanations of this organizational behavior was provided by Howard Bowen, an economist who also had been president of the University of Iowa and Grinnell College, in his 1980 book, *The Costs of Higher Education*. According to Bowen's "revenue theory" of higher education costs, colleges and universities in the United States were guided by five "natural laws," whose cumulative impact was to promote ever-increasing expenditures, namely due to the quest for excellence, prestige, and influence. His third and fourth laws can be combined and summarized as, "Colleges raise all they can—and spend all they raise."

One possible inference from this general observation might be that, therefore, colleges and universities' spendthrift inclinations extend to endowments—leading to continual pressures to draw from endowments to meet immediate expenses, whether it be to balance a budget in lean times or to pursue new, ambitious projects in times of optimism and growth. The ostensible danger of such practices would be that a president and board of trustees could be selfish or myopic by exhausting the endowment during their own tenure, leaving the institution at risk for future generations. But has this happened? In fact, a close reading of Bowen's book indicates that in the United States, endowment practices represent a significant exception to the rule of raising all the money one can and then spending all that one raises. As Bowen noted, "An exception to this is the endowments that are raised where the endowment principal is not spent, but the annual income is."[12]

If endowment management has been the fiscally constrained exception to the general rule of increased spending by colleges and universities, what have been the consequences for institutional priorities and planning? Has the maintenance and growth of perpetual endowments tended to make colleges socially responsible in honoring their charters to benefit the public good? Has cautious endowment spending fostered responsible decisions in colleges and universities over all? Whereas Henry Hansmann asked, "Why do universities have endowments?," a subsequent question is, "Why do colleges and universities ascribe to the principle that maintaining perpetual endowments with marginal annual spending from endowments is sound higher education policy?"

Controversies in Context

During the years 2005–2008 the national press along with those scholarly journals and specialized professional publications dealing with philanthropy and public policy gave considerable attention to the issue of placing limits requiring colleges and universities to spend their endowments at a substantial annual rate so as to provide an antidote to accumulating substantial institutional assets.[13] Focus was primarily on the practices at Harvard University and other visible, affluent institutions with substantial endowments. The bulk of the attention was visible and volatile, as it emphasized the role of government *regulation* and *requirements* in endowment spend down. Most conspicuous were the US Congressional hearings chaired by

Senator Charles E. Grassley (R) of Iowa between May and October 2007, which led some members of the Senate Finance Committee to consider possible legislation that would "tax certain elements of university endowments and put restrictions on the offshore hedge-fund investments that some endowments make."[14]

Less strident and more sanguine were committee deliberations leading to requests for numerous colleges and universities to file reports on their practices and track records. The question that emerged from the hearings was, "How long should gifts just grow?" The implication was that, "Trillions of tax-free dollars earning double-digit returns are inciting calls to speed up spending."[15] The issue was contentious throughout American higher education (and its related foundations of the nonprofit sector) because it brought into question an essential, historic and defining feature of responsible foundation stewardship: the sanctity of perpetual endowments. Closely related to this concern was the objection by national higher education associations and lobbying groups to any measures that would allow government regulation on how an academic endowment is spent.[16] The arguments gained momentum, as within higher education representatives from institutions with small endowments emphasized that their conduct (and plight) was markedly different from the options and opportunities facing Harvard and a relatively few universities with large endowments.[17]

Most of this debate focused on accountability and potential changes in tax policies and requirements to prompt colleges and universities to increase substantially their percentage and amount of endowment spend down annually. Building from this, historical research adds another dimension. In contrast to congressional hearings and proposed *punitive* or *coercive* legislation, we consider the present and past proposition that academic institutions in their role as eleemosynary institutions (i.e., as legally chartered nonprofit charitable organizations) opt voluntarily to spend down endowments. And, by extension, for many cases, it includes consideration that boards and donors may wish to plan for deliberate dissolution of funds or foundations to coincide with a fixed, finite target date for addressing solutions to specific foundation programs and agenda items.

The groundswell of articles and reports dealing with limited life span and philanthropic endowments published from 2007 through 2009 were not isolated.[18] In fact, they are best depicted as the latest examples of a theme that tends to resurface periodically. For example, about a decade ago several articles brought attention to donors and foundations that had, indeed, committed to devoting their resources to specific projects to be completed in a set, relatively short period. Waldemar Nielsen, a highly respected scholar and analyst of the nonprofit sector, wrote specifically in 1996 about "The Pitfalls of Perpetuity."[19] In 1997 Julie Nicklin of the *Chronicle of Higher Education* wrote several lengthy articles that showcased foundations that were on schedule to spend down and close out, with special attention to note that the Markey Trust had given $500 million and was deliberately closing down.[20] In a similar vein, Nicklin brought attention to the case of the Whitaker Foundation's mandate to meet its appropriation goals and then go out of business. A few years later Diane Granat wrote about what was hailed as the "Give While You Live" phenomenon among donors.[21] Hence, the recent interest in the topic was in fact a resurrection of a persistent strand of planning in American philanthropy, not merely an example of spontaneous combustion sparked by the inordinate investment returns of the years 2003 to 2008. These relatively recent works and articles were the legacies of such classic works as Jesse Brundage Sears's 1922 pioneering study for the United States Commissioner of Education, *Philanthropy in the History of American Higher Education.*[22]

Exhibit A: The Case of Contemporary Harvard and Its Endowment

Near the end of his 1922 study, *Philanthropy in the History of American Higher Education*, Jesse B. Sears speculated that because of the funds then being given to colleges and universities for permanent endowments, there soon would come a day when those institutions would no longer need income from other sources.[23] To subject this projection to historical analysis, we opt to focus on an atypical institution that provides what might be termed a "best case scenario" for endowment growth: Harvard University.[24] Looking back, Sears's optimism seems quaintly naïve. While endowments continued to grow, no doubt exceeding Sears's wildest imaginings, there seems today to be an inverse relationship between the size of a college's endowment and the amount it charges students in tuition and fees, that is, the larger the size of the endowment, the greater the charges to students. An important historical reminder is that about a century ago some private universities—namely, Stanford and Rice—charged their students no tuition, relying on endowments to keep prices low and to keep the institution competitive with rival institutions, such as the public University of California, whose tradition of charging no tuition to in-state students extended for over a century.[25] At most historic institutions on the East Coast, annual tuition and fee charges between 1890 and 1910 were deliberately kept low, showing little change from a typical charge of $150 per year over two decades—a price that would be about $3,500 in 2010 when indexed for inflation.[26] The complication for contemporary policy deliberations is that the rationale and guidelines for endowment usage designed to keep tuition prices low as set forth by founders at Rice and Stanford in the late nineteenth and early twentieth centuries have tended to fade from higher education memory in the early twenty-first century.

One explanation for this institutional behavior comes from labor economist Ronald Ehrenberg in his 2000 book, *Tuition Rising: Why College Costs So Much*. According to Ehrenberg, the pursuit of prestige and excellence, especially in attracting talented students and faculty, is the paramount dynamic in driving the budget of an academically strong institution. To echo Howard Bowen's "revenue theory," a highly ranked university will spend to keep pace or go ahead of those benchmark institutions with which it competes for talent.[27] There was little incentive to reduce costs, especially when the guiding principle, as noted by economist Charles Clotfelter, is "Buying the Best"—the strategy he identified in 1996 as the crucial explanation for the escalation of costs at elite colleges and universities.[28] However, as Howard Bowen noted, since universities are constrained by custom and regulations to draw substantial resources from endowment funds, the need for fresh resources often comes from raising tuition and mandatory fees charged to students. In other words, escalation of the costs of a college education increasingly were met by raising the price—rather than drawing from endowment resources. Documentation of this sustained trend comes from year-by-year tracking of college tuition price, either through the consumer price index (CPI) or the Higher Education Price Index (HEPI), both of which indicate that college prices consistently have increased at an annual rate higher than general inflation since 1985. In 2010 the price for attending an academically selective residential campus as an undergraduate ranged from about $50,000 to $60,000 per academic year.

Even when Harvard's endowment hit its pre-recession peak of just under 37 billion dollars in 2008, the university gave no indication that it would ever consider eliminating charges to its students. Harvard was not alone, of course, in maintaining silence in response to a growing number of calls from various sectors of society for well-endowed colleges and universities to eliminate or at least reduce student charges. It was simply the most prominent and frequent target of those appeals since it had by far the largest endowment. The silence was rather deafening to a public increasingly frustrated by the rising cost of higher education, whose tuition charges have long outstripped increases in the consumer price index. Congress soon took notice, especially Sen. Charles Grassley, ranking Republican on the Senate Finance Committee. What offended Grassley most was the clear indication that Harvard was spending less than 5 percent of the value of its endowment each year (known as its "spend" or "payout" rate). He was keenly aware that since 1969, America's foundations have been required by law to spend a minimum of 5 percent (actually, it was originally 6 percent, but the amount was later reduced to 5 percent) of the value of their endowments annually. Grassley protested that if American colleges and universities did not want their endowments to come under similar federal mandates, they had better start acting as if they were more mindful that those funds had received privileged tax treatment because of their charitable nature.[29] In response, Harvard and a handful of other wealthy institutions quickly announced plans to eliminate student loans from their financial aid awards. While this was not quite the response that many had hoped for, it was enough at the time to forestall further action; then, along came the Great Recession and the issue became moot for the time being.

The privileged tax treatment that college and university endowment funds receive is twofold.[30] In the first place, donors who made the original gifts (assuming they were made since 1917) received a charitable deduction from their income taxes for those contributions. (In many instances, the favorable treatment was threefold because the income tax deduction for gifts of appreciated securities and other assets is calculated at their current fair market value, not their cost basis.) Then, because colleges and universities are tax-exempt, the income from their investment of those funds is free of taxation. This means that a university, such as Harvard, when it was spending less than 5 percent of the value of its endowment annually, was simply putting more money back into investments in order to grow its endowment at a faster rate. What was wrong with this scenario was that the favorable tax treatment given to charitable contributions was based on the historic understanding that these funds were to provide a *public benefit*.

Historically colleges fulfilled this obligation by providing an affordable education, often to students who were financially needy. This would be accomplished either by keeping the price of college low and/or by awarding ample financial aid to applicants. Our emphasis is that, in fact and fairness, the public derives little or no discernible benefit from the accumulation of charitable funds. Colleges and universities may have increased their prestige as a result of having larger endowments, but the public has received no benefit from the accrued bragging rights of higher education institutions in which endowment figures have become a construct or proxy to suggest a measure of institutional strength.

College and university administrators did not readily admit that at least part of the motivation to increase the size of their institution's endowment was based on the desire to enhance its prestige. Instead, they explained that they need to grow the size of their endowments aggressively in up markets so that they will have a greater cushion when the next inevitable economic downturn occurs. The most recent recession would appear to be a good case in point for this argument except for the fact that those funds received favorable tax treatment because they provide a public benefit *now*, not just in the future. Many arguments about making sure that we do not sell the future short by failing to maintain the current purchasing power of the endowment seem to suggest that there is no good reason to believe that the economy will grow in the future as it has in the past, nor that gifts will continue to be forthcoming in the future as they have been in the past. In fact, there is good reason to believe that both economic growth and charitable giving will continue in the future. In light of the steep increases in tuition and fees over the past decade, there is a compelling argument for maintaining that today's gifts should take care of today's needs and future gifts should take care of future needs. Moreover, looking at this issue from the perspective of mission, one might question whether it is better to return a dollar to the endowment so that it will be available for future spending rather than invest that dollar in today's student.[31]

Although Harvard and other prestigious colleges and universities were unwilling to consider using endowment earnings to eliminate or lower tuition charges, the university's records indicated that university leaders were willing to engage in risky investment behavior in an effort to ensure continued high growth rates. When the recession hit, Harvard's endowment quickly lost more than 10 billion dollars—27 percent of its value. This steep loss has been blamed on equally steep allocations of the investment pool to what are known as alternative assets, which are more speculative and harder to value.

If arguments for spending at least as much of a university's endowment as is required of a foundation appear overly theoretical, consider the possibility that any university with an endowment payout rate of less than 5 percent really does not need a larger endowment—or an endowment as large as the one it already has. Clearly, a spend rate of at least 5 percent would mean that more money could be awarded to needy students or applied to academic programs. Many—if not most—colleges and universities with smaller endowments are of necessity having to spend 5 percent or more of their endowment's value annually just to meet their obligations. Moreover, there is reason to believe that huge endowments encourage inefficiency and waste. Before the onset of the Great Recession, one faculty member at a well-endowed Midwestern liberal arts college told a *Chronicle of Higher Education* reporter that he believed it was not a good thing for endowment earnings to provide more than 40 percent of an institution's annual operating budget. He had seen the poor decision making that results from access to too much easy money: mediocre ideas get funded because it is easier to give in than to say no, and since the funds are available, why not?[32]

Also, the record of spending in big-time varsity athletics, has demonstrated that easy money in large quantities encourages waste. Detailed economic analyses from such independent commissions as the Knight Foundation, for example, indicated that by 2009 university-increased spending on intercollegiate athletics had for years surpassed percentage increases in institutional spending for educational programs—a phenomenon that led university presidents to acknowledge that they as institutional officers had little or no control over this syndrome.[33] For data to support this concern one need only look at the salaries of football coaches of big-time programs, whose compensation in 2010 surpasses on the average more than one million dollars per year. At the same time, salaries of presidents at some of the best-endowed colleges and universities along with the number of high level administrative positions have increased at a far greater rate than the number of and salaries for tenure track professors.[34] During the same period the amount of money that has been devoted to expanded staff at some of those colleges continues to surpass percentage increases for instruction and educational programs.[35] It also is illustrated by spending on elaborate campus amenities to attract affluent applicants.[36] These concessions to student consumerism tended not to be paid by increased spending from endowments—but rather, by raising the price of tuition and fees paid by students—a strategy that transfers disproportionate burden of costs on to students from modest income families.

The reliance of American colleges and universities, both independent and state-supported institutions, on ongoing charitable contributions from the public is a good thing. This dependency has created bonds between those institutions and their constituencies. It has also called forth higher levels of accountability and transparency in American higher education. Adequate endowment funding to meet legitimate needs is a good thing. As Henry Hansmann of Yale Law School concluded in 1990, too much money in the hands of nonprofit leaders presented a great a temptation to use it unwisely—potentially harming America's philanthropic tradition and causing public skepticism about all of higher education.[37]

Rediscovering the French Connection

To induct the significance of recent events and the case study of contemporary Harvard University to general, enduring policy deliberations, it is useful to reconstruct and analyze important historical precedents for national public policies *requiring* foundation spend down. To paraphrase the language of early economists, we want to identify significant historic episodes in which government officials sought to bring to life the so-called dead hand of permanent endowments. If one aim of historical policy analysis is to reduce the myopia of contemporary deliberations on this issue of practices in colleges and universities in the United States, then this is done by bringing attention to some overlooked strands in national policies and laws implemented earlier and elsewhere. The base from which we start is the work of economist and government official A. J. Turgot in late eighteenth century France.[38] Not only was Turgot influential throughout Europe and the American colonies as an economist, he also was effective in shaping some crucial regulations for France's economic policies for several years. Central to his writings and policies was prohibition of perpetual endowments for foundations because they drained both the national economy and the vitality of the foundation leaders. Although influential two centuries ago, this legacy has been often forgotten or neglected recently in the United States. To fill in these gaps we propose to track down and critically analyze policy analysts and policy makers who followed Turgot, especially in the nineteenth century and over the next two centuries and who, from time to time, brought variations of his work into economic and legislative planning.

The research problem is that American legal and social institutions overwhelmingly bear the influence of Anglo-Saxon precedents. To explore some alternative policies in addition to customary reliance on Anglo-Saxon legal precedents, it is illuminating to look to France for potential models. One particularly interesting example is the context of Turgot's economic theory and policies in eighteenth-century France. The problem was that although the monarchy was committed to modernization and industrialization as part of concerted economic planning and growth, all this was stymied by the lack of fluid capital. Turgot analyzed incomes and expenditures within France and concluded that churches held a disproportionate amount of wealth, whether in currency or real estate, in the form of endowments. Nothing moved. Hence, Turgot's response was to rail against the "dead hand" of endowments. His antidote for the gridlocked nationwide economy was to put a term limit of five years on all endowments. It was the eighteenth-century equivalent of "use it or lose it." And, as a national policy it was effective in energizing the economy.[39]

In contrast to Turgot in France, in England neither the Crown nor Parliament considered enacting comparable measures. Consider the case of Henry VIII and his contentious battles with the Church— what we know as the Roman Catholic Church. A standard interpretation is that Henry VIII broke from Rome over papal objections to his annulled marriages in his literally unfertile attempts to sire a legitimate male heir. But what is overlooked is that whatever problems Henry VIII had with his wife—or, rather, wives—he had equally strong and perhaps even more monarchal headaches with England's lethargic economy. One of his bold moves was to seize all church and monastic lands.[40] The rationale was that they represented holdings of wealth that were inordinate—and largely inactive in terms of national economic activity—and also exempt from taxation. It came dangerously close to hoarding. Had Henry VIII's financial advisors thought along the lines of Turgot in France, Henry probably could have avoided much of the strife over religion and the church—and might have reduced problems in England's domestic economy that persisted into the nineteenth century.

France under Turgot in the eighteenth century avoided a great deal of this economic misery that persisted for the English monarchy. In contrast to France, it would continue to drain England. A pivotal character and policy in American colonial history was George Grenville and his imperial economic plan, first as Treasurer of the Royal Navy and then as England's Prime Minister, who came to be known as the "Boy Wonder" of finance. He endorsed: an aggressive imperialism in which high taxes on goods in the colonies, including America, bailed out the Mother Country. The infamous Stamp Act was the most conspicuous attempt—and, one that most taxed the patience as well as pocketbooks of American colonists. Nowhere was the convergence of Great Britain's quest for revenues from its colonies more consequential for American higher education than in the case of the chartering of The College of William & Mary in Virginia in 1692. When a delegation from Virginia petitioned the Crown for a royal charter and financial support for a proposed college that would educate future civil leaders and provide Christian education that promoted salvation, the initial response was bleak. The Crown's Attorney General, preoccupied with budget problems, had little interest in diverting royal monies to educational and charitable endeavors, especially in the colonies. He curtly replied to the Virginia petitioners, "Souls! Damn your souls! Raise tobacco!"[41] Fortunately for the development and funding of higher education in the New World, Queen Mary interceded to convince her husband, King William, that granting a royal charter for the college in Virginia was a worthy deed. All parties went away happy, as the Virginians returned home with a precious royal charter for the new college, along with generous subsidies from excise taxes—making it the wealthiest of the eight original colonial colleges. The Crown in turn gained a supply of colonial revenues, as Virginia tobacco became one of its most enduring, bountiful sources of sales and taxation revenues. The limit to this story, however, is that it was exceptional; that is, it was one of the few ventures of the English Crown into chartering and funding colleges throughout its colonial empire.

This legacy was consequential for colleges and universities, whether in colonial America or during the period of the new United States. First, it meant in part that England's reliance on imperialism rather than limiting endowments within its borders continued England's financial problems. Its international political significance was that the emphasis on severe colonial taxation was a pivotal development that led to the American colonies' revolt—and eventually creation of the new United States. A secondary corollary was that it ended up being decisive in shaping the legal environment of higher education in the young United States, where colleges received a charter but little guaranteed recurring annual financial appropriations from their state legislatures. It represented a marked reversal of the Crown's historic policies toward the ancient English universities of Oxford and Cambridge in which receipt of a royal charter included a pledge of continuing generous royal financial support. In contrast, in the United States each college had to scramble to make ends meet each year through a combination of donations, bequests, and tuition payments. There was no national ministry of education comparable to the Crown, as charters were the purview of each state. Such was the situation that eventually gave rise to a pivotal confrontation over control of colleges—the 1819 Dartmouth College case. According to the legendary account of the trial, in the closing argument Dartmouth alumnus and attorney Daniel Webster, tearfully pleaded to Chief Justice John Marshall and the Supreme Court, "It is, sir, but a small college...But there are those who love it."[42] One of many consequences of this case and its favorable decision for Dartmouth College was to reinforce and define what are called *eleemosynary* institutions in American life. These are charitable entities that, by dint of their chartered mission, gain privileges and exemptions so that they can do their good works.

Colleges and universities have gained immensely from being included in this category—which at the time included such private voluntary associations creating orphanages, work farms, libraries, schools for the blind, and other charities. The other side of the compact was that such a privileged organization was required implicitly and explicitly to demonstrate its fidelity to its chartered, special purpose. And, it was expected to record and document its sound stewardship of resources—with special attention to truly spending monies for the right reasons on the right activities and constituencies. Colleges had complex identities under this rubric. They were recipients of philanthropy; and, at the same time, they often were also expected as part of their charter to act as *dispensers* of philanthropy—primarily through the requirement that they provide financial aid for needy students. In other words, creating these tax-exempt privileged institutions as charitable foundations meant that it was blessed to give *and to receive*. What has happened over time is a tendency, whether by accident or design, for colleges to emphasize for themselves the role of being an object of and recipient of, philanthropy. But, look again at the other side of the equation: their responsibility to distribute (i.e., spend) for educational and philanthropic purposes was integral to the deal. In other words, colleges and universities' perpetual endowments in the United States had the potential to be a microcosm variation of the dormant wealth represented by church endowments of eighteenth-century France.

An Implication and Application: Colleges and the Frustration of Restricted Scholarship Endowments

One example of the dysfunction of the historic restrictions on spending is to consider, for example, that within virtually every college and university in the United States, there is a place where the sanctity of perpetual endowments provides an annual nuisance, if not a source of frustration. Here the objects of analyses are the numerous endowed student-scholarship funds that carry with them the particular conditions and terms of the benefactors. As Michelle York reported in the *New York Times* in 2005, "Every year, millions in scholarships and financial aid are awarded at more than 4,200 colleges and universities. But other scholarships amounting to perhaps several million dollars more are tied up in endowments that have rules so obscure and restrictive that they are rarely tapped—even as the costs of higher education soars."[43] Illustrative of this syndrome is a scholarship fund restricted to the sons and daughters of Spanish-American War veterans. This might have made sense in 1910. What a difference a century makes! If a Director of Financial Aid actually did receive a student application to receive such a scholarship today, the only logical response would be to be incredulous and skeptical—mainly because such an applicant probably would be at least one hundred and twenty years old. This is an extreme case, but illustrates the serious point that the conditions placed on the perpetual scholarship endowment had eventually rendered it useless. Worst of all, it was dysfunctional because the scholarship monies were tied up and could no longer be awarded to needy students. A more recent, documented example comes from the University of California, San Diego where the Malcolm R. Stacey Memorial Scholarship is restricted to "Jewish orphans interested in pursuing a graduate degree in aeronautical engineering." After ten years without attracting qualified applicants the scholarship endowment had grown to $400,000.[44] The irony is that this inutility raises the prestige of the university by keeping both endowment and interest intact while at the same time decreases the role of the university in providing worthy financial aid to needy students.

There are other variations on the theme of scholarship endowment stagnation when requirements include arcane conditions of geography, field of study, or other nonmeritocratic features. College and university officers do have a ready potential solution to break the legal stranglehold of perpetual scholarship endowments—the doctrine of *cy pres*. According to this principle (translated as "so near…"), if a college can demonstrate to the courts that it has made good faith effort to abide by the terms of the restricted scholarship, followed by reasonable attempts to get in touch with heirs of the original donor, to change the restrictions, the court can grant a petition allowing redefinition of the trust terms. Having done so, the college may bundle such dormant scholarship endowments and request that the court henceforth allow the college to administer the scholarships in a sound, reasonable manner. The doctrine of *cy pres* gives the legal instrument to alter the perpetuity feature of the "dead hand" of endowments. Unfortunately, many colleges today do not pursue such remedy. According to Henry Hansmann's 1990 article, "Why Do Universities Have Endowments?," the utility of the *cy pres* solution often has been ignored by college and university trustees.[45] A more recent analysis by Theodore H. Frank in 2008 noted that *cy pres* settlements often were problematic.[46] For assorted reasons, these kinds of cases indicate that perpetual endowments can be counter-productive to the general aim of providing charitable resources and student financial aid because the burden and nuisance of having college legal staff pursue remedies has tended to create an inertia that allows the dysfunction to persist.

Decentralization and Endowments: Foundations and Associations within the University

Most comparisons and compilations treat a given college or university as a single entity, especially when it comes to estimating the size and relative rank of endowments. However, in recent years there is good reason to supplement this portrayal by disaggregating a college or university into its components. This may represent the influence of the historic adage on getting and spending that often is invoked as Harvard's dictum, "every tub on its own bottom." We are, of course, familiar with the discrete units of academic organizations—schools, colleges, and departments. And, certainly since about 1980 each dean, whether it be the College of Business, Agriculture, Arts and Sciences, or Engineering, devotes substantial time to fund-raising, probably has a sophisticated, expensive development staff, and operates its own arrangement of special funds or endowments. The result is that now many universities adhere, at least in principle, to a goal of decentralized funding. In practice, decentralization usually is combined with allowance for cross-subsidies in which, at the discretion of the president or provost, some funds can be transferred to shore up units that are operating in the red. In general, however, deans and vice presidents are urged to be self-supporting. The most recent example of the implementation of this principle is in the managerial policy known as "RCM"—an abbreviation for "Responsibility Centered Management." Under this arrangement, a provost monitors each constituent unit to see whether it is a net-giver or net-taker in terms of university general funds.

Encouragement of this kind of decentralized arrangement has grown to new levels and complications due to the increasing popularity of a new unit—the academic "center" or "institute." Furthermore, many universities have added within their overall structure numerous privately incorporated associations or foundations—for example, the University Research Foundation, the State University Athletic Association, or a University Research Park. Furthermore, each college or program has its own "Friends of the…" arrangement, usually incorporated as a tax-exempt nonprofit organization. Add to this the distinct entities of dedicated scholarship funds—each with its own endowment, conditions, and restrictions. The appeal of multifaceted programs and fund-raising entities may be likened to crabgrass—they sprout across the campus landscape. And, each center or unit is a hardy perennial that is difficult, if not impossible, to eliminate even when it fails to be self-supporting.

This arrangement may work well in an extended period of financial growth. It is a form of internal patronage and accommodation that is tempting for a provost or president to approve. However, today it has become problematic. Consider, for example, a 2009 report by the Education Advisory Board's University Leadership Council, titled *Competing in the Era of Big Bets: Achieving Scale in Multidisciplinary Research*.[47] Its strong message is that the proliferation of these numerous sub-units has become counterproductive. They are expensive to run; they are difficult to monitor; and often end up obligating a university to enduring, perhaps permanent, subsidies. One defense of this practice is that many university-based research institutes and centers are funded by sponsored research grants, often from federal agencies. According to this explanation, when external grant funding runs out, a research institute is closed. However, this strict discipline is not always followed. Furthermore, many research and development units are funded in part by endowments and private gifts, especially at their founding—as indicated by the numerous research units and centers "named" in honor of a philanthropist or donor. Center directors may intend eventually to land externally-sponsored research grants—but that is an aspiration that tends to come after start-up operations.

This kind of intra-institutional activity is a prime area where at least consideration of term limits on the life span of an endowment would make good sense both in terms of effective contributions to scholarship and service—and to sound stewardship of institutional resources and governance. Why should a research center for a particular topic or project be presumed to exist forever? Might it not make more sense to establish a reasonable life span and focus resources—rather than string them out indefinitely?

The Timeliness of Endowment Research and Reconsideration

The dramatic vacillations in the financial health of colleges and universities during the first decade of the twenty-first century suggest the need for careful reconsideration of customary practices and prohibitions put into place centuries ago to promote the well-being of academic institutions. A few years ago—in 2008—many universities and their related foundations and not-for-profit institutions enjoyed high percentage annual returns on their endowments. For those institutions that had hired experienced hedge fund managers with an enterprising bent, the returns over four or five years had been generous—sometimes as high as 10 to 20 percent per year. This was an "embarrassment of riches" in which the quickly increased resources led soon thereafter to questions internally and externally about a given foundation's rate of and calendar for distribution to central services and programs. Problems of policy and practice were in the main regarded as the problems of prosperity—that is, making good decisions in an era of abundance. If a foundation board and executive director were to have a headache, this would be the complex yet delightful problem to have.

Suddenly and, in many cases, unexpectedly, declines in the stock market around July 2008 changed the atmosphere and environment of both foundation analysis and foundation behavior. A prosperous foundation in, for example, 2006, whose board worried that an annual spend-out of more than 5 percent per annum might be perceived as risky stewardship now had to deal with the news that with or without increased endowment expenditures, by 2009, endowments had plummeted as much as 25 to 33 percent in less than a year. Furthermore, the unpredictability of stock portfolios for nonprofit organizations were exacerbated by the real and symbolic shocks that surfaced in December 2008 with revelations of the fraudulent promises and practices of Bernard Madoff. The consequences of the bogus investment schemes had disproportionate impact on numerous donors and recipient educational and charitable foundations and represented the second of a double whammy on the customary generosity of nonprofit organizations in the United States. As Diana B. Henriques outlined in painful detail in the *New York Times*, one crippling effect of the Madoff scheme was that it "kept rippling outward, across borders."[48] Colleges and universities were particularly at risk. It meant substantial loss of resources for program support plus the crisis of confidence that diffused beyond the literal financial losses. The fluctuations between 2007 and 2009 reinforced the need for universities and donors to think critically about trajectories of time and money in fulfilling college and university goals.

Most likely, many established colleges and universities will resist any attempts to be subjected either to government requirements or even suggestions of voluntary decisions to behave as a provider as well as a recipient of philanthropic largesse. Furthermore, colleges and universities that are energetic and effective in acquiring private donations that build the institutional endowment will nonetheless still claim that a large endowment provides little relief in meeting year-to-year expenses. One finds in 1994, for example, that a development officer for the University of Pennsylvania claimed that even though the university had just completed a successful billion dollar fund-raising campaign, the institution really was on a tight budget.[49] This explanation echoed and illustrated the primary theme of Howard Bowen's "revenue theory"—that is, regardless of how much resources come in to a university, the university will spend it—and probably claim the need for yet more funding. In a similar vein, even the wealthiest universities have sometimes relied on accounting tricks to project an image of chronic financial woe. In 1992, for example, Harvard's annual report taken at face value would have led one to conclude that the cupboard was bare. This was not necessarily the case, however, according to one financial analyst who pointed out the peculiar message Harvard's reports were broadcasting to the public. Despite a multibillion dollar endowment, its annual operating budget was reported as $42 million in the red. One reason for this profile was the university's use of "fund accounting" reports, leading to the expert interpretation that Harvard was "managing its bottom line in such a way as to appear poorer than it really is. The university is in the midst of a plan to reportedly raise $2.5 billion on top of what is already the world's largest private endowment. Harvard is a bit like the rich man who wears scuffed shoes and a frayed collar when he visits his doctor."[50] Perhaps a keen stethoscope of institutional and policy analysis will allow higher education analysts to be alert to what constitutes genuinely healthy conduct by generously endowed universities of the United States.

If this institutional conduct were not sufficiently suspect to give pause to major university's depiction of—and approach to—their use of resources, including endowment wealth, events of the past decade have suggested what truly is a world turned upside down. Or, stated another way, it has been a strange world in which university values about stewardship have been inverted so as to be wrong-headed. A decade ago Yale's chief investment officer, David Swensen, wrote the influential book, *Pioneering Portfolio Management*—with the interesting subtitle, *An Unconventional Approach to Institutional Investment.*[51] According to Andrew Delbanco's essay review in *The New York Review of Books*, Swensen's principal case to his professional academic investment managers was that he had discovered no less than the formula to assure university endowments high yields with low risks.[52] Indeed, this worked—for awhile. Perusing the annual editions of the *Chronicle of Higher Education's* special Almanac year-by-year over the past decade, one does indeed find a three- or four-year run in the middle of the decade where numerous universities reported annual endowment growth of 10 percent, 15 percent, and even 20 percent. But when one looks closely at subsequent trends, one finds that by 2008 and 2009 the double digit numbers are intact, except that by these years they had turned from gains to losses.

The irony of this historical analysis is that philanthropy and higher education, including the wise and sound stewardship of endowments, evidently has come to mean in the twenty-first century that it is imprudent for a university to spend 10 percent to 15 percent per year on academic improvement and enhancements to assure quality and affordability. Evidently, however, it was all right—or, at least, understandable and forgivable, for the same institution to lose 10 percent to 30 percent on its endowment through risky investment strategies. Are US universities off course in their gyroscope of values and priorities and goals when it is acceptable to lose a lot of the endowment due to greed and risk-taking investments, but off base and spendthrift when "investing" in the present and future by spending substantially more than the customary albeit arbitrary limit of 5 percent spend-down per year to solve problems and provide solutions to educational concerns? That is the devil's dilemma of endowments and philanthropy for American higher education in the twenty-first century.

Conclusion: Policy Reconsiderations for Higher Education as a Public Good

The larger and longer term question that surfaces from this historical analysis is the question of whether and how colleges and universities in the United States serve the public good. The numerous privileges that the federal and state governments have granted to academic institutions, including tax exemptions, originally were provided with the understanding that colleges and universities would attract and educate a succession of learned individuals who would serve civil society. Implicit and explicit in this compact was the condition that higher education would be accessible and affordable to talented yet financially needy youth.

The problem is that the cautious stewardship of institutional wealth in the form of perpetual endowments appears to be either indifferent or counter-productive in prompting colleges and universities to carry out this societal role. If this shortfall is sufficiently grievous, then historical analysis provides to present-day policy makers within institutions and in external governing bodies the justification to reconsider whether the presumption of permanent endowments and low endowment spending have ceased to demonstrate their efficacy in assisting colleges and universities to serve the public welfare. If not, the historic policy of perpetual endowments warrants review as prelude to drafting a thoughtful new deal.

The historical data on prices and costs of going to college over the past 30 years indicate that an institution that accumulates a large endowment does not necessarily increase its accessibility and affordability to prospective students. Nor does a large perpetual endowment provide any demonstrated safety net when a college or a university may face hard times. To the contrary, restrictions on spending give no reason to believe that any financial crisis would provide the necessary key to unlock legal restrictions on endowment spending that would dissipate the capital. In other words, the pledge of stewardship to provide safety for tomorrow is a false promise because "tomorrow" never comes. Perhaps most counter-productive is the recent tendency for a large endowment to become a symbolic indicator of institutional prestige, an indulgence whose unexpected consequence has been to impede investment in timely, needy educational services.

A proposal for reforming the "dead hand" of endowments would be for college and university boards and presidents to adopt voluntarily an increasingly diversified approach to fund-raising and, then, to the subsequent management of these private donations. Instead of presuming or insisting that a philanthropic gift be placed in a perpetual endowment, college officials would have to work with donors to reach a mutual agreement on a range of options that would best serve the institutional and public goals of higher education. Gifts for some projects may, indeed, best be placed in a perpetual trust. Other gifts, however, might be sought and then administered with realistic appraisals on solving a problem or providing a service in some finite period, whether it be five or ten or one hundred years.

The simultaneous self-reform for campus leaders would be to unlearn the presumption that to spend more than the accrued interest of an endowment is bad practice. It would also include reconsideration of the customary belief that to spend more than about 5 percent of an endowment in a single year is inappropriate. Institutional discipline and accountability would no longer be defined automatically in terms of preserving a gift forever. The new deal would be to invoke the discipline of thoughtfulness; that is, responsibility for scrutinizing each philanthropic gift in terms of its distinctive combination of time, money, and goal.

5

Government Relations and the Nonprofit Sector: Legislation and Policies in Philanthropy and Higher Education

Colleges and universities, along with the private foundations discussed in chapter 3, join with numerous other institutions including many art museums, libraries, performing arts groups, symphonies, research centers, social service agencies, and hospitals as members of what is called the *nonprofit sector*. It is a distinctively American phenomenon that is not readily found nor even understood in many other nations. This chapter deals with how government at the federal, state and local levels views this collective institutional category in terms of rights, responsibilities, and regulations. And, by extension, it includes how business corporations as leaders in the national economy and as patrons of educational and charitable activities, interact with the government and with the nonprofit sector.[1]

One of the formal concepts that characterize the nonprofit sector is the so-called 501(c)(3) status conferred by the Internal Revenue Service to qualifying organizations. Within this group there are two categories—first, organizations that are "public charities" and, second, those that are "private foundations." Taking stock in 2014 some of the defining benefits associated with 501(c)(3) organizational status are as follows: exemption from federal income tax; exemption from state and local property taxes; eligibility of donors to declare a tax deduction for their donations. The three primary questions covered in this chapter are as follows: First is the historical question, "How did this status and sector evolve?" Second, "What are the exceptions and details associated with this?" And, finally, "What are the prospects for continuity and change in the benefits and obligations of the non-profit sector in the future?"

For those who work in colleges and universities the understandable tendency is to see the campus as the center of the organizational universe. But in the United States the larger picture is that colleges and universities coexist with numerous other educational and service institutions. This has deep historical roots, namely the fundamentally American belief that individuals had the *right* to assemble and create *voluntary associations* based on some mutual interest. It also includes formalizing the rights and protections of associations that had formal status as *corporations*. This latter achievement was confirmed in the 1819 *Dartmouth College* v. *Woodward* case heard by Chief Justice John Marshall and the Supreme Court. The key term invoked by attorney Daniel Webster representing Dartmouth College was *eleemosynary*.[2] It refers to a private charitable institution chartered by the government. Its main feature was that it protected such institutions from arbitrary political interference or hostile takeovers in large part by recognizing the sanctity of an institutional charter. It did *not* provide exemption from federal income taxes for the obvious albeit often overlooked reason that there were no federal income taxes levied at that time—and there would not be any for another century. Yes, the *eleemosynary* category included colleges—but not exclusively so. Colleges were folded into the flock of numerous charitable organizations. Since this landmark decision, how these interdependent components interact in cooperation and competition with one another has been defined by evolving public policies at the federal, state, and local levels.

Historically the United States Congress has been reluctant to intrude into higher education affairs such as hiring, employment, academic freedom, promotion and tenure of faculty, admission of students, degree requirements, land use, or revenues.[3] What this means pragmatically and concisely is that government usually does not levy taxes and also tries to minimize regulations to which other organizations, especially business corporations, would be subject. It means also that colleges are given substantial autonomy in overseeing their internal affairs. In the late nineteenth century when Congress started to create national legislation such as the Sherman Anti-Trust Act and other measures to curb business monopolies, higher education institutions were explicitly and implicitly exempted. Later, in the half century from 1930 to 1980 when there was increasing federal legislation directed at companies and the commercial workplace, colleges and universities usually were given exemptions or extensions. For example, a college did not have to comply with working condition regulations that were mandated for factories. A college did not have to pay property taxes or payroll taxes even when it was a landowner or employer. After enactment of federal income taxes in 1917, academic institutions did not have to pay income taxes regardless of their revenues from various activities. When social security taxes were introduced in the 1930s they were mandatory for businesses as employers and for their employees, but not for colleges. The United States Supreme Court's 1954 decision in *Brown* v. *Board of Education* had immediate jurisdiction over local public school systems but was untested and unclear on its implication for racial desegregation in colleges and universities. Passage of Affirmative Action standards for businesses with federal contracts in the 1960s did not apply to colleges and universities. In the 1980s college and universities applied for and received reprieves and exceptions for compliance requirements associated with the Americans with Disabilities Act. In other words, there was a tradition in which colleges and universities were viewed by the federal government as privileged enterprises distinct from commercial corporations. And, this status usually saved colleges and universities a great deal of time and money so that they could devote primary attention to their central *educational* missions of teaching, research, and service.

What about the parallel policies and practices for higher education's companion institutions, the philanthropic foundations? As presented in chapter 4, between 1900 and 1920, private philanthropic foundations also were treated as special entities not subject to federal regulations that applied to business and industry. Unlike colleges and universities, however, the rights and benefits acquired by foundations usually were punctuated by periodic, recurrent public outrage because the source of the foundation wealth was indelibly linked to what was called "tainted money" of the Captains of Industry and massive business and corporate earnings. Public misgivings toward John D. Rockefeller and his company, Standard Oil Trust, were sufficiently strong that in 1910 the proposed Rockefeller Foundation was denied in its application to the United States Congress for a *national* charter.[4] This strong statement of populist reform was largely a symbolic act, as the Rockefeller Foundation was readily able to procure a state charter and then proceed with its national plans and projects. It did signal that the American public—and, some factions in Congress—had grave concerns about an arrangement that allowed wealthy business corporations to use their industrial profits to take on the guise of caring philanthropic institutions.

The large foundations, indeed, have faced periodic and recurrent congressional and public skepticism. Landmarks in the pattern of public resentment toward foundations took place in the1930s, then again in the early 1950s, and followed by conspicuous congressional investigations as part of the 1969 Tax Reform Act and its sequel legislation of 1985.[5] Such episodes of concern, although serious and warranted, were bumps in the road but not barricades to the legitimization of philanthropic foundations as favored institutions. The net result was that starting around 1910 this status *both* for colleges and foundations became increasingly valuable. They showed similarity and partnership in the Progressive Era when Congress followed the implorations of presidents Theodore Roosevelt and Woodrow Wilson to press for legislation such as income taxes and corporate taxes. The crucial codicil was that colleges and foundations were exempted from these taxes. Over time this led to the identification by the late twentieth century of a loose federation of educational and philanthropic institutions more or less familiar to us today as the nonprofit sector.

This arrangement in part reflects a national heritage of federal restraint. In other words, if an activity or enterprise was not explicitly mentioned in the United States Constitution, it was considered by default and design to be outside Congressional oversight, left to state or local governments and to the private domain. Although this scenario has endured in general, over time colleges and universities have gradually yet persistently come under increased purview of Congress and federal legislation—and, in some important cases, as the object of federal financial support.[6]

A record of voluntary cooperation and compliance with federal, state, and local agencies on the part of colleges and universities has been the American tradition of compromise. It is an approach that has allowed public affairs to avoid or at least reduce overexpansion of the federal government into civil society, especially in higher education. This arrangement was illustrated by Congressional reliance on regional accrediting associations rather than federal agencies to oversee the appropriate mission and operation of colleges and universities after World War II as a part of assuring public trust in the administration of new government programs. It was a mutually agreeable strategy evident in negotiations between the federal government and academic institutions in establishing conditions for distribution of federal student aid, ranging from the 1944 GI Bill to the 1972 Pell

Grants in the half century following World War II. This has been the tradition that led in 1952 to the National Collegiate Athletic Association (NCAA) rather than a federal agency to be named by the United States Congress to take responsibility for the collective conduct of intercollegiate sports programs.[7] Congress and, then, federal agencies usually have not intruded into university affairs until— or, unless—voluntary compacts and working relationships have broken down.

At times colleges, foundations, and business corporations intersected in public policies. An important innovation that surfaced between World War I and World War II was the federal government's favorable rulings on relations between private business and private colleges. This started around 1936 and gained momentum as an important addition to the philanthropy of higher education with sustained, systematic contributions from business corporations.[8] According to historians Merle Curti and Roderick Nash, the first step in this extended campaign was led by Frank Abrams, Corporate Executive for Standard Oil of New Jersey in 1948. He urged companies to make charitable contributions to private colleges and universities. Soon thereafter, however, Abrams's efforts were stalled when his company's legal counsel warned that the state's corporate charter forbade such contributions to higher education unless all stockholders approved. But this restriction was removed when the State of New Jersey amended its corporation law to "empower corporations chartered in the state to contribute, as public policy, to educational institutions." Elsewhere, other New Jersey corporate boards tested the restrictions. In one high stakes court case dealing with the constitutionality of corporate gifts to private colleges, the board of the A. P. Smith Company made a contribution to Princeton University—which was promptly blocked by stockholders who argued that the state amendment was unconstitutional if applied to an historic, existing corporate charter. Fortunately for independent colleges, the courts upheld the company's right to contribute to private higher education. As a superior court judge in New Jersey wrote in his 1951 opinion:

> I am strongly persuaded by the evidence that the only hope for the survival of the privately supported American colleges and universities lies in the willingness of corporate wealth to furnish in moderation some support to institutions which are so essential to public welfare and therefore, of necessity, to corporate welfare...I cannot conceive of any greater benefit to corporations in this country than to build and

continue to build, respect for and adherence to a system of free enterprise and democratic government, the serious impairment of either of which may well spell the destruction of all corporate enterprise.[9]

This opinion carried the day in the court's decision. As such, it cleared the way for a period of generous support of independent colleges from corporations and foundations. Not only were corporate barriers to donating to higher education removed, incentives to do so were enhanced. Heretofore, when corporations contributed to independent colleges, their company initiatives usually had been confined to scholarships for the children of employees. There was little consciousness among executives or board members about long-term or large-scale support of colleges as an endangered, important national resource for the public good. However, this changed dramatically in the early 1950s when major corporate leaders, including Frank Abrams of Standard Oil and Alfred P. Sloan of General Motors, worked persistently among chief executive officers and board members of companies nationwide to overcome the conventional view that a corporation ought not, need not, support independent colleges and universities unless there was some direct benefit to the company.

This informal movement eventually led to creation of formal agencies that provided the dynamic structure and leadership for systematic, ongoing financial support of independent colleges as a collective entity. The landmark event was the founding of the Associated Colleges of Indiana in 1948, called the "first of the regional college fund-raising cooperatives." Its founder was Frank Sparks, the founder and former executive for the Indianapolis Pump and Tube Company who at the age of 40 had earned a PhD in order to fulfill his own self-imposed criteria as what was entailed to be qualified to serve as a college president. As president of Wabash College in Indiana from 1941 to 1956 he combined his commitment to his own campus with attention to the larger sphere of higher education philanthropy and the business community.

After World War II Sparks led an ambitious plan to create a "Greater Wabash" that had far greater implications as a model and precedent for public policies and academic institutions nationwide. It was foremost a model of a small college's self-revitalization. Sparks as a college president emphasized multiple initiatives. These included healing schisms between college officials and old-guard alumni; reconstructing the Board of Trustees into a powerful body of prominent, wealthy individuals; recruiting nationally distinguished professors to the college; renovating and expanding the campus and physical plant; and, attracting sustained large scale financial support. The convergence of these emphases would, then, give Wabash college national visibility as a "pillar of strength" in the private sector. And, the aim was for the college to be associated in the public mind with the philosophy of independence and self-reliance characteristic of the American private business sector. Philanthropic support from alumni, citizens, and private foundations were integral to this plan.

President Sparks's vision for his own Wabash College provided a base for his larger commitment to the character and health of all independent colleges in Indiana and nationwide. It sprang from his concern after World War II that the recent, growing entrance of state and federal government support of higher education also carried the threat of government control of higher education. He wrote, "Federal aid to education almost certainly will mean the disappearance from our educational system of the independent, privately financed, liberal arts colleges." President Sparks talked with leaders from business and industry as well as with board members and presidents at other colleges in the state. He gained a strong ally in the president of Earlham College. Their efforts were persuasive and led to creation of the Associated Colleges of Indiana, the first cooperative statewide association of independent colleges in the nation—which stood as the enduring, formal product of Sparks's ideas and groundwork. This pioneering association in Indiana fostered counterparts elsewhere, particularly in Ohio, Michigan, New York, and California. The hallmark of the associations was their partnership of college presidents and corporate leaders. Historians Merle Curti and Roderick Nash observed that Sparks's campaign emphasized that "liberal arts colleges preserve freedom; they produce many essential scientists and business executives; tax laws make it inexpensive to give, since corporations could deduct up to five percent of their net income for contributions to charitable institutions and causes."[10]

Creation of state associations to support independent colleges eventually led to national initiatives. The Council for Financial Aid to Education was incorporated in 1952 "with funds supplied by the General Education Board, the Alfred P. Sloan Foundation, the Carnegie Corporation, and the Ford Foundation's Fund for the Advancement of Education." Similarly, in 1957 business and academic leaders formed the Informal Committee for Corporate Aid to American Universities. And, as noted earlier in chapter 3, the Council for Financial Aid to Education reported in 1962 more than $42 million in corporate contributions.

One interesting unforeseen consequence of the successful efforts of private businesses working to support private colleges and universities was that ultimately it benefitted *all* colleges and universities, whether private (independent) or public (i.e., state supported). This would become especially evident by the 1970s as state universities stepped up their own private fund-raising campaigns. Another significant result of these cumulative efforts was that *donors* to colleges and universities who filed itemized tax returns were allowed to declare college gifts as income tax *deductions*. This allowance gave colleges and other nonprofit sector organizations added magnetism in attracting donations from an expanded, diverse constituency. And, contrary to the fears of business leaders and private college presidents following World War II, the expansion of government programs of student financial aid did *not* necessarily freeze out the private or independent colleges. For example, the landmark 1972 higher education reauthorization bill that included creation of Pell Grants and other federal student aid and loan programs included eligibility for students enrolling at independent colleges and universities, thanks to the effective and persuasive information provided to Congress by such analysts and advocates as Virginia Fadil Hodgkinson and the National Association of Independent Colleges and Universities. At the state level, eventually 30 states approved portable scholarships for state citizens enrolling at independent colleges and universities within the home state—a program often called a TAG, short for "tuition assistance grant."

Meanwhile, the large philanthropic foundations once again faced periodic criticism from the general public and from the United States Congress. As noted in chapter 3 most prominent were the Congressional hearings about the new Ford Foundation. Another extended round of hearings started a decade later, and concluded with the Tax Reform Act of 1969 in which the large foundations received a scolding of sorts for alleged political lobbying as well as being disingenuous in shifting of business and philanthropic funds as a tax ploy. In looking over these periodic congressional hearings the irony is that the private foundations were at one time championed by Democrats and, later, by Republicans—a vacillation that had the net effect of neutralizing partisan attacks and, thus, over the long haul allowed foundations to gain Congressional acquiescence if not applause for their varied activities. Where the famous foundations lost ground was in their declining relative financial strength whenever federal agencies entered into some shared area of research and development, such as the health sciences and medicine. To exacerbate this schism, in the period between 1970 and 1990, the established foundations' endowments were eroded by declines in the value of their stock market holdings.

The success of colleges and universities as part of the nonprofit sector to gain federal tax exemptions along with tax incentives has been integral to the flourishing of higher education nationwide. The price of this success was excess, as the nonprofit sector became a relatively easy mark for groups that sought inclusion. This kind of opportunism was fostered by default because oversight and regulation by the Internal Revenue Service has been light. Good documentation of this dual trend was provided in 2009 with the study by Rob Reich, Lacey Dorn, and Stefanie Sutton, *Any Thing Goes: Approval of Nonprofit Status by the IRS*, conducted for Stanford University's Center on Philanthropy and Civil Society—itself a nonprofit organization whose founding grant came from the Hewlett Foundation.

Many of the peculiar and eccentric qualifying organizations represent petty larcenies—convenient tax write-offs and other perks for recreational and self-indulgent hobbies or pursuits devised by individuals who banded together to apply to the IRS—and were granted 501(c)(3) status. Some extreme examples cited in the Stanford study included "Promise Land Ranch, Inc." of Charlotte, Tennessee which states, "We exist to provide healing and hope to hurting individuals. We accomplish this by meeting people in their time of need, accepting them as they are and providing a safe environment for them to share their pain. This may be through organized retreats, or trips to other countries, or just a coffee at Starbucks." Elsewhere, the "Renegade Roller Girls of Oregon" reported revenues of $40,000 in 2007, of which $20,000 was spent on administrative expenses and $1,000 was donated to other public charities. "Geekaid of Michigan" was inspired by a group of friends who held a private party in 2005 and, later, as an approved organization stated, "Today GeekAid is all about bringing together individuals passionate about art and technology, and understand that we must encourage and foster that passion whenever the opportunity arises. We also feel strongly that you should have fun doing it." In Chicago, "Sin for Charity" undertakes no charitable activity itself other than staging events to raise money for other public charities and is classified as a "Human Service Organization." Nationwide one finds numerous local chapters of the "Sisters of Perpetual Indulgence Inc.," an international order of drag nuns that "raises money and awareness for causes within their community."

In Florida, "CrossHeir Outfitters" describes itself as "an awesome new ministry, ordained by God and Fueled by the passion of a Few good Bubbas wanting to see simple blue-blooded American country boys come to the knowledge of the saving power and life-changing experience with our Lord and Savior Jesus Christ." In conjunction with outdoor product companies this group provides an "enclosed ministry trailer" that will change the lives of Bubbas everywhere. In New Castle, Delaware, a federally approved tax-exempt nonprofit was "Ghostface Ryders Incorporated" whose main goal was "to change the game and bring innovative ideas to the world one bike at a time... while achieving family unity among motorcyclists."[11]

In 2008 the IRS approved 501(c)(3) status for 56,190 organizations out of an applicant pool of 57,401 applicants—an acceptance rate of over 97 percent.[12] Most were classified as "public charities" (just under 73 percent)—as distinguished from a "private foundation" (just under 12 percent). The cumulative cost of these numerous nonprofit organizations is the loss of federal tax revenue—an amount that is difficult to estimate let alone ascertain. Perhaps more serious has been the creation of grey area of kinds of activities allowable under the auspices of a nonprofit organization. These tensions point to some popular, erroneous misunderstandings as to what a nonprofit organization is—and what it is not.

The popular image of a "nonprofit organization" is one that receives its tax breaks because it provides social services or educational programs, often relying on volunteers and probably characterized by thrift and dedication of its board and paid staff. A good illustration of this implicit personification is conjured by a corporate announcement by the Kentucky Utilities Company in a newspaper with the engaging headline, "Your nonprofit helps others. Now we'd like to help you." The accompanying illustration features volunteers serving holiday season meals at a homeless shelter, and is followed by the invitational caption to readers, "Learn how your nonprofit can earn rebates of up to $50,000 per facility for energy upgrades."[13]

The newspaper features were genuine and represented the American philanthropic tradition at its best, including corporate and nonprofit collaboration, with thanks for a job well done. Unfortunately, it was incomplete. As reported by a 2012 article in the *New York Times,* contrary to popular perception, the "bulk of charitable giving is not earmarked for the poor."[14] It hardly makes good sense or good policy to presume that only programs or services for the poor should qualify for tax-exempt status. Yet the popular image does draw into bold relief some major splits within the nonprofit sector in terms of an organization's intended services and constituencies. Perhaps more problematic for reconsideration than the skewed public imagery is that in fact, although many (perhaps most) nonprofit organizations are involved in service and educational programs, there is no legal standard that precludes a nonprofit organization from paying its staff high salaries just as there is no implicit or explicit requirement that a nonprofit organization be lean or impoverished. Technically and legally a nonprofit organization is one that does not pay stock dividends to investors. The Internal Revenue Service's reference materials for IRS form 990 tax return instruction lists over 500 entries for types of exempt organizations, clustered into 20 major categories. Beyond this taxonomy the more salient question for public policies and nonprofit organizations is determining thoughtfully which kinds of activities are worthy—and which are not.

The politicization of nonprofit organizations and their accompanying vague, sometimes dubious aims and nomenclature are captured in high stakes battles over legislation, such as the partisan debates about federal minimum wage laws in 2013 and 2014. Central to the policy discussions is a nonprofit research organization, the Employment Policies Institute.[15] A criticism of the Employment Policies Institute is that it presents itself as a research institute and does, indeed, sponsor research papers and policy supports, including some research grants awarded to university-based professors. The complication is that they do it "with the gloss of research." As a reporter from the *New York Times* commented on a front-page headline story of February 10, 2014: "Just four blocks from the White House is the headquarters of the Employment Policies Institute, a widely quoted economic research center whose academic reports have repeatedly warned that increasing the minimum wage could be harmful, increasing poverty and unemployment. But something fundamental goes unsaid in the institute's reports: The nonprofit group is run by a public relations firm that also represents the restaurant industry, as part of a tightly coordinated effort to defeat the minimum wage increase that the White House and Democrats in Congress have pushed for."

Other participating nonprofit research groups in this legislative issue include the Center for Consumer Freedom, the Center for American Progress and the Economic Policy Institute (note the singular "Policy," as distinguished from the "Economic Policies Institute"). In other words, a mix of conservative and liberal groups that appear to be systematic research and analyses centers are disingenuous in their reliance on advocacy for external donor groups in business and industry. Research papers with the stamp of approval of nonprofit research centers often become central to lobbying. It resurrects a perennial concern about whether this is appropriate for the nonprofit, tax deductible groups to operate. One resolution or acquiescent explanation is to shrug one's shoulders and hope that on balance one gets counter valence, in which several points of view on an issue each invokes its selected research papers, with the result being a peculiar, diverse marketplace of ideas. Such an explanation raises additional questions and concerns about the propriety of relationships, direct and indirect, among business, legislation, and the nonprofit centers.

Business corporations throughout the twentieth century were subject to concerns, even accusations, about what was termed the "Curse of Bigness." For higher education in the late twentieth and early twenty-first centuries, the comparable concern was that spending of colleges and universities and national headquarters for nonprofit agencies were subject to a "Question of Bigness." From time to time there have been "bad apples" of abuse and even illegal conduct that bring alarm and shame to nonprofit organizations, including colleges and universities. In 1996 William Aramony, chief executive of United Way of America (UWA), was sentenced to six years in prison for fraud and financial mismanagement, grounded in high salaries and a lavish life style funded by UWA. Beyond personal indulgence, the fall out was consequential nationwide, as contributions to United Way local chapters declined substantially.[16] The conspicuous counterpart for higher education took place in 1997 when the Regents of the State of New York removed 18 of 19 trustees at Adelphi University from office for violations of self-dealing and failing to provide proper oversight of the university president's extravagant salary and spending.[17]

These highly publicized cases were exceptional—and dealt with illegal actions that led to criminal charges. High presidential salaries usually were more a question of whether board and administrative actions were *appropriate* as distinguished from those that were *illegal*. College and university boards were entrusted to have autonomy in determining salaries and compensation of presidents and other high-level administrators. Established colleges and universities dismissed the foibles and indulgences of nonprofit organizations as discussed in the Stanford University report, *Anything Goes* as not germane to *their* legitimate, serious academic business. Nonetheless the prospect of excess and abuse among colleges and universities persisted sufficiently to raise concerns among some articulate, thoughtful higher education and nonprofit leaders who had some fears that they might be susceptible to losing their tax benefits.[18]

Colleges started to confront public concerns about scandals and spending associated with nonprofit organizations. On December 7, 1994, the president of Duke University, Nannerl O. Keohane, wrote an op-ed piece in the *Chronicle of Higher Education* directed at undergraduates and recent alumni with emphasis on what the nonprofit world *should* be if it were to be true to its principles and public trust. She noted, "If a handsome income is your goal in life, you should be in some other line of work." The need for her message was that colleges and universities had themselves often strayed with excessive emphasis on fund-raising and with paying some campus employees extremely high salaries. Keohane noted, "We in higher education are certainly guilty of some of these offenses, some of which antagonize those whose loyalty we prize most highly—our alumni." Her elaboration on this point was as follows:

> We are held by the public, by the government, and by one another to a different standard from the for-profit-world, and this is as it should be. We must carefully consider our stewardship of the financial resources entrusted to our care and give an open and accurate accounting of how those resources have been used...And we must be particularly careful about the salaries we pay our senior executives. In a business operated for profit, if a leader succeeds in bringing significant added value to the enterprise and is clearly responsible for making large amounts of money for the company, a generous salary and bonuses strike most of us as fair...Non-profits are, and should be different. No matter how much added value any of us might bring as leaders of non-profit organizations, the value should redound to the benefit of the organization and not to us personally...It is easy for us, and for our boards of directors, to look to the corporate world for comparisons, to be tempted to reward strong leadership in the non-profit world in the same way. But this is a dangerous temptation, and, in the end, it will bring us to grief. We should resist the growing tendency to look at our salaries as though we were each in daily readiness to be recruited to Wall Street if the price were right.[19]

Twenty years after publication of Keohane's op-ed piece, higher education trustees and leaders were reading but not heeding her message. To the contrary, college and university boards tended to go in the opposite direction in compensation for presidents, vice presidents, and deans. Few academic leaders and boards would disagree with

Keohane's argument in general—at least, not in the public forum. However, putting her principles into practice remained uncertain if not unlikely. Most boards would justify and rationalize high salaries for administrators at their particular campus, invoking "market forces" and the need to build up compensation in order to retain a particular president for many years to come. In 2011 the median presidential compensation at 500 independent colleges and universities was $301,299 in base salary. Nor do such reports include deferred compensation, club memberships, retirement packages, interest-free home mortgage loans, paid premiums on insurance policies and health plans, vacation houses, performance bonuses and a host of other financial benefits.[20] One hundred and eighty independent institutions reported presidential compensation packages over $500,000 per year. Forty-two presidents received annual compensation surpassing $1 million per year.[21] During the academic year 2011–2012 the highest paid presidents at state universities—including base salary plus other forms of compensation—were the president of Auburn University at $ 2,542,865; the president of the Ohio State University at $1,899,420; the president of George Mason University at $1,869,369; the president of Ball State University at $984,647; and the president of the University of Michigan System at $918,783.[22]

The median annual compensation for university presidents was over $400,000. In some states where the governor has imposed a cap on a state university president's salary, the university's internal private foundations have provided supplements that go beyond the official state salary ceiling. One is hard pressed to identify rhyme or reason in the presidential salary distribution according to criteria such as institutional prestige, size, location, or affiliation. Perhaps the soundest generalization is that a president is paid what her or his particular board of trustees chooses to pay, quite apart from external standards or benchmarks. Contrary to Keohane's suggestion that academic leaders eschew comparing their professional positions (and compensation) with Wall Street, one finds over the past decade that university trustees referred to university administrators in business and corporate language. Standard usage in the academic lexicon is that the university president is the academic "CEO." The provost is the "CAO" (Chief Academic Officer) and the vice president for business affairs is the "CFO" (Chief Financial Officer).

A graphic, recent example of dubious excess that captures these concerns comes from Brandeis University where in January 2014 university trustees paid its former president $4.9 million—a package that included $811,000 for untaken sabbatical and $4.1 million in deferred compensation over his 17 years as president.[23] His base salary in 2011 was $627,000. Ironically, shortly after the board made public announcement about its payment to the ex-president, the same board announced new compensation policies that, according to one reporter, were "designed to assuage campus outrage and perhaps prevent this from happening again." United States Senator Chuck Grassley (R-Iowa) commented, "It's surprising to see nonprofit employees paid like Wall Street Bankers...as Brandeis makes improvements, other colleges could and should follow the example, even though it seems like too little too late in this case."[24]

Elsewhere in universities one finds what Keohane probably would call "handsome income" for athletics directors and especially for head coaches in such high profile sports as football and men's basketball. The highest annual salary packages for coaches in 2013 are $4 million to $5 million per year. Fifty years earlier, the highest paid college basketball coach in the nation earned $45, 000.[25] The highest annual salary for John Wooden, basketball coach of UCLA whose teams won ten consecutive NCAA championships was $35,000 in 1975, his final season before retirement. Head football coaches in the NCAA Division I programs in 2012 earned mean base salaries above $1 million—even though most of these athletics programs lost money. Numerous assistant coaches have base salaries in the range of $200,000 to $600,000 per year. At those state universities which are the home of the highest coaching salaries, the matter-of-fact explanation is, "Hey! These are from private funds!" Left out of the justification is that the "private funds" are part and parcel of the nonprofit, tax exemption criteria—and, hence, subject to public standards and trustee stewardship. Herein rests the essential issues of the nonprofit sector as to what is appropriate in terms of the letter and spirit of the law. The data suggested that there was an academic version of "Anything Goes!"

This is not to say that college and university boards of trustees have not partially and selectively heeded Keohane's advice about salary sacrifice for *some* academic employees. Rather, they have been frugal in other areas of campus expenditures outside the realm of leadership salaries. Increasing reliance on adjunct instructors and elimination of tenure track faculty appointments constitute a substantial source of costs savings. Yet these take place close to the core of the educational mission at the same time that the supportive "shell" of administration tends to soar both in salaries and in the number of newly created positions. Studies by the Delta Cost Project in 2011 indicate that each year public universities spend a declining percentage of revenues from tuition and state student subsidies for *educational* programs.[26] Who is to say that the president is paid too much or paid too little with an annual base salary of, for example, $750,000 per year? Trustees of a college or university seldom face constraints or curbs in their institutional decisions about administrative compensation.

Higher Education as part of the nonprofit sector increasingly faces public questions and even crises of confidence when one considers the constellation of *external* organizations that are indelibly linked with colleges and universities. The National Collegiate Athletic Association (NCAA), for example, is approved as a nonprofit 501(c)(3) tax-exempt organization. Incidental to this categorization is that its annual revenues, including television, other broadcasting, and other programs were $757 million in 2010–2011.[27] Much of its staff time and work are devoted to promoting highly commercial intercollegiate sports tournaments. In April 2010 the NCAA signed a 14-year contract for $10.8 billion with CBS and Turner Sports for broadcast rights to the NCAA men's basketball tournament. The president of the NCAA in 2013 has an annual salary of $1.7 million. The NCAA notes that 96 percent of its revenues (i.e., $727 million out of $757 million) go back to member institutions. Breaking down that total, 60 percent ($454 million) is transferred to universities who are members of the NCAA's big-time category, known as Division I programs. Most of this is distributed to six programs, as follows: academic enhancement programs receive $22.4 million; the basketball fund is $180 million; grants to various Division I conferences constitute $8 million; grants-in-aid for student-athletes at Division I programs receive $111 million; the student assistance fund accounts for $40 million; and, the sports sponsorship program annual appropriation is $55 million. The size of the NCAA annual budget combined with its focus on commercial broadcast of intercollegiate games provides an interesting case study of what does—and does not—constitute an educational and charitable nonprofit organization.

Analyzing the size and scope of the NCAA starts but does not exhaust the question of whether big-time intercollegiate athletics should be considered an educational and charitable activity or, perhaps, a major business enterprise. The NCAA budget does *not* include the ticket sales and broadcast revenues from regular season football and basketball games offered by the various conferences (e.g., the Big Ten, the Southeast Conference, the Atlantic Coast Conference, the Big East Conference, the Big Twelve, or the Pac Twelve, et al.) and their universities for football, basketball, and other revenue-producing sports.

A large American university is a sufficiently complex organization that it creates within its structure a microcosm of the national non-profit sector. A flagship state university, for example, includes numerous nonprofit corporations—and, in many cases, may also include some commercial and business-for-profit corporations as well. The nonprofit corporations typically include a University Foundation (UF), a University Research Foundation (URF), probably abbreviated as the URF, a university athletics association (UAA), an alumni association, an incorporated university hospital, and a university medical services foundation. Furthermore, such internal units as the university art museum, the university symphony, the university library, and each academic college may have their own nonprofit charitable corporations dedicated to specific fund-raising, such as "University Art Museum Associates" or "University Library Associates." Each of these can be a distinct nonprofit corporation with varying degrees of self-determination and autonomy from the university as a whole, including such features as its own board, membership roster, mailing list, donor prospect files, alumni rolls, membership fees, endowments, reserve funds, and, of course, its own 990 Form to be filed each year with the IRS.

Nonprofit corporations within a university set up for fund-raising in some instances can be problematic for a university board of trustees. For example, during the years 2003–2004 the University of Georgia was involved in a contentious dispute with its own University of Georgia Foundation which is in charge of fund-raising, receipt of donations, and management of the university's $400 million endowment.[28] It also has a subsidiary, the UGA Real Estate Foundation. Some of the entanglements causing tension included the practice of the Foundation paying more than half of the university president's salary. Power to pay also could mean the power to withhold or reduce presidential compensation when foundation trustees were dissatisfied with the president, quite apart from the university regents' decisions. These family quarrels became severe, leading the university regents to declare a "divorce" from the Foundation.[29] After a trial separation, the university regents and the foundation board eventually reconciled—but this left unanswered questions for all colleges and universities questions about authority and autonomy within the university.[30] To add to the discomfort of propriety for nonprofit trustees, newspaper articles indicated that 27 out of 55 trustees of the University of Georgia Foundation were employed by commercial firms that had engaged in $30 million in business with the Foundation or the University in the preceding three-year period despite a state law and federal tax codes that restricted "self-dealing" by directors of nonprofit organizations.

Trustees for nonprofit organizations faced another challenging situation in addition to growing scrutiny about conflicts of interest and business dealing. Namely, should directors of nonprofits be allowed to be compensated for their board service by the nonprofit organization? It was another example of the nonprofit sector drifting toward mimicking business corporations, where substantial compensation was standard practice. One highly publicized case involved The Horace W. Goldsmith Foundation in New York City.[31] It also led to the public report that some other foundations, such as the Duke Trusts, paid directors. The disheartening feature of these episodes is that they brought into the public spotlight the disparities between nonprofit board members and most institutional employees. For example, one foundation paid a board member $126,000 per year for service in addition to reimbursement for travel and lodging. The board member's salary as a CEO was several million dollars per year. Hence, the payment as a trustee was miniscule in comparison—yet far more than most full-time employees of a foundation or a university earned. Nonprofit organizations that chose to pay board members faced another public relations headache: namely, its dysfunctional consequences for volunteerism. IRS regulations allow individuals to deduct the cost of goods donated to a charity. However, one strict condition is that a volunteer is *not* allowed to deduct the expense of one's time devoted to a nonprofit organization.

Separately incorporated fund-raising foundations within state universities also have had persistent problems with their status as part of a public institution. If a state university's fund-raising foundation is the repository for donations to the university along with other revenue streams such as endowment earnings, what are its public responsibilities? This was the litmus that surfaced with increasing frequency. Indiana University's IU Foundation in 1996 and the University of Louisville's University Foundation in 2004, for example, resisted newspaper reporters' open records requests for information on donors. Foundation resistance was based on their claim that they were *private corporations* and, hence, not subject to open records laws. Eventually such claims were defeated in the courts or in outside settlements, usually on the grounds that the private corporation exists only to support the university, a public institution.[32]

Over time the IRS has looked with increasing frequency and scrutiny at the actions of donors. Senator Charles E. Grassley, Republican from Iowa, prompted the Senate Finance Committee in 2005 to investigate a particular practice of creating what is called a "supporting organization." This is a nonprofit organization set up by a donor to hold a large sum of money without directing its resources to any particular charitable organization. The incident that brought renewed attention from Congress and from the IRS involved George B. Kaiser, an Oklahoma oilman who, according to the *New York Times* reporter Stephanie Strom, had "set aside roughly $1 billion for charitable endeavors" from his personal fortune estimated at $4 billion. In exchange for having relinquished personal control of the $1 billion endowment, he was able to deflect taxes on much of his own income for several years. The rub was that evidently he had only set aside $3.4 million for charitable giving in the "separate organization" whose board appointments were donor-controlled. The concern of the IRS is that this provides a vehicle more focused on advantageous family estate planning than in making donations to educational and service-oriented nonprofit institutions. The Commissioner of the IRS noted that his agency was taking the case seriously because it was symptomatic of a growing number of comparable abuses.[33]

An area especially pertinent to philanthropy and higher education fund-raising shaped by changing government relations has been that of the rights of donors to colleges and universities. The traditional base was that Congress and the Courts tended to give strong support to colleges in matters of gifts and bequests. In contrast, since 1980 one finds a groundswell of cases where the burden of proof has shifted so that colleges and universities who had accepted gifts from donors were required to explain if and how they had carried out the conditions of the gifts. Recent notable examples: first, the Bain gift to Yale; second, the family bequest for Princeton's Woodrow Wilson School of Public Affairs; third, the historic donation to create Sophie Newcomb College as part of Tulane University; and, fourth, Fisk University's selling part of its art collection donated to the university by Georgia O'Keefe.

Whereas the Woodrow Wilson School disagreements over focused spending percolated over several decades, some disputes over major donations have boiled over quickly. In 1995 courts ruled that Yale University had to return to alumnus donor Lee Bass his 1991 gift of

$20 million that had been designated for creation of an intensive one-year, two-credit course that was proposed to analyze all aspects of Western history. Donor Bass argued successfully that Yale's actions such as creating endowed professorships and other projects had not fulfilled the conditions of his gift. Press coverage was not favorable to the university, as one editorial gave Yale an "F" in ethics while *Time* magazine's coverage described "four years of fumbling" as a formula for "How to Lose $20 million."[34] There was credence to the sensational headlines, as Yale was operating at a deficit and, after the payback to alumnus and donor Lee Bass, the university still had to fulfill its obligation to pay the salaries of the appointed new endowed professorships. This was not a high point in the responsible steward-ship of wealth and resources in American higher education.

In 2010 the Tennessee attorney general's office opposed Fisk University's plan to sell an art collection of 101 works given by artist Georgia O'Keefe to Fisk in the 1940s and 1950s. The state's objection was made "on the grounds that it violated the artist's wishes that the works be displayed together and not sold."[35] The compelling situation in response to the attorney general, according to university officials, was that Fisk was in financial trouble, could no longer afford proper presentation and care of the valuable collection valued at $74 million. Fisk University needed to lower its operating expenses and at the same time also needed the sales money for the institution to survive. The compromise resolution allowed Fisk University to sell part of the collection for $30 million on the condition that $20 million be put into an endowment to ensure the artwork's future care. Although the compromise was acceptable, the case raised questions about how an academic institution balances complying with a donor's intent while monitoring the overall funding and functions of the university.

What happens when a family whose 1961 large donation to create and endow the Woodrow Wilson School of Public Affairs at Princeton concludes that university officials have not adequately com-plied with the donors' intent? The answer was an expensive, draining, and highly publicized quarrel between prominent alumni and their alma mater. This was the principle issue in the Robertson family's six-year dispute with Princeton that ended in December 2008 with a settlement in which Princeton was allowed to retain academic con-trol over the School and its $900 million endowment—but agreed to pay the donor family $90 million—with $40 million to cover legal fees and $50 million for the Robertsons to create a new, distinct foundation committed to education for public affairs professionals.

Over several years the Robertson family was concerned that graduates of the Woodrow Wilson School were not going into the foreign
service or diplomatic corps, as was the original intent of the bequest
and the School. Princeton officials responded that professional fields
had changed and the Woodrow Wilson School was being resilient in
responding to the changing environment and definitions of government service and public affairs. The out-of-court settlement spared
both sides an expensive trial and did allow the university to retain
control over the academic program, including its curriculum and
faculty appointments. It represented a significant example of the
potential for disagreements by donors, at great cost to all parties.[36]

Another variation on the theme of donor concerns over university
compliance with major gifts took place at Tulane University in 2008.
A descendent of the founding benefactor of Sophie Newcomb College
of Tulane University sued the university to reopen the women's college which had been folded into the coeducational overall university.
University officials defended their action noting that the merger was a
necessary decision in the aftermath of the damage caused by Hurricane
Katrina. Furthermore, the university argued, they claimed to have
maintained compliance with the historic bequest by expanding and
funding opportunities for women within the new configuration of
Tulane University.[37] What this meant was that henceforth there was a
single undergraduate college and it was coeducational, enrolling both
men and women students—named Newcomb-Tulane College. And,
starting in 2006 the Newcomb Institute maintained some of the traditions of the original Newcomb College and provided an array of programs and guest speakers—none of which were directly connected to
granting of academic credit or degrees. A court ruling in 2011 upheld
the university's merger and collegiate reforms.

Most of our attention has dealt with *federal* policies involving colleges and the nonprofit sector. And this is reasonable since in most
cases state and local governments have tended to defer to and adopt
the IRS 501(c)(3) designations as proxies to qualify for state and local
exemptions. But this has not been a static arrangement. It has been
under review with some changes mainly because state and local governments have become strapped for cash. This is evident and not surprising in small "college towns" such as Champaign-Urbana, Evanston,
Princeton, and Bloomington where, respectively, the University of
Illinois, Northwestern University, Princeton University, and Indiana
University are dominant. Less obvious is that the prevalence of a university in the local community also extends to some major metropolitan

areas. Cities such as Boston, Providence, Baltimore, Pittsburgh, and Cleveland local governments have pushed for reconsideration of property tax exemption for colleges and universities that are the community's largest employer and landowner.[38] In 2012 the mayor of Providence noted that Brown University received $38 million in property tax exemptions—an amount that the city could recover only from the revenue collected from its 178,000 taxpayers. It includes critical analysis of college and university land use. Is a university's golf course truly used for educational purposes? Also central to this reconsideration of tax exemptions are hospitals that represent an important area of overlap among the nonprofit sector and universities.

Cities which are strapped for tax revenues have questioned whether hospitals, especially university hospitals, are fulfilling their obligations as charitable organizations. The city of Pittsburgh filed suit challenging the University of Pittsburgh Medical Center's tax-exempt status, "saying that the medical center should pay some payroll taxes and more property taxes, estimated to total about $20 million annually." The city's lead lawyer on the case wrote to the city solicitor, "Its commitment to charity is dwarfed by its preoccupation with profits."[39] According to reports, the university hospital had excess operating revenue of nearly $1 billion and reserves of more than $3 billion. Twenty of its executives were paid salaries of more than $1 million annually. The city attorney claimed that the university hospital spent only about 2 percent of its net patient revenues on charity care. The upshot was that with the University of Pittsburgh hospital, along with counterparts at the Johns Hopkins University and Case Western Reserve, critics argued that these hospitals do not deserve their tax-exempt status. In some cities, such as Boston, estimates are that well over half the land is owned by tax-exempt nonprofit organizations—a situation that shrinks the traditional revenue sources for public schools. The upshot is that colleges and universities will be increasingly hard-pressed to defend and maintain their customary local tax exemptions.

An interesting new wrinkle in these "town versus gown" disputes over taxing colleges is that the recent case of Princeton University has extended the concerns from the university as a large land owner and employer—and user of city services—is the new, uncharted area of a university as a commercial entrepreneur. In 2013 the slogan in the public forum and lawsuit was, "Why Shouldn't Princeton pay taxes?" Proponents argued that revenues that Princeton University had gained from spin-off companies and intellectual properties payments for royalties related to patents and commercial products called for a reconsideration of traditional tax exemptions. In 2011 Princeton university took in over $115 million from patents, of which $35 million was given to various faculty members.[40] The plaintiffs did not begrudge the university and its professors these revenues, but did want them subject to comparable taxation as other businesses and citizens would face. The university countered that already its $7 million per year tax payments to local government made it the largest taxpayer in the borough and city. Furthermore, Princeton and other universities involved in high stakes research and development were merely following the guidelines and incentives from the 1980 Bayh-Dole Act that allowed organizations, including universities, to partake of patent royalties that were in part the result of large scale federal research sponsorship—reform legislation intended to promote research institutions to enhance national economic development. The response from the plaintiffs was that perhaps it was time to reconsider the character of research universities—which were behaving now as if they were for-profit enterprises, far from their historic stature as educational, charitable institutions requiring exemptions and protections.

At the federal level, colleges and all nonprofit organizations have faced increasing scrutiny, including audits, from the Internal Revenue Service for revenues generated by sponsored activities that are not related to the institution's central educational mission. This is the "unrelated business income tax," often referred to be its acronym, UBIT. It has included findings that colleges sometimes fail to pay sufficient employment taxes. Thirty colleges were audited by the IRS in 2010 and found growing incidence of tax underpayment from supporting organizations which were charities that collected and then channeled money to a university.[41]

On balance, over the past century nonprofit tax-exempt organizations including colleges and universities, have been granted formidable legal protections and benefits—and most of these remain intact. However, since about 1970 these have faced erosion and a growing amount of critical review. It has led university presidents such as Derek Bok of Harvard to speak and write publicly to decry what he and his fellow university presidents see as a drift toward government overregulation of higher education.[42] In 1979 sociologist Nathan Glazer concluded that there had been a gradual yet persistent change in tax policies, in which colleges and business corporations had in large measure traded places in the lens of federal agencies.[43]

Whereas a college in 1914 was exempted because it was a special type of institution with a rare educational mission and in need of protection if it were to survive, in the late twentieth century its special status meant that it was expected to be on the vanguard of social justice and to comply with increasingly rigorous standards of accountability and organizational behavior—including the aforementioned initiatives to have colleges and their affiliated units pay taxes. The irony was that in the meanwhile businesses which historically had been expected to pay high income and property taxes were increasingly granted deferments, exemptions, and subsidies. A good recent illustration of this reversal was that in December 2013 the governor of Connecticut announced that the state was providing the commercial sports network ESPN a $25 million incentive package to persuade the company to remain in Connecticut.[44]

The corollary is that many colleges and universities that were among the largest employers and landowners in a community were now increasingly expected to pay taxes reminiscent of traditional expectations of a factory or manufacturing company. Ironically, ESPN was a large, profitable corporate enterprise yet had come to adopt some of the terminology traditionally associated with academic institutions— such as calling its headquarters a "campus." If this was not a world turned upside down, it was at least one in which public policies had undergone significant reversal and crossover. One interpretation of these changes is that higher education as an enterprise has come to be regarded by government as a "mature industry," with a decreasing need for special treatment and exemptions or direct subsidies and support as a fragile, small, and beleaguered charity.[45] Acknowledging this change in higher education, one also must note that the features, including the nonprofit tax exemptions, of academic institutions have been magnetic to a host of new enterprises. The convergence of these multiple streams of organizational and legislative developments probably signals the emergence of a new hybrid American institution— the entrepreneurial and lucrative nonprofit organization in specialties ranging from health professions to technological innovations. In short, the lines of education, service, and commerce have become increasingly blurred in what has been termed a postindustrial economy.

Resolution of these changes in academic institutions, new start-up enterprises, and in government policies remains unclear. More certain is that various levels of government will repeatedly question and revisit the tax exemptions and privileges that fostered philanthropic support of higher education. A good, recent example was in February

2013 when a Congressional hearing dealt with a new volley of tough questions on tax breaks for charities. Nonprofit organizations understandably were concerned that any congressional action that would limit a charitable tax deduction would diminish incentives for donors to make gifts. The president of Southwestern University in Texas, Jake B. Schrum, speaking on behalf of the Council for Advancement and Support of Education, told the Congressional panel, "Charitable gifts help institutions fund scholarships for low-income students, recruit top-notch faculty, and strengthen academic programs." This testimony summarized and reinforced the traditional justifications for protecting and nurturing nonprofit organizations.[46] At the same time, it coexists with a chorus of criticisms and concerns as presented in this chapter. The uncertain and unpredictable consequence is that college and university presidents and their boards will be asked to explain and negotiate with Congress and with federal agencies—and, by extension—to taxpayers and potential donors, as to what optimal, fair policies are—and ought to be.

6

Professionalization of Philanthropy: Fund-Raising and Development

The practice of philanthropy includes both the raising and the giving of money. Indeed, one could argue that it always has. While money is sometimes given without having been asked for, such giving tends to be episodic and small scale. Moreover, it tends to resemble almsgiving or charity more closely than the organized giving and receiving of money that is the practice of philanthropy. While charity performs an important function in relieving human misery, philanthropy requires giving on a larger, more sustained scale as it addresses the root causes of social ills and seeks to reform society in order to enhance the quality of life for all of its members.

One of the findings of Curti and Nash in their research on the role of philanthropy in shaping the American system of higher education is that philanthropy has to be stimulated.[1] It should not be surprising, therefore, that the origins of the profession of fund-raising are ancient. James Howell Smith, author of *Honorable Beggars*, reports that the origins of fund-raising as a profession can be traced back to the time of the large medieval charities that sprang up in Northern Italy. Smith notes that they frequently had "a permanent officer designated as the financial agent, or proctor, whose duty it was to travel over the domain pleading for gifts and bequests."[2]

Likewise, it is instructive to note that in the first systematic effort in North America to raise money, the Massachusetts Bay Colony sent three clergymen to England in 1641 to solicit money for Harvard College.[3] While the colony's leaders might have been tempted to rely solely on letters or the brochure (*New England's First Fruits*) that was later developed and sent to assist the three fund-raisers in making a case for support, they knew instinctively that middlemen, who could engage in face-to-face fund-raising with prospective donors, were needed to generate funds of the magnitude being sought.

For those who do educational fund-raising, it is worth noting that the four hundredth anniversary of the profession is approaching. Much has changed in the past four centuries and especially in the last four decades. For one, educational fund-raising is now regarded as a profession, even if it is deemed "a peculiar calling" as noted by Mark Drozdowski, who for some years has written a column called "The Fund Raiser" for the *Chronicle of Higher Education*.[4] While theological training does not prohibit modern-day entry into the profession, which has no specific educational requirement, it also does not provide the clear advantage that it did in the seventeenth century. Today's educational fund-raising professional, or development officer, is more likely to have graduate training in higher-education administration, nonprofit management, or philanthropic studies, or an MPA, MBA, or JD degree. If she has no graduate degree, she may have received certification through the Association of Fundraising Professionals (AFP). Chances are good that today's fund-raiser specializes in annual giving, foundation relations, corporate giving, planned giving, major gifts, or campaign fund-raising, instead of being the generalist of a few decades ago. More important than academic degrees, today's fund-raising professional will have a skill set that equips her for success in her area of specialization.

To a large extent, the trend toward specialization within fund-raising reflects the fact that the field has become more complex, thus requiring specialized knowledge. The trend also is a by-product of professionalization within the nonprofit sector, triggered by passage of the Tax Reform Act of 1969 and accelerated by the founding of Independent Sector in 1980. Between those events, the Council for Advancement and Support of Education (CASE) was created in 1974 by the merger of the American Alumni Council (AAC) and the American College Public Relations Association (ACPRA). CASE is the professional organization to which most American colleges and universities belong, as do their individual staff members in fund-raising, alumni relations, communications (media relations, publications, and marketing), and government relations. By encouraging professionalism in these fields, CASE has also fostered specialization.

In a more subtle, but no less real, way, the movement toward the professionalization of development reflects the fact that there is a great deal of competition among American colleges and universities. They compete in a very intentional way for students, faculty, fund-raising dollars, and prestige. The intensity of this competition is often cited as a key factor contributing to the widely recognized quality of American higher education.[5] It also contributes to the high cost of attendance, but that is a topic for another day.

Using insights from the field of organizational analysis, especially that branch known as the new institutionalism, scholars have noted that competition in higher education has caused colleges to become more alike instead of more distinctive. Imitation rather than innovation characterizes most colleges and universities. Thus, if College A has three master's-degree-holding grants writers in its foundation relations office and two attorneys providing leadership for its planned giving program, then College B will seek to emulate A, especially if A's development operation generates greater revenues than does B's.

Competition and imitation have led to burgeoning staff. The development office of 40 or 50 years ago was modestly staffed, if it existed at all, and was not a high pressure, results-oriented operation on most campuses. Today, all that has changed dramatically. The development staff of large Research I universities often number 250 or more. Many small liberal arts colleges have 20 or more people on their development staff. The results these staff generate also have grown dramatically. According to *Giving USA 2013*, giving to higher education in the 2011–2012 fiscal year totaled $31 billion.[6] A recent report from the Council for Aid to Education announced that the total had risen to $33.8 billion in 2012–2013.[7]

One of the truisms of American higher education is that the most successful colleges and universities are those that are the most accomplished in fund-raising. The story of how educational fund-raising has evolved since 1641 is an interesting one that will be briefly reviewed in the next section.

Focus on Understanding and Support

Much like the medieval charities that hired a person to travel about the countryside pleading for gifts, America's early-college leaders realized that the dependence of their schools on philanthropy was so great that engaging a person to focus on raising funds would be necessary. Although presidents, trustees, and officials of the sponsoring denomination, where there was one, continued to raise funds for the early American colleges, hiring a college agent quickly became common practice. This practice persisted well into the twentieth-century on many campuses.

In a 1958 essay, social historian Merle Curti credited the American bent toward efficiency in all things with giving rise to the professional middlemen of philanthropy. Furthermore, he credited the college agent with being the model. "The prototype," wrote Curti, "was the lean and tireless agent that the nineteenth-century college hired for a pittance to travel over the land begging for contributions to keep the wolf from the classroom door."[8]

The college agent as educational fund-raiser remained a remarkably stable model for many years. In truth, before the industrialization that became widespread in America following the Civil War, there was not a great deal of money available to be raised. Most of the gifts gathered by college agents were small in value and in the form of what donors had to give, which in many instances was livestock or farm produce—"corn not cash," as one historian put it.[9]

Industrialization greatly expanded the United States economy and pumped money into society, creating a few vast fortunes while also putting more cash into the hands of the average citizen. With this infusion of wealth came a shift in American philanthropy toward larger gifts. Some of these gifts were substantial enough to create new colleges that extended educational opportunities to women and to people of color, especially freed slaves in the South. Other gifts were large enough to provide for the creation of research universities; some had been colleges with classical curriculums before being transformed, while in other instances, wholly new institutions were established.

During this same era, college agents played a vital role in the survival of the 182 colleges (out of an estimated 700) that were founded between the American Revolution and the Civil War and still in existence by the midpoint of the twentieth century.[10] More often than not, the big events in philanthropy, including those in support of higher education, were the result of initiatives by church officials, college presidents, or philanthropists themselves. Perhaps the most famous of the church officials whose work had a major impact on both higher education and American philanthropy was Frederick T. Gates, who became chief philanthropic adviser to John D. Rockefeller Sr. When Gates first met his future employer, he was executive secretary of the recently formed American Baptist Education Society. In that role, he solicited Rockefeller for funds to found the University of Chicago. Having gained Rockefeller's confidence and trust in their work on that project, within a few years Gates was hired by Rockefeller to take charge of his philanthropic giving.[11]

In this role, Gates shielded Rockefeller from what had become a daily onslaught of funding requests and fund-raisers, many of whom were ministers appealing to Rockefeller's devout Christianity. Most importantly, Gates brought organization and effectiveness to the giving away of millions of dollars. In the process, he helped shape American philanthropy, especially as it relates to foundation giving and higher education.

Having been a highly effective fund-raiser himself, Gates was interested in seeing the vocation become more professionalized. His advice to those working in the field ranged from matters of personal hygiene to etiquette to technique. Smith reports that on one occasion, Gates advised a solicitor to: "Appeal only to the noblest motives... [The prospect's] own mind will suggest to him all the more selfish ones, but he will not wish you to suppose that he thought of these."[12]

The fortunes made possible by industrialization and an expanding economy gave rise to a new philanthropic vehicle, that uniquely American invention known as the foundation. The foundation is a practical response to the challenge of putting large amounts of money to work in service to the public good. The invention of the foundation reflects American concern with achieving efficiency through organization. Two of the most successful pioneers of business organization, Andrew Carnegie and John D. Rockefeller Sr., were leaders in implementing this new approach to giving. They were the kind of big-picture thinkers capable of envisioning "an unlimited agenda of works, in which participants redefined goals as circumstances changed," which Zunz has identified as the real genius of the foundation.[13]

About the same time that the first foundations were beginning to crop up, colleges began to discover and tap into a source of regular, ongoing financial support that, even though it had long existed, had been largely overlooked—their alumni. Organized giving and receiving took a major step forward in 1890 when a few Yale graduates established the Alumni Fund, the forerunner of the annual fund that is today a staple of educational fund-raising. Efforts to organize and sustain supportive relationships with alumni quickly became such a widespread practice that by 1927, the American Alumni Council had been formed as a resource and collective voice for the many institution-specific alumni associations.[14]

The availability of greater wealth in society, the advent of foundations, and the eagerness of alumni to band together to support and promote Alma Mater combined to gradually reshape the agenda and redefine the role of the college agent. In short order at some of the more prominent schools, organized fund-raising campaigns became the norm. Although occasionally designated for endowment growth, most of these campaigns were for capital funds to finance new construction; today, even though most campaigns are comprehensive efforts with multiple funding priorities, only some of which are related to capital projects, they are still most often referred to as capital campaigns. Harvard's 1906 campaign, which generated $2.4 million from more than 2,000 donors, marked the first time an institution of higher learning had raised as much as a million dollars at one time, according to Curti and Nash. Interestingly, in that same year, Harvard's class of 1881, in conjunction with its twenty-fifth reunion, made a gift of $113,777, the income from which was to be for unrestricted purposes.[15] Thereafter, the fund-raising staffs at many colleges, especially in the Northeast, began focusing greater time and attention on reunion-class giving.

The rapid expansion of giving to colleges and universities after the turn of the twentieth century paralleled trends in the greater society. Progressive Era civic and political leaders promoted the idea that every citizen is responsible for the public good. Campaigns to build new YMCA facilities created new opportunities for giving that, while still rooted in Christianity, broadened the purposes to be served by the average person's giving to include community improvement as well as church and denominational causes. And efforts such as the Christmas Seals campaign to fight the scourge of tuberculosis gave Americans the opportunity to join with others across the nation to strive for improvement in the quality of life for all citizens. In his 1965 classic, *Fund Raising in the United States*, Scott Cutlip characterizes the Christmas Seals campaign as "a lucrative device for raising millions with penny contributions."[16] The genius of the Christmas Seals campaign is that it gave people of all ages and all socioeconomic levels the opportunity to participate.

In Cutlip's analysis, it was the 1908 Christmas Seals campaign that was the turning point in the acceptance of mass philanthropy by the American population. Timing is everything, it is said, and the 1908 Christmas Seals campaign was perfectly timed to establish the idea that America would be a nation of givers. Philanthropy would not be a mere pastime nor an exclusive obligation of the wealthy; rather, it would be a widespread activity in which the majority of Americans would participate. At a time when Carnegie, Rockefeller, and others, such as Julius Rosenwald and Mrs. Russell Sage, were attracting much attention for putting millions into their foundations, average

Americans also were investing in a better society. Fund-raising's greatest contribution to American society is the democratization of philanthropy that it made possible.[17]

While the Christmas Seals campaigns regularized mass philanthropy, it was fund-raising for war relief during World War I that revealed its potential scale. In May 1917, the American Red Cross organized a drive that raised over $114 million to support European war relief. The following year, $169 million was raised in another drive for the same purpose. During the second decade of the 1900s, federated campaigns also became a regular feature of civic life; today most federated community campaigns operate under the banner of United Way of America. Mass philanthropy had become so well integrated into everyday life in this country by the 1950s, according to Zunz, that "one could identify the season by the door-to-door collection in progress."[18]

The origins of the intensive fund-raising drive that is today associated with higher education also can be traced back to the first decade of the twentieth century. Although it became known as the "Ward method," the approach was the product of a collaboration between Lyman Pierce and Charles Sumner Ward, two highly successful YMCA fund-raisers. Their work together began in 1905 when the YMCA's international headquarters sent Ward to Washington, D.C., to assist Pierce in finishing a campaign to build and furnish a new building. Cutlip credits the two with producing the modern fund-raising campaign, including the following techniques: "careful organization, picked volunteers spurred on by team competition, prestige leaders, powerful publicity, a large gift to be matched by the public's donations, careful records, report meetings, and a definite time limit."[19]

More important perhaps, Cutlip credits Pierce and Ward with introducing a definite system of raising money that would replace the begging that had characterized the approach used by philanthropic organizations up to that time.[20] Pierce and Ward's approach is also credited with being the first to demonstrate that "fund-raising success depended as much on 'method' as on the personalities of the individuals involved."[21] The campaign approach brought method to the madness of soliciting philanthropic gifts, influencing all of fund-raising to become more orderly, systemized, and results-oriented.

The "Ward method" was first applied to higher education in 1914 when the University of Pittsburgh hired Charles Sumner Ward to conduct a campaign. Ward brought a number of people into that campaign who later would become some of the biggest names in professional fund-raising, including Carlton and George Ketchum and Arnaud Marts.

Spurred by the success of World War I fund-raising, several professional fund-raising firms opened in the years immediately after the war's end. Ward and Harvey J. Hill opened Ward and Hill Associates, a professional fund-raising firm in 1919. Soon thereafter, they were joined by Lyman Pierce and F. Herbert Wells, and the firm became Ward, Hill, Pierce & Wells.[22]

John Price Jones, a Harvard alumnus who had worked in professional fund-raising, was hired by his alma mater after World War I to run its Harvard Endowment Fund Campaign. Against a goal of $10 million, the campaign succeeded in raising $14.2 million. Subsequently, Jones founded his own company.[23]

The stock market crash of 1929 and the ensuing Great Depression put tremendous strain on the finances of philanthropic organizations while simultaneously making fund-raising much more difficult. In that environment and with little regulation of fund-raising, high pressure tactics and unethical practices became a growing problem that threatened to taint everyone in the field. In response, representatives of nine major firms met in 1935 to create the American Association of Fundraising Counsel and to establish a fair practice standard. Arguably, this event signaled the professionalization of fund-raising. Without question, it was a major step in that direction. Nonetheless, as Zunz has commented, "it would take another twenty years before social critic Vance Packard would actually popularize the term 'fund-raiser' in his 1957 book, *The Hidden Persuaders*."[24]

On most campuses, the role of the college agent changed dramatically after 1900 as fund-raising became a more orderly, organized, and regular activity. Nonetheless, there was still no consensus in higher education about what to call the work of the agents. For the most part, "fund-raisers" were people who worked for consulting firms (for-profit organizations) that provided counsel to colleges on how to organize and conduct campaigns; in some instances, they placed members of their staff on campus for a period of time to direct a campaign.

Writing in 1969, Harlow J. Heneman, himself a fund-raising consultant, said that as recently as ten years earlier, many college presidents refused to have a person identified as a "fund-raiser" among their senior officers. These presidents, according to Heneman, considered fund-raising to be demeaning or undignified. This did not mean, however, that their institutions did not engage in fund-raising.

Rather, the responsibility was assigned to people whose job titles were in public relations or alumni relations.[25]

Heneman's assertion is supported by the fact that the two professional organizations for people working in external relations (excluding admissions) were the American Alumni Council (AAC), founded in 1927, and the American College Public Relations Association (ACPRA) which originated in 1917, although it was 1946 before that name was adopted. There was no organization of fund-raisers until 1960, when the National Society of Fund Raisers (now the Association of Fundraising Professionals or AFP) was established with assistance from the American Association of Fundraising Counsel (AAFRC), which had been established in 1935 and (since 2006) is now the Giving Institute: Leading Consultants to Non-Profits. Although the membership of the Association of Fundraising Professionals (AFP) is broad-based and open to anyone working in philanthropic fund-raising, many college and university fund-raisers belong to AFP.

The term "development" did not come into use until the 1920s when Northwestern University established the nation's first Department of Development. Comments made by R. L. Stuhr, and incorporated by Worth and Asp into their historical sketch of "Development and Fund Raising," suggest that Northwestern's Department of Development was created to increase the university's likelihood of achieving its long-term goals.[26] Although no one office acting alone can accomplish such a broad mandate, Northwestern's leadership realized that it was less likely to achieve its vision for the institution if responsibility for doing so was not assigned to someone and to a department he or she would direct. At the time, Northwestern was planning a campaign, but its leaders also knew that no single fund-raising drive, regardless of how successful, would be sufficient to fulfill its aspirations, which were not limited to funding although dependent upon it. Northwestern's Department of Development was created to give long-term continuity and clarity to efforts to build acceptance for the institution, recruit students, and obtain financial support.[27]

Its original use notwithstanding, "development" over the years has come to be used interchangeably with "fund-raising." Even so, the terms are not really synonymous. In his 1966 classic, *Designs for Fund-Raising*, Harold Seymour wrote, "the word 'development'... should not be taken merely as another word for raising money, but as a broad term for the planned promotion of understanding, participation, and support."[28] Fund-raising is asking for money; it is episodic. Development cultivates and sustains ongoing relationships that often extend over decades, between an educational institution and its constituencies. The distinctions between the two concepts may be subtle, but they are important to the long-term success of people who accept the challenge of raising the funds necessary to advance a college or university toward its goals.

Although "development" made its debut in higher education in the 1920s, it did not gain widespread usage until after World War II. Even in that era of unprecedented pressure to raise funds, however, acceptance of the term, as well as the concept it embodies, was gradual and uneven. In a survey of its membership in 1952, the American College Public Relations Association found only 13 institutions where a person held the title "director of development."[29] Likewise, in 1955, an American Alumni Council survey, 65 years after the Yale Alumni Fund was organized, revealed that fewer than one-third of colleges and universities had made serious efforts to cultivate alumni philanthropy.[30] Even as late as the 1967–68 academic year, Leslie discovered that 19 percent of co-ed colleges, 4 percent of men's colleges, and 43 percent of women's colleges had no fund-raising staff designated as such.[31] Nevertheless, the pattern was set and change—even among the holdouts—came rapidly in the 1970s as inflation and a slowing down in the growth of other revenue sources made fund-raising a continuous activity and forced alumni fund-raising efforts to broaden into total institutional development programs.[32]

As "development" was emerging as the term of choice in the 1950s, there remained many questions about how the alumni relations, public relations, and fund-raising functions should be organized, as well as uncertainty about their rightful place in the academy. To address these concerns, the American Alumni Council (AAC) and the American College Public Relations Association (ACPRA), with support from the Ford Foundation, undertook a joint study in 1957. This study culminated early in 1958 with a conference involving college presidents, trustees, development officers, and others at the Greenbrier Hotel in West Virginia. The Greenbrier Conference of 1958 proved to be a significant moment in the professionalization of development. The most important outcome of the AAC-ACPRA study was the recommendation of what Leslie has called "an umbrella concept." Alumni relations, public relations, fund-raising, and other related functions (government relations at state institutions, student recruitment, and—where applicable—the university press) would be grouped together under the umbrella. All functions under the umbrella would report to a single officer, in most cases, a vice president for development, who would coordinate their efforts and report directly to the president of the institution. In the years following the conference, the title "vice president for development" became a staple in higher education.[33]

While the umbrella concept was the key recommendation coming out of the AAC-ACPRA study, the most important outcome of the Greenbrier Conference was that, thereafter, the development office and the development officer would have a clear and legitimate place in the organizational structure of higher education administration. While the generosity of donors would continue to be the center of attention in educational philanthropy, presidents and trustees would no longer feel a need to hide from the fact that their colleges employed people whose job it was to cultivate donor interest and ask for gifts.

The proceedings of the Greenbrier Conference of 1958 were recorded in a publication titled *The Advancement of Understanding and Support of Higher Education.* As the title suggests, the idea of calling the umbrella "institutional advancement," instead of "development," was already starting to take hold. The momentum behind this transition accelerated in 1974 when the American Alumni Council (AAC) and the American College Public Relations Association (ACPRA) merged to form the Council for Advancement and Support of Education (CASE). From that time forward, "institutional advancement" has been regarded as the broader concept, and "development" has been taken to mean "fund-raising" when used in connection with higher education.

A. Westley Rowland, general editor of the *Handbook of Institutional Advancement*, has defined "institutional advancement" as encompassing "all activities and programs undertaken by an institution to develop understanding and support from all its constituencies in order to achieve its goals in securing such resources as students, faculty, and dollars."[34] The subtitle of Rowland's *Handbook* provides a good list of the functional areas included within institutional advancement. The subtitle is as follows: *A Modern Guide to Executive Management, Institutional Relations, Fund-Raising, Alumni Administration, Government Relations, Publications, Periodicals, and Enrollment Management.* Although not specifically named, media relations is also part of institutional advancement and, at some schools, strategic planning is as well.

Between the Greenbrier Conference and the creation of CASE, there was a decade-long series of Congressional hearings that culminated in passage of the Tax Reform Act of 1969. The philanthropic community was shaken up by passage of this legislation in ways that it had never been shaken before. After all, when the federal income tax laws were passed earlier in the century, provisions were made that not only exempted nonprofit organizations from taxation but also allowed for the deductibility from taxes of gifts made to those nonprofits that are considered to be charitable. These provisions remained intact and unchallenged when the Internal Revenue Code of 1954, which created the current nonprofit classification system (i.e., section 501), was enacted. Accordingly, the nonprofit sector, as it is now known, was ill-prepared for the often contentious nature of the Congressional hearings leading up to the Tax Reform Act of 1969 or for what they revealed about public misunderstanding and mistrust of the sector in general and of foundations in particular.

Whereas no distinctions among foundations had existed before, the Tax Reform Act of 1969 created four categories of foundations: private, corporate, operating, and community. A further distinction was made in that community foundations were declared to be public charities and exempt, therefore, from the payout requirement imposed on the others. Special annual filings were also mandated, and rather onerous penalties were established for foundations failing to meet payout requirements.

The Tax Reform Act of 1969 also contained provisions creating several new instruments, or vehicles, for charitable giving. These instruments enabled individuals to give assets to 501(c)(3) organizations and obtain immediate tax benefits while also retaining income from the assets given. Throughout the 1970s and much of the 1980s, these new vehicles for charitable giving were known as "deferred gifts." However, as planned giving evolved into a distinct component of the overall development program at most colleges and universities, these newly emerged giving vehicles became known simply as planned gifts.

While much of the Tax Reform Act of 1969 is now regarded as positive, it introduced an unprecedented level of complexity into fundraising, the management of charitable assets, and the administration of foundations. This complexity required new levels of training and professionalism of everyone working in educational fund-raising. From that point forward, there was a growing tendency for development personnel to become specialists in a single area such as planned giving, foundation relations, corporate giving, annual giving, or major gifts fund-raising (which is supported by specialists in prospect research). This movement toward specialization has contributed to the growth of the development staff of most colleges and universities; it has been sustained by the fact specialists are able to raise more money in their areas of expertise, which translates into an overall increase in funds raised. It is further sustained by the fact that organizations such as CASE, AFP, and a growing number of universities offer specialized training in these areas of fund-raising.

An important role of any professional organization is to set standards for the ethical conduct of its members. CASE did this in 1982. In 1993, CASE and the other professional organizations involved in philanthropic fund-raising (American Association of Fundraising Counsel, Association for Healthcare Philanthropy, and the Association of Fundraising Professionals) took the concern for ethics and fair play an important step further by adopting a common Donor Bill of Rights, which is readily available online.

Educational fund-raising did not become an organized activity until the turn of the twentieth century. The degree of organization and the professionalization of the people did not undergo dramatic change until after World War II. Since that time, however, progress on both fronts has been rapid. Especially pivotal moments in the professionalization of educational fund-raising were the Greenbrier Conference of 1958 and the founding of the Council for Advancement and Support of Education (CASE) in 1974. Two post-World War II trends are evident in this brief historical sketch: educational fund-raising has become more professionalized and there has been a growing focus on raising funds through well-organized development programs. A third trend, which will be discussed in the next section, is the shift toward major-gift fund-raising that has come to characterize the field over the past two decades.[35]

Given all of the change in the role, one is tempted to comment that the development officer of today would not recognize the college agent of an earlier era—and vice versa. However, it is entirely possible that the kind of people who choose this peculiar calling for their life's work has not changed much over the centuries. They are the kind of people who believe in the mission of higher education and the good that philanthropy makes possible and embrace their work as a form of moral action. And in that sense, they might well recognize one another, although the college agent of old would likely be astounded by the number of women who are working in the field and who hold positions of leadership today.

The Development Office

There is considerable difference, of course, between the organizational charts of a liberal arts college with a dozen professionals on its development staff and a large research university with three hundred. Much of the difference, in fact, is in organization. While there are variations in approach, the work of educational fund-raising is the same regardless of the setting.

One of the main differences between smaller and large institutions is in the connections and communications among staff members. Typically, in smaller colleges and universities all of the development staff is housed in the same building, which enables frequent interaction among the whole staff. In many—if not most—large universities, each college or school has one or more development staff members who report directly to the dean of that unit and may be housed with the unit rather than with development colleagues. If that unit happens to be the medical school or the college of health sciences, it can have quite a large development staff devoted to meeting its specialized fund-raising needs. Also, at schools with large NCAA Division I athletic programs, there most often is a fund-raising staff that reports directly to the athletic director.

The size of the staff in these satellite development offices depends on a combination of that unit's funding needs and the opportunities for raising funds to support it. Moreover, in most universities today, there is an expectation that the deans of the separate colleges will be engaged in raising funds. The development staff assigned to the unit works with that dean to arrange appointments with prospective donors and the director of development for that college often accompanies the dean on such calls. Another factor determining the size of the development staff in each college or school within the university is the portion of the overall goal of the university's comprehensive campaign assigned to that area. With an increasing number of billion-dollar-plus campaigns, the figure can be substantial.

As the word "satellite" implies, even the largest universities have a central development office. In state institutions, the central development office often is the foundation office, since state institutions frequently establish separate 501(c)(3) entities to raise and receive funds for their support. Whether the chief officer's title is president of the foundation or senior vice president for development, there invariably is an individual charged with setting the tone and direction of the university's overall development program. This person works closely with the university president to ensure that his or her priorities are being addressed and that messages from the development office to the institution's constituencies are consistent with the president's statements about the school and its future.

With so many players involved, coordination of effort requires a great deal of the senior development officer's time and attention. In large settings, special care must be taken to ensure that donors are not solicited by multiple units of the university. This can be more challenging than it appears at first glance. If a wealthy alumnus and former football player is a graduate of both the college of arts and sciences and the law school, whose major gift prospect is he—the college of arts and science or the law school, or is he the province of the athletic association? What if his spouse is a graduate of the music conservatory? What if their daughter is a student in the school of engineering? The details get complicated rather quickly, and if care is not taken, a single prospective donor might be solicited by two or more development officers or deans in a short period of time. An important role of the central development office is to make sure such does not happen.

Generally speaking, the central development office is in charge of those aspects of the fund-raising program that support the overall institution. The annual fund is a good example. Also, rather than each college having its own staff of people with expertise in prospect research or planned giving, those people usually are in central development where they can support the major gift officers in all of the satellite operations. Additionally, in order to ensure that every gift is processed, properly recorded, and—most important—acknowledged, gift processing and record keeping are central development office functions.

Preparing for, announcing, directing, and celebrating periodic efforts to raise substantial sums of money—known as campaigns— is also a central development function. These days, "extraordinary" may be a better word than "substantial" to describe the fund-raising goals of campaigns. With 80 campaigns either under way or already completed at or above a billion dollars, the billion-dollar campaign has become commonplace in American higher education. The size of a campaign goal, aside from intended uses of the funds raised, has become a benchmark in the competition for prestige that is a hallmark of the American university system. Among smaller schools, especially selective liberal arts colleges, the competition is no less intense, even though their goals are smaller since they have fewer alumni, parents, and friends. Overall, the current benchmark of highest prestige is a goal of five hundred million dollars or more. Assuming that the US economy continues to generate wealth at the rate it has since World War II, it is only a matter of time before this benchmark moves up to the billion-dollar level.

As is implied by the heavy reliance on terms such as "typically," and "generally speaking" to describe the organizational structures of university development programs, there are many variations in today's mega-university. There is no one-size-fits-all correct way of organizing a large development program. The important thing is for the form to follow function and for the form to fit the specific environment. Each institutional environment is a bit different from all others. In the sections that follow, some elements common to all comprehensive development programs will be briefly reviewed. The reader should bear in mind that in smaller operations, it is common for multiple functions to be assigned to a single development officer. One good example is the combination of corporate and foundation giving programs under a single director of corporate and foundation relations. Another is for combined responsibilities for stewardship and prospect research to be assigned to one individual.

Annual Giving—Annual giving is both the foundation upon which the development program is built and its leading edge. Annual giving traces its roots to the work of the college agents and the actions of those forward-thinking alumni who established the Yale Alumni Fund in 1890. Another part of its heritage at many schools is the Alumni Loyalty Fund that commonly was run by the alumni office in the years before there was a separate development office. Yet it also is the place where new technologies such as social media, e-solicitations, and online giving are making their mark.

In a very important sense, it is the annual giving office that teaches philanthropy to rising generations of alumni donors. This is done through the phonathon, which typically employs student callers, and especially through the senior class gift programs that most schools run. An important objective of the senior class gift program is to instill a habit of giving to the institution before students leave campus. Today, stories abound about the modest size of the first gift made to Johns Hopkins University by alumnus, business entrepreneur, and former New York mayor Michael Bloomberg, who—in the intervening years—has committed more than a billion dollars to his alma mater.[36] Many schools have their own story about a major donor whose giving started out small and grew large.

There is a huge difference, of course, between having wealth and being philanthropically inclined. Prospective major gift donors often first demonstrate a willingness to give generously to a college or university through their annual gifts. Any donor regularly giving a thousand dollars or more through the annual fund merits a closer look to determine if she is a prospect for a major gift to the institution. If not, perhaps that person would be willing to serve as a volunteer leader for her class's next reunion class gift, if she is an alumna. As discussed earlier, reunion class giving programs can be traced back to the twenty-fifth anniversary reunion gift of the class of 1881 to Harvard.

Except at institutions that have a separate staff in charge of reunion class giving, it is typically managed by the annual giving office with assistance from major gift officers who may have as their prospects people who are in classes with milestone reunions on the horizon.

One of the great frustrations of development officers is the failure of donors to make gifts every year. Part of the magic behind the name "annual fund" is the hope that it will encourage donors to give annually. To further encourage them, many schools have found ways to recognize donors who make gifts in consecutive years, sometimes including the number of years of consecutive giving after the individual's name in the donor report.

In addition to consecutive giving, colleges and universities want to encourage their constituencies to increase the amount of their giving over time, if not annually. Toward this end, a series of gift clubs or donor recognition societies has been established at most schools. Typically, these clubs start at the 100-dollar level and move up from that point to multiple thousands. In more recent years, colleges and universities also have established cumulative or lifetime giving societies to recognize donors whose giving totals a hundred thousand dollars or more. The idea is to encourage both regular giving and substantial giving over the course of the donor's lifetime.

Typically, annual giving programs generate gifts that relieve the annual operating budget. A few schools count only unrestricted gifts in their annual funds, but most count any gift that is budget-relieving and likely to be repeated annually. Direct mail, phonathon, electronic solicitations, and face-to-face fund-raising are the solicitation techniques used to generate gifts to the annual fund. Alumni, the parents of currently enrolled students, and non-alumni friends, some of whom are likely the parents of former students, are the primary constituencies solicited for annual fund gifts. Although not typically among the primary audience to which annual fund appeals are addressed, in some instances corporations and foundations make recurring gifts that are counted in a school's annual giving results.

Corporate Giving—Corporate giving to higher education has a rich history. Although a change in the tax laws in 1935 first allowed corporations to make charitable gifts from their taxable income, no specific mention was made regarding contributions to higher education. On that basis a group of A. P. Smith Company stockholders in 1951 mounted a legal challenge to the board of director's decision to make a gift to Princeton. In his decision that was announced in 1953, Judge Alfred P. Stein ruled such contributions "necessary to assure a 'friendly reservoir' of trained men and women from which industry might draw."[37] Corporate giving to higher education flourished in the years thereafter.

Two other events in the history of corporate giving are particularly noteworthy. In 1952, the Council for Financial Aid to Education (CFAE) was founded. Curti and Nash declare CFAE, which is now CAE (Council for Aid to Education), to have been the most influential fund-raising organization to come into being after World War II.[38] While the council has compiled an annual survey of all giving to education (VSE or Voluntary Support of Education) since 1957, it has taken a special interest in corporate philanthropy.

The other event was the decision made in 1954 by General Motors to match employee contributions. This decision launched the corporate matching gifts programs that for most of next half-century were a particularly important source of support for higher education. Unfortunately, in the past 15 years, more and more corporations have discontinued their matching gifts programs.

Moreover, in the twenty-first century, corporations have become much more strategic in their giving, and their giving is tied more closely to their marketing. Still, corporations remain an important source of funding for research. Accordingly, research universities typically have people on their development staff with expertise in corporate giving. Schools located in metropolitan areas with concentrations of major corporate facilities or headquarters offices may also have corporate giving officers. Many others combine corporate giving with foundation relations since both require a grants-writing approach to solicitation.

Foundation Relations—As the number of foundations continues to grow, so too does the importance of foundation support of higher education. There are now an estimated 80,000 foundations in the United States, and they were the largest source of support for higher education in 2012. In fact, foundation giving exceeded alumni giving by nearly 20 percent ($9.2 billion from foundations versus $7.7 billion from alumni) in fiscal 2012.[39]

Although there was much concern at the time that passage of the Tax Reform Act of 1969 spelled the doom of foundations in America, that did not happen. To be sure, there was a decade-long period of adjustment when the number of foundations decreased by 2,000 (from 24,000 in 1969 to 22,000 in 1980). However, over the next two decades, the number soared, exceeding 50,000 by 2000.[40] Clearly, the pace of growth continues to be quite robust despite the widespread growth of donor advised funds (DAFs) which provide an alternative to establishing a foundation for wealth holders who wish to set aside funds for later distribution to charitable organizations.

No college or university can or should ignore foundations as a source of financial support. Nonetheless, it is important to be realistic about what foundations will support, which pretty much excludes operating costs. Most foundation grant making is project-focused; this orientation is captured in the claim that foundations provide the venture capital for social progress. The type of projects that any one foundation chooses to fund is in keeping with its mission. The good news is that information about the missions, interests, and funding priorities is readily available online, in print, or both. This means, however, that foundation relations staff members must be good researchers as well as good writers.

As the significance of foundation support of higher education continues to grow, assuming that it does, it is likely that the size of the foundation relations staff and the role they play in the overall development program will also grow.

Planned Giving—Although it is sometimes said that the Tax Reform Act of 1969 created planned giving, that is not really true. While it may be true that the Tax Reform Act of 1969 mandated the hiring of specialists in planned giving, it did nothing to alter the fact that bequests are at the heart of a planned giving program as they long have been. *Giving USA 2013* reports that bequests to philanthropy in 2012 exceeded 23 billion dollars.[41]

Because bequests are so important to endowment growth, it is somewhat surprising that it was not until 1924 that Cornell launched the first organized bequest program in American higher education.[42] Whether or not an institution's leaders feel that it has sufficient in-house expertise to offer gift annuities or to promote giving through lead trusts or unitrusts, even the smallest colleges ought to promote giving by bequest and through life insurance.

Alumni are especially good prospects for planned giving. But, in actuality, any individual who has demonstrated a belief in the work and mission of the institution through her or his giving ought to be invited to consider a planned gift that would represent that person's ultimate gift to the college or university. With planned giving, in particular, the ages and stages of a donor's life make a difference. Young donors are generally more focused on starting families and getting established in their careers than they are in planning their estates or securing income for their retirement. For these and other reasons, planned giving opportunities are generally promoted through articles in the college magazine and special newsletters targeted to an older segment of the mailing list.

Planned giving, even if is limited to a wills and bequest program, is a way for colleges and universities to participate in and take appropriate advantage of the ongoing transfer of wealth from one generation to the next. It also is an attractive and cost effective way for a college to provide assistance to its donors in their estate planning. Various planned giving vehicles, especially gift annuities and unitrusts, can be used by donors to provide themselves and their spouses with income during their lifetimes while making an often substantial gift to their college or university.

Despite the attention focused on deferred gifts, not all planned gifts are deferred. Some, such as gifts from individual retirement accounts (IRAs), which Congress has made possible through special legislation in recent years, provide immediate support. The real meaning behind the term is that sophisticated legal counsel and professional estate planning often are required in order for the donor to make the gift he or she intends for the institution.

Because special knowledge is required, not every development officer is equipped to do planned giving nor is everyone temperamentally well suited for this kind of work. Although having a background in law can be very helpful, one does not have to be a lawyer. But if the planned giving staff does not include a lawyer (or lawyers), the staff must have ready access to a firm that has expertise in these matters.

While there are special considerations to be taken into account in establishing a planned giving program, no development program is comprehensive or complete without one.

Major Gifts and Campaign Fund-Raising—Forty years ago, the conventional wisdom about campaign fund-raising was that in order to maintain the required level of intensity, a campaign could not last longer than three years. Two other basic assumptions were that donors would not make pledges lasting more than three years and that 80 percent of the money raised would come from 20 percent of the donors (fund-raising's parallel to the Pareto principle). In the 1990s, as campaign goals grew much larger, there was a shift toward a five-year campaign schedule and a pledge period that extended over five years.

By that time, conventional wisdom said that 90 percent of the funds pledged would come from the top 10 percent of donors. After the turn of the twenty-first century, the size of campaign goals skyrocketed, campaigns became seven-year efforts, and donors were increasingly encouraged to pledge over whatever number of years would enable them to make their optimal gift. Also, there was a growing awareness that fewer than 5 percent of the donors would account for 95 percent or more of the campaign goal.

As campaigns became more frequent, seasoned development officers and other higher education leaders began to realize that it was not just during campaigns that a small number of donors accounted for the vast majority of the money given to higher education—the same thing was true year in and year out. While it had long been known that higher education receives a majority of the largest gifts made in America each year, many people were surprised by the mounting evidence that 5 percent of donors regularly contribute almost 95 percent of all gifts to higher education.[43] The response, naturally, has been a growing focus on major gift fund-raising. Whereas, in the past, colleges and universities would release all campaign staff once a drive was over, they began to keep at least a core group of them to continue essentially the same work between campaigns. Members of the major gifts and planned giving staff often work together; both are supported by prospect research, which has become a continuous activity instead of something done in preparation for a campaign.

Campaigns with ambitious goals cause donors to raise their sights, which is necessary to generate the funds needed for capital improvements and endowment growth. Thus, it remains important to have campaigns, even though colleges and universities are increasingly in continuous campaign mode.

Like campaign fund-raising, major gift fund-raising is done face to face. Major-gifts officers help maintain strong and supportive relationships with major-gift donors between campaigns. They also work with the prospect research staff to identify new prospective major-gift donors and, then, to build relationships with them.

In the September 15, 1995, issue of the *Chronicle of Higher Education*, Rita Bornstein, then president of Rollins College, was quoted as saying: "The art of fund raising is understanding an institution and being able to interpret that institution to the outside world to stimulate giving. Fund raising is more than asking for money. It's connecting with the external world."[44] This is indeed what the work of development, and especially major gift fund-raising, is all about.

Conclusion

In 1973, the Council for Financial Aid to Education declared that American higher education was "elevated to excellence" by philanthropy.[45] There can be little doubt this is true. The partnership between philanthropy and higher education has made possible an excellent system of higher learning in the United States. It has created educational opportunity for countless young men and women whose lives have been enriched and whose contributions to society have been greater. It has made possible breakthrough research in medicine and science. It has strengthened the economy and enhanced the quality of life for all Americans. The heroes of this partnership are the philanthropists, the many people who have given of their resources to fuel the advancement of learning in America. But the middlemen—the honorable beggars, college agents, and development officers—who stimulated their generosity have made a vital contribution as well.

7

Colleges and Their Constituencies: New Directions in Philanthropy

In 2000 Harvard political scientist Robert Putnam attracted widespread national attention for his provocative book, *Bowling Alone*.[1] His concluding observation was that by the late twentieth century there were alarming signs that Americans had ceased to be a nation of joiners. Membership in the kinds of voluntary associations that had characterized US civic and public life for centuries, such as those described in chapter 2, summarizing Alexis de Tocqueville's accounts of American society in 1831, appeared to be declining.[2] If this were so, it would have, of course serious, consequences for philanthropy that customarily has depended on public-minded voluntary collaborations of groups of private citizens.

Putnam was accurate, even perceptive, for identifying changing trends in participation associated with certain kinds of groups. He noted declining membership and vitality of service clubs such as Benevolent and Protective Order of the Elks, Veterans of Foreign Wars (VFW), Rotary Club, Lions Club, and Optimists. Did this necessarily mean that Americans of the 1990s were withdrawing from groups and, literally or figuratively, eschewing membership in bowling leagues in favor of "bowling alone?" Voluntary associations, including nonprofit organizations, often reflect generational experiences and behaviors. One explanation for the apparent decline was that the men and women who had come of age in World War II were now either retired or deceased. Little wonder that the crowds at VFW Halls on Saturday night or the Rotary Club luncheons on Tuesday were marked by empty seats. At colleges and universities, professors may not have been "bowling alone," but there were signs that now they were "eating alone." Faculty clubs that had been the focal point of campus camaraderie and gossip had all but disappeared.[3] Although such associations and organizations may have seemed to be enduring "pillars of the community," they were indelibly linked to a specific generational age group. Many made faint effort to recruit new members by expanding their missions or protocols.

To counter and supplement the older generation of associations, what stands out since around 1980 has been the proliferation of philanthropic support and service organizations tied to both public and private institutions. The designation "Friends of the…" became a conspicuous feature in a growing number of activities in American civic life. Tax shortfalls or legislation such as California's Proposition 13 passed into law in 1978 may have reduced biennial state and local funding to schools and public libraries. But some of the slack was taken up by a spirited proliferation of new incorporated groups, such as "The Friends of the Community Library." Colleges and universities were especially fertile ground for the sprouting of numerous "Friends" groups—each dedicated to its chosen area, ranging from the university art museum to the children's hospital. Community social events increasingly centered on wine-and-cheese receptions that were both a fund-raiser and source of involvement for donors and recipients alike. Furthermore students at numerous campuses took the initiative to create service-learning groups whose activities provided a dramatic, enduring surge of energy and innovation for college- and university-based philanthropy. Also, the increasing diversity of the American college and university campus was giving rise to a large number of new associations and groups that reflected the changing constituencies in matters of gender, race, ethnicity, religion, and sexual orientation.

These transformations have provided yet the latest chapter in what historian Peter Dobkin Hall and fellow scholars have been documenting to explain the invention of the nonprofit sector over three hundred years.[4] It has never been static, never homogenous, and usually marked by contradictions, rivalries, flux, and disagreements within its own broad boundaries. So, perhaps Americans were bowling alone—but this may well have been a respite from getting ready to prepare a report at the annual meeting of the Friends of Historic Preservation or attend an exhibit and fund-raising event at the Friends of the College Art Museum. Illustrative of national developments that echoed these grass roots initiatives was the founding in 1980 of Independent Sector—a Washington, D.C.–based association that brought together representatives from a wide range of philanthropic and service groups.

An interesting example of the mix of continuity and change in American philanthropy comes about from an unexpected case: the rise and demise of the monumental Crystal Cathedral in Orange County, California. In chapter 4 about endowments our analysis suggested some of the pitfalls of counting on perpetuity. For over four decades the Crystal Cathedral had embodied the ultimate combination of religion and self-promotion amidst a prosperous commercial culture. This mega-church, founded by the Reverend Robert Schuler, commanded a striking physical presence with its towering glass edifice combined with the largest religious television-viewing audience in the nation. Members of the nondenominational congregation totalling 1,800 had accepted the invitation to make donations for inscribed granite stones on its "Walk of Faith" as memorials that were supposed to last forever. For all this prominence and prosperity, in 2010 the Crystal Cathedral declared bankruptcy due to overreaching projects and extravagant spending by its leadership. Its imposing glass building and campus were purchased by the Roman Catholic Diocese of Orange County. Soon thereafter donors were notified that their memorial granite markers that honored loved ones would not last for perpetuity—as promised.[5]

The Crystal Cathedral was an exceptional case, both in its dramatic ascent and financial success followed its equally dramatic implosion. It did have direct implications for higher education because by 2012 numerous colleges and universities were facing a reckoning with their degrees of construction debt. According to Moody's, overall debt levels at 500 colleges and universities more than doubled during the period 2000 to 2011, as the total reached $122 billion. The Ohio State University, for example, reported $2 billion in construction debt. Troubling data showed that income from gifts and investments declined more than 40 percent relative to the amount colleges owed. What one reporter called a "spending binge," often on lavish buildings to attract students, now meant that those same students were stuck with picking up the bill via special student fee levies. Fitness centers with climbing walls, student unions with elaborate facilities, and dormitories with single-occupancy suites represented the kinds of expensive construction projects that were escalating college indebtedness.[6]

In contrast to campus construction financed by borrowing, some universities enjoyed unprecedented good fortune—such as the University of Southern California which featured a full-page announcement in the *New York Times* for its 2014 "historic $50 million gift to establish the Michelson Center for Convergent Bioscience. Thanks to Dr. Gary

Michelson, "a visionary philanthropist and retired orthopaedic spinal surgeon," USC now had the 190,000 square-foot facility for state-of-the-art research that had potential to transform the biological sciences into "quantitative and predictive sciences, fast-tracking the detection and cure of diseases."[7]

These varied examples provide a good illustration of the character of philanthropy in the early twenty-first century as one of the perils and problems of prosperity. A primer and preview on this comes from American popular culture, whether in, namely, the 1958 hit rock n'roll song, *Money*; or, the long tradition of self-help motivational speakers who have exhorted Americans that acquiring wealth can be one's destiny, all the way to the Hollywood movie *Wall Street*'s hyperbolic mantra that "Greed...is Good!"

These vestiges of belief and advocacy from popular culture at first glance may appear to be unrelated to established groups as foundation officials or a university board of trustees. On closer inspection, they sing a similar song. Few American nonprofit organizations would disagree with this candid revelation about the perpetual need for money. According to the Harvard view book of 1963, "Wealth, like age, does not make a college great. But it helps." Fifty years later, Harvard along with all colleges and universities reaffirmed that money mattered. As Scott Jaschik commented in his 2013 article, "Rich Harvard, Poor Harvard":

> Harvard University recently announced an 11.3 percent return on its endowment, which was valued at $32.7 billion on June 30. That's the largest endowment in higher education. The university also recently announced a $6.5 billion fund-raising campaign—the largest ever in higher education. But an interview released by the university Friday with its chief financial officer, Dan Shore, focused on financial pressures on the university. He said that the university has a $34 million deficit. And while that's small in the context of the university's $4.2 billion budget, he said that "the path toward our ability to thrive in the future requires that we not wait until the deficit gets even bigger before we start to act, because then it will require us to be in a much more reactive position." He also noted uncertainty about federal support, on which Harvard relies for research.

Jaschik went on to note, "In language that is similar to that used at many less wealthy colleges, Shore also said that Harvard can't simply add expenses. 'The campaign helps, but, fundamentally, we can no longer live in a world where things continue simply to be additive,'"

Shore said. "The next new and exciting thing that we think it's important to do can't simply be layered on top of all of the other things that we've been doing. It's just not a sustainable model. And I think the entire higher education industry is feeling the need to move away from that way of doing business."[8]

George Bernard Shaw once responded to the claim that "money is the root of all evil" with the rebuttal that "*lack* of money was the root of all evil." The implication for the philanthropy of higher education is that money alone is not a panacea for problems. Indeed, at many colleges and universities acquiring a lot of additional money might simply mean expanding and extending rather undistinctive programs and bad practices—a situation that reinforces complacence without encouraging earnest innovation or reform. Hence, the crucial distinction is that getting money has to be accompanied by wise discretionary choices on how and where to spend. Stewardship of college and university wealth, then, endures as the historic challenge facing higher education and philanthropy, whether in 1636 or 2014. The past is prologue for a challenging, exciting era in American higher education of the twenty-first century. And, this overarching challenge can be parsed into some particular topics that have come to the fore recently in a series of episodes and cases that illustrate perennial dilemmas. As the concluding chapter of this book, the present chapter on new directions in philanthropy provides grounding and interpretation of several essential themes and principles.

First, research on philanthropy and institutional conduct has been increasingly sophisticated and pragmatic in applications to institutional planning and decision-making.[9] In December 2013 a study sponsored by Indiana University's Lilly Family School of Philanthropy and the fund-raising consulting company of Johnson Grossnickle and Associates issued a report with the major finding that a college or university was more likely to receive multi-million dollar gifts from donors if students and alumni reported a great campus experience that fostered loyalty and affiliation; a long-serving president; institutional maturity; a strong national ranking; a high percentage of tenured professors; a relatively large endowment; regional location, with metropolitan and Northeastern sites being most favorable; and, a pattern of thoughtful growth.[10] How colleges and universities opt to respond to this "data driven" directive will be crucial to survival and flourishing in the future.

Second, philanthropy in the United States is being shaped by a new generation of philanthropists—an interesting mix of distinctive large donors along with a formidable change in giving patterns according to age and demographic profiles. On August 5, 2010, for example, "in an unprecedented show of generosity, a band of forty American billionaires have pledged to give at least half their fortunes to charity."[11] Led by Warren Buffett and Microsoft co-founder Bill Gates and Melinda Gates, the roster included television mogul Ted Turner, Oracle co-founder Larry Ellison, and Hollywood movie maker George Lucas, among others. To probe this groundswell of robust philanthropy that has emerged in the early twenty-first century, it is useful to look specifically at two influential individuals who have led by example— George Soros and Michael Bloomberg.

George Soros, who made his fortune as an international financier is a citizen of the United States who fled his native Hungary during German occupation in World War II. He found sanctuary in England where he studied at the London School of Economics and, then, moved to New York City in 1956. His commitment as a philanthropist since 1979 has been to promoting democratic institutions and a genuine civic society—goals pursued internationally through his Open Society Foundations to which he has contributed $8 billion.[12] His philanthropy is pertinent to higher education on several counts: first, his reliance on and belief in the efficacy of colleges and universities to educate and to carry out programs associated with civic society; second, his interest in reforming universities worldwide, as suggested by his showcase School of Public Policy at the Central European University in Budapest. Third, he has provided funding and leadership for the Soros Justice Fellows Program. Fourth, a number of his initiatives have dealt with the commitment to encouraging the founding and development of private higher education and philanthropic organizations in Eastern Europe and other regions which heretofore have had little tradition of a nonprofit or independent sector.

Michael Bloomberg, who completed his third consecutive term as mayor of New York City in December 2013, personifies an American success story built on a combination of intelligence, education, and energy that became the basis for making a fortune in financial software development that now is estimated to be worth $34 billion. Most pertinent for this book is that Bloomberg, whose philanthropy has touched numerous projects, places particular emphasis on support for education. Recalling the preceding mention of the 2013 Indiana University study of what makes a college attractive to donors, Bloomberg is unabashed in his generous praise for his undergraduate alma mater, the Johns Hopkins University. Along with his success as a student and, later, as an entrepreneur, the striking feature of Bloomberg's story is his gratitude to Johns Hopkins for the opportunities its student life and residential campus provided him to be a leader and participant in a range of activities, including having served as president of his senior class, his fraternity, and the campus-wide Greek fraternity council. In contrast to a boring high school, Bloomberg blossomed in the stimulating academics and campus from which he graduated in 1964. Starting with a $5 dollar donation he made as a young alumnus in 1964, Bloomberg's total gifts to his alma mater have surpassed $1.1 billion—ranging from bricks and mortar donations to endowments for the School of Public Health and numerous other areas.[13]

Although a great deal of attention gravitates to such charismatic, large donors and to their foundations, it is crucial to keep in mind that large gifts coexist with and sometimes may be matched in total dollars by the cumulative philanthropy of relatively small gifts by thousands of individual donors who are affiliated, for example, as alumni. In 1992 individual contributions represented 82 percent of all philanthropic dollars.[14] The topic that ties together these disparate threads is that of colleges and their constituencies. Our analysis of philanthropy and higher education is characterized by close attention to historical developments. However, it is neither antiquarian nor backward looking in tone. Rather, our concluding commentary emphasizes the importance of college and university leaders to rely on the historical data to look *forward*—to acquire a working sense of how the profile of donors and their philanthropic choices are *changing*. And, the crucial corollary is that academic and campus traditions also must change in harmony with new generations of constituents. This includes changes *within* established institutions, as the composition of their students, faculty, staff, and board increasingly reflect the growing inclusion of heretofore small groups.[15] A significant example of these changes is the undergraduate-enrollment data from the University of California, Berkeley, for Fall 2012 displayed according to race and ethnicity: 44 percent Asian, 14 percent Hispanic, 4 percent African American, 10 percent international, and 32 percent White.[16]

The changing composition of students, alumni, and donors reflect features of age, race, religion, gender, political perspectives, physical conditions, and sexual orientation. A positive sign of change is, for example, when a campus organization for Islamic students introduces fellow students from the entire campus to the historic notion of *zakat*—the requirement of giving to the less fortunate. All the more encouraging and enlightening is when one learns from students at Hillel that they invoke the Hebrew word, *tzedakah*—translated as "charity."[17]

Also encouraging among the recent changes has been the emergence of organized, articulate groups representing issues traditionally ignored—such as students who are deaf or have severe hearing loss who heretofore had been marginalized or underserved by colleges and universities.[18] Often overlooked is the rapid pace of demographic change, as each campus undergoes an annual turnover of about 20 to 25 percent of its student population—an institutional dynamic that increases the urgency for university leaders to be cognizant of new groups.

Complacence or being oblivious to change is anathema to creating a vital and well-funded college or university. Major foundations, for example, have noted clearly over the past decade that their generous support of higher education has dwindled and diverted because many colleges are perceived by the foundations as having the goal of remaining the "same, except with more financial support."[19] Additional concerns by foundations were that colleges and universities tended to show a lack of common goals for innovation, little systematic innovation, few measurable results, and imperceptible needs. The message was that the burden of proof rested with colleges and universities if they sought support from foundations.

Diversity in higher education also plays out in the special missions and constituencies of many colleges. This has been a major source of diversity and complexity when one looks at institutions and donors. It has, at very least, two significant variations. One, it refers to growing diversity *within* institutions. Two, it refers to diversity *among* institutions in the panorama of American colleges and universities. This phenomenon has become sufficiently pronounced if not pervasive that researchers in philanthropy have identified what are called "minority serving institutions."[20]

Historically Black colleges and universities (HBCUs) suffered for years from misrepresentation as institutions that were financially mismanaged and also lagging in philanthropic initiatives. However, recent research by such scholars as Marybeth Gasman and Noah Drezner have presented fresh data which amend the earlier, erroneous characterizations. Gasman's study of the United Negro College Fund relied on archival sources from a variety of organizations to tell the story of one of the most remarkable and successful initiatives over a half century. The slogan, "A Mind Is a Terrible Thing to Waste!"

gained nationwide recognition.[21] Compelling as that campaign was, it was only part of the organizational saga of innovation in fund-raising that included initiative by wives of corporate executives in New York City, resilience to assert the importance of HBCUs in the wake of the *Brown* v. *Board of Education* decision by the US Supreme Court in 1954, and other challenges that had faced this institutional group. Gasman and Drezner also have brought belated attention to the Oram Group—a "maverick" in American higher education funding for its commitment to working with the Black college community during the 1970s.[22]

To speak of women as a minority in higher education is both bittersweet and inaccurate. If there is a cumulative story of success in expansion and achievement it is the role of women as students, faculty, administrators, trustees—and, as philanthropists. An excellent work that recognized and researched this topic is Andrea Walton's anthology on women and philanthropy.[23] A significant insight offered by several contributing authors to that anthology is that the contribution of women directly and indirectly, formally and informally, to philanthropy in higher education often has been woefully underacknowledged. For starters, one might consider the royal charter for a college in Virginia in 1693, named in honor of King William *and* Queen Mary. Indeed, reading through transcripts and records, one finds that Queen Mary was the proactive, prime mover in gaining both a charter and funding for the new College, with King William's attitude ranging from indifferent to acquiescent. One reason that the contribution of women as college builders and supporters has been understated is that often their contributions were in terms of time, service, and informal influence. In other words, for women philanthropy often has meant myriad contributions along with money. A good example of this distinctive role has been that of "Sisters in Service"—African-American sororities whose members as students and alumni have a strong tradition of commitment and organization in educational and service activities.[24] Even women's roles in philanthropy as donors have been integral—as suggested by Jane Stanford's support for the founding and, then, financial survival of young Stanford University. Among the great foundations, Olivia Slocum Sage, widow of railroad financier Russell Sage, used her inheritance of $70 million to fund numerous college projects and, most enduring and influential, to found in 1907 the Russell Sage Foundation which was committed to substantive pioneering initiatives in social work. And, after its founding, its effective leader was Mary E. Richmond.[25] Elsewhere in the prestigious network of major foundations, a woman—Sydnor H. Walker—was an early and long-time leader of Rockefeller support for social work, social sciences, and universities in the South.[26] Yet another example of a woman as a college founder and donor, Scripps College—a member of California's Claremont Colleges—was founded in 1926 by Ellen Browning Scripps who believed that "the paramount obligation of a college is to develop in its students the ability to think clearly and independently, and the ability to live confidently, courageously, and hopefully." Scripps, a newspaper editor and journalist who inherited her family's publishing fortune, devoted herself to other philanthropic projects, including the funding and founding of the Scripps Institute of Oceanography.

In addition to these forgotten or underappreciated pioneering women, the statistical profile is that by 2011 women represented almost 60 percent—that is, approximately 12 million out of 20 million of all undergraduate enrollments. Furthermore, women's academic achievement was high, as they received a disproportionate percentage of conferred bachelor's degrees and academic honors.[27] Whereas in 1969 women constituted a small percentage of enrollments at medical schools and law schools, this changed persistently starting around 1974 so that by 2011 about half the students in these advanced professional schools were women. Between 2000 and 2013 six women had served as president of an Ivy League university, including Brown, the University of Pennsylvania, Harvard, and Princeton—a change that was historically remarkable and institutionally beneficial. It has followed that women as alumnae of undergraduate colleges and advanced and professional degree programs gained an increasing share of leadership roles in business, law, medicine, and higher education. This in turn has meant that women as alumnae have increasing stature and representation as donors and board members in higher education. To *not* acknowledge and incorporate such changing composition into revising campus events, traditions, ceremonies and development activities would be myopic and irresponsible.

Since a student's satisfaction with her or his college experience is a strong predictor of future-giving to Alma Mater, development officers are wise to consider the growing body of research literature on the priorities, values, and decisions of young alumni. Scholars such as Travis McDearmon provide systematic data base analysis from which one can discern substantial trends.[28] In addition to the patterns of giving by recent college graduates, there are interesting findings when one analyzes the larger sphere of young women and men who have inherited substantial wealth from their families. Typically in their mid-20s, this group has been called the "Trust Fund Progressives." Their collective profile indicates a strong commitment to become involved in philanthropy sooner rather than later, and to give away a sizeable part of their inheritance at an early age. The explanation is that they have an "urge to redistribute" wealth and are "looking to level the playing field in some small way" today.[29] These promising, intriguing trends are not always completely compelling or persuasive. For example, in 2010, Mark Zuckerberg, the young and wealthy mastermind of Facebook held an unabashedly self-serving press conference and then an appearance on the Oprah Winfrey television show in which he announced his matching gift of $100 million to Newark, New Jersey Public Schools—a benevolent gesture that seemed to emphasize instant public relations over thoughtful planning for genuine innovation.[30] This was an example of philanthropy as opportunism, all the more dubious in that its eventual distribution of funds was devoted to fulfilling existing financial obligations for payments—items that were overwhelmingly "business as usual," as distinguished from thoughtful innovation or reform.

The preceding analysis has emphasized the importance for colleges to be aware of and responsive to diversity, especially the emergence of relatively new organized affiliations and identities among alumni and supporters. To another extreme, college and university leadership—including presidents, vice presidents for development, and boards of trustees—need to pay attention to the very different problem of overemphasis in selected, established areas and their alumni constituencies. Foremost in this category is intercollegiate athletics. It is a higher education activity that personifies the problems of popularity and imbalance—along with changing generational patterns of involvement.[31] A vice president for development most likely welcomes fund-raising by the intercollegiate athletics association or department for the obvious reason that it tends to bring in a lot of money, and this can be included into the total fund-raising revenue for the university-wide development office. That benefit, however, is incomplete because it also creates serious questions of propriety and priorities for an educational institution and related tax deductions.

One perennial question that surfaces is whether a big time, successful football or basketball program induces donations to educational and academic programs. Numerous studies indicate that the correlations and causations are equivocal at best. A good resolution would be for academic leaders such as the president or provost to persuade big donors to athletics to consider the overall future of Alma Mater and double the proposed gift, with half going to educational programs.[32] Such gestures would demonstrate genuine commitment to the partnership of athletics and academics with the added appeal of making a sports booster a true campus hero. It would require commitment on the part of a president to assert total institutional vision and priorities as distinguished from acquiescing with predictable partisan giving patterns.

Big time college sports comes to the fore as a divisive as well as a harmonizing element in the life of a college or university. About a decade ago the University of Illinois faced tension, even paralysis, in a generational conflict over the traditional athletics mascot, "Chief Illiwinek." The split was largely between older alumni versus young alumni and current undergraduates.[33] It was a symbolic clash that drained donations, tested loyalties—and even led an excellent chancellor to leave for another presidency due to frustration at the gridlock. One concession to change at many universities is that seating capacity at football stadiums has been reduced in part because a declining number of undergraduates each year want to go to games. In short, the status of intercollegiate sports as a campus and truly *student* activity becomes less clear, in favor of a spectator event for older alumni and many fans who have no other connection with the campus. It has implications for donors and public policies. Why, for example, should a donor who makes a gift for renovation of luxury suites at a stadium receive a tax deduction?[34] Such a situation becomes especially troubling because its connection with educational mission is vague and uncertain.

A graphic, documented example comes from a recent episode involving a complex mix of intercollegiate athletics as the object of support from interdependent civic, educational, and philanthropic organizations along with private donors. The situation is thus: A group of three private donors gave $3.1 million to refurbish the luxury locker rooms at a civic arena that is owned and operated by a nonprofit organization, which we will call "The City Center." However, the executive director of the City Center noted to local reporters that the gift did not come directly to the City Center. It was deliberately funneled by the donors through the local Community Foundation "because the City Center Corp. is a not-for-profit organization, rather than a charitable entity, so donors could not receive deductions for any donations made directly to the center." The three major donors refused to comment on their contribution, which now was tax deductible because it had gone through the Community Foundation. A conservative estimate is that the donors are in the 33 percent tax bracket, which means that this cost tax payers over $1 million.

The details of the conception and design of the new locker room complex is described as follows: it is for exclusive use by the local university men's varsity basketball team. Most of the fund-raising was done by the university basketball coach who also commissioned the architectural design and was not competitively bid, although other contracts were bid by the City Center Corporation. According to one reporter, "The new complex includes a new State U Fund booster room that allows top boosters to see the players through glass as they walk into the arena," an area that the Coach "described on his Web site as 'very NBA-ish.' He called the entire complex 'the gold standard.'" The newspaper article continued, "The new space at the arena is lavishly decorated and includes much of the original flooring from the 2012 NCAA Championship game in New Orleans," which the local university had won. At most the locker rooms will be used 30 times per year—and exclusively by the university basketball team. Within its confines, "individual seven-foot-tall granite showers sit next to hot and cold tubs for players after games." The major donors refused to comment on this initiative. The complexity of the situation is that simultaneously it is apart from and a part of the state university's high profile activities. Also curious is the lack of inclusion with university officials such as the vice president for development, the director of athletics, or the president.

What about the role and image of the Community Foundation, the charitable organization through whom the donations were funneled? This case was not low profile since it was the single largest donation the Community Foundation received during the year 2013. Its webpage emphasizes "charitable causes in our community," with the mission of enhancing "the quality of life in our region."[35] Its photographic images depict underserved and needy groups—children from low-income groups, the elderly, and service organizations dealing with such basic needs as food and shelter. Its website provides the following commentary in its "About Us" section, noting that the Community Foundation is

> where people go to give—of their passion, money and ideas—to enhance the quality of life in our region. We help individuals, families, businesses and nonprofit organizations establish charitable funds, guide their resource to support causes they care about, meet community needs and make a difference. We also lead, convene and facilitate on important community issues.

In describing "How We Work," the website notes that "community foundations are public charities created by a collaboration of local citizens with a common purpose—to improve the quality of life in their region. The Community Foundation is one of nearly 700 community foundations across the nation. We are a unique tax-exempt nonprofit that enables individuals, families, businesses, and other nonprofit organizations to establish permanent charitable funds to meet current and future community needs. Overseen by a volunteer board of community leaders and run by professionals who are experts in local philanthropy, we invest and manage these charitable funds. In addition, we convene community leaders and volunteers to help people come together, to have the greatest collective impact for good."

On balance, the donation and arrangements are legal. However, for universities and community nonprofit charitable organizations, the crucial issues in the twenty-first century are *appearance* and *appropriateness*. The arrangements appear to be disingenuous. How is this a *charitable* endeavor that leads to "the greatest collective impact for good"? Also conspicuous is that the role of the university is unclear. Its men's basketball team is the major attendance attraction but neither the university nor its athletic department owns the arena—it rents from the civic center corporation and, by extension, from the city. Its employees and university donors are involved—but technically the flagship state university is a step removed. Its men's basketball coach and its major donors to university athletics programs are involved, but evidently the university is not. For a discerning taxpayer, all this raises questions about the *appropriateness* of the arrangement. What civic or community service goal has been fulfilled? What educational goal has been pursued? And, most problematic, which public trusts have been evaded? Such are the unanswered questions that ultimately will surface when colleges and universities seek tax benefits, donations, or other support.[36] All this can be problematic for a campus— and for all nonprofit organizations dependent on trust and goodwill, as well as government tax exemptions.

This specific case leads to a persistent question facing donors in determining what project or organization should be the beneficiary of their philanthropy. The deliberations often played out as family quarrels within a community, as exemplified by concerns that donations to food banks and homeless shelters were at low ebb while at the same time support for a civic art museum was soaring. Or, within a university, fund-raising for the School of Law and the School of Business were abundant, where the College of Education received little attention. Variations on this theme repeatedly kindled debates over not only how much should be given—but also, to whom?

A controversial answer to this question was provided by Peter Singer, a professor of bioethics at Princeton, in his 2013 op-ed essay in the *New York Times*, "Good Charity, Bad Charity."[37] He opened with the argument that a dollar donated for curing blindness is a dollar better spent than one for a new wing of an art museum. Singer's approach had some initial appeal because it appeared to offer an algorithm of working through choices logically and, perhaps, ethically. It was a false promise because its shortfalls were multiple. First, if extended it would tend to suggest that the most worthy charity would (or, should) receive all donations—a "winner takes all" syndrome. Medical and health services would tend to trump cultural activities. But his opening example was simplistic based on a false dichotomy that was needlessly limiting. It provided little systematic guidance on how should one, for example, choose between building a new wing for a hospital clinic and laboratory for ophthalmology as distinguished from paying the costs of administering established treatments for blindness?

Second, Singer's essay seems to have an inherent bias that literal immediate life and death matters that one would associate with, for example, medical research or health care, are paramount. For starters, this overlooks an essential, fair tenet of support for the arts and humanities—namely, that they are activities without which life is less worth living. Even if one were to concede that matters of health warrant top priority, ultimately final choices are based on untestable or negligible differences. Furthermore, to brush aside theater, dance, rare books, or humanities curricula as relatively unessential is at best an absurd concession made temporarily for the sake of plumbing the depths of Singer's argument. In fact, in a metropolitan area such as greater New York City, the real life tension and debates often deal with donor favoritism for high profile performing art centers and art museums, with less urgency in their giving for food banks, half way houses, refuge centers for battered women, and daily basic needs of meals and shelter.

The question still remains from Singer's op-ed essay about hard choices and "right" choices *within* health and medical orbits: namely, how does one "know" or "choose" that support for kidney research is more or less urgent than research on cardiology and hearts? Singer tends to forget that philanthropy by definition is a *voluntary* act—and that imposing a strict imperative on donor choices is anathema. It also comes across as moralistic and self-righteous rather than ethical in tone.

Leaving the Singer case, a particularly grave concern for philanthropy associated with higher education involves clarity and transparency. Since, as noted earlier in this book, colleges and universities often are a large landowner and employer within a metropolitan community, they have acquired a burden of perception on sources and distributions of their resources. Sponsored research in the form of federal grants already skew the external funding toward the medical and health fields. Grants from the National Institutes of Health and, to a lesser extent, from the National Science Foundation are dominant. In contrast, grant funding from the National Endowment for the Humanities and the National Endowment for the Arts is miniscule. Private fund-raising and philanthropy, then, become more flexible and discretionary in their objects of support, with potential as the margin of difference in funding worthy fields that may—or may not—have high priority in federal grants. Hence, a fundamental question for a university is whether their fund-raising is appropriate, especially in trying to carry out *all* missions and commitments to which a campus is pledged. A university is, on close inspection, a microcosm of the myriad activities and services competing for support within the larger society. As such, it too is the setting for discussions over priorities such as health versus arts, and arts versus basic human services.

Beyond such specific cases, a large question that accompanies the success of philanthropy in the United States, including for higher education, is the persistence of criticisms about dysfunctions and abuses of charitable giving. Ken Stern, former chief executive of National Public Radio, received national attention for his article on "The Charity Swindle"—namely, laxness in accountability for how charities actually spend the monies they collect.[38] Stern's focus was on the case of the US Navy Veterans Association, a charitable group founded in 2002 that had raised about $100 million, but with little records to show that it went to the proclaimed needy constituencies. Lack of accountability was fostered in part by an understaffed Internal Revenue Service which was unable to audit or monitor its giving. According to Stern, "Everything about the Association turned out to be false: no state chapters, no members, no leader with the name redolent of naval history."

A problem more subtle than outright fraud has been concern over the relative ease with which donors and receiving organizations can receive tax exemptions. Ray D. Madoff, a law professor at Boston

College, has written about "how government gives" tax breaks, with the concern that "many charitable deductions do not serve the public good."[39] Madoff wrote, "The government does its own charitable giving, in the form of tax deductions. When an individual makes a donation to a qualifying organization, the federal government essentially pays a portion of that donation: a $1,000 donation from a donor in the highest tax bracket costs that donor only $604. The federal government kicks in the remaining $396 in the form of a reduction in taxes." Madoff estimates that such tax benefits represent about $40 billion per year in forfeited tax revenues. The abuse is that "the federal government too often provides the deductions for donations that offer little or no benefit."

In the wake of the widespread collapse and sustained poor showing of university investment portfolios since 2008, some critics have raised questions about whether universities and their affiliated investment officers have strayed from adhering to the so-called prudent investor rules.[40] With signs of investment portfolio recovery by 2014, however, yesterday's mistakes and abuses probably will fade from public concern.

Perhaps the most troubling criticism of contemporary American philanthropy comes from Peter Buffett, son of the famous financier and philanthropist Warren Buffett, who brings attention to what he calls the "Charitable-Industrial Complex."[41] Peter Buffett grounds his commentary in the examples of well-intentioned donations—such as "campaigns for distributing condoms to stop the spread of AIDS in a brothel area unexpectedly ended up creating a higher price for unprotected sex." The unsettling insight of Buffett's article was his allegation that a great deal of charity is dysfunctional due to its unintended consequences—in which a well-intentioned contribution that was supposed to solve a social problem fell short in its primary goal and upset the ecology of a community to make matters worse. Beyond such examples, Buffett expresses concern over the unchecked growth of the nonprofit sector, noting that "between 2001 and 2011, the number of nonprofits increased 25 percent. Their growth rate now exceeds that of both the business and government sectors. It's a massive business, with approximately $316 billion given away in 2012 in the United States alone and more than 9.4 million employed." His overarching criticism is that the practice of "conscience laundering" has served to simultaneously assuage concerns about accumulating wealth, yet not effectively solving the social problems exacerbated by growing inequalities of wealth within communities and nations.

Peter Buffett's commentary is strong and extreme. It echoes earlier criticisms by others that large charitable institutions can become powerful economic bullies.[42] Whether or not one is persuaded by his wholesale complaints and concerns, there are some intermediate, more moderate or preliminary responses that might reduce if not eliminate some alleged abuses. One is that philanthropic ventures can and should be subject to rigorous evaluation, including Peter Buffett's warning about unintended consequences. On the other hand, even if planning and evaluation are thoughtful and thorough, one may not be able either to track or then eliminate all unintended consequences.

An historic example that comes to mind is the response of social reformer turned novelist Upton Sinclair to public opinion and reform legislation following publication of *The Jungle* about Chicago's infamous meat-packing industry. Sinclair's intent as author and reporter was to expose the squalid working conditions and low wages of slaughter house workers, most of whom were immigrants or newcomers to Chicago. To his surprise, the response of American readers and, eventually, members of Congress, was shock over the unsanitary conditions involved in meat packing and making sausages—response that was sufficiently strong that it led to congressional creation of agencies for inspecting meat and packing houses. Sinclair's bittersweet comment was that "he had aimed for America's heart, but hit her stomach." Comparable ironies and shortfalls may accompany any attempts at reform or innovation by nonprofit organizations. A troubling feature of Peter Buffett's reform recommendations is that they would result either in paralysis and a fear of any intervention—or, for Americans to abandon completely the contemporary charitable foundation and activity enterprise—a response that is unlikely and unrealistic.

A second reform might be for Congress to revisit IRS qualifications for conferring tax exemptions to, respectively, donors and for educational and charitable organizations, including colleges and universities, who receive donations. Even though Peter Buffett's wholesale denunciation of the United States's philanthropic and charitable enterprise is sufficiently bombastic that it will be defused and even denied, his op-ed article along with a persistent flow of articles and reports that criticize the status quo in philanthropic activities and their adjacent public policies, college and university boards, and leaders would do well to be cognizant of this public awareness and critical scrutiny.

Criticism of higher education has led to some intriguing challenges and changes among philanthropists. For example, high-tech entrepreneur Peter Thiel, himself an alumnus of Stanford University, has used his substantial individual wealth to provide funding for what might be termed his "case against college." Thiel's highly publicized new program started in 2011 with awards of $100,000 to 24 selected high school seniors *not* to attend college. His rationale for the fellowship program was that "some entrepreneurial students may be better off leaving college" in order "to develop their ideas more quickly than they would at a traditional university. Its broader aim goes beyond helping the twenty-four winners, by raising big questions about the state of higher education."[43]

Thiel and other current advocates for the case against college may be correct in pointing out that a Bill Gates or a Steve Jobs did not need a college degree to be successful. What this ignores is that the overall strength of American higher education in the twentieth century was less spectacular yet important—namely, to educate for civil society and expertise. It was true not only for preparing young people for law and medicine, but also pharmacy, engineering, physics, biology, chemistry, mathematics, teaching, social work, clergy, nursing, accounting, forestry, public health, and other professions—and at the same time helping to educate them to be concerned, informed citizens—that would lead and staff new organizations in the public and private sector and as concerned, informed citizens.

This issue brings to mind the memorable 2005 Stanford University commencement speech made by the late Steve Jobs, chief executive officer of Apple, in which graduating seniors were urged to "find what you love."[44] Jobs emphasized at the start of his talk that he had *not* graduated from college. Even though this speech is often cited as lending credence to the recent case against college, careful reading suggests that it is not especially persuasive in its logic and examples. First, Jobs did not opt *not* to go to college. Nor was he excluded from college. He went to Reed College and dropped out—a very different life choice than not going to college at all. Second, even after dropping out, he stayed close to the Reed College campus—its students, faculty, resources, and opportunities—all to his educational and vocational gain. Third, his explanation for dropping out—disorientation and uncertainty—probably were signs that a liberal education was prompting him to consider and confront complex questions of purpose and place. Perhaps Reed College was "doing its job" for Jobs?

Furthermore it was conveniently safe that Steve Jobs gave his inspirational talk to graduating Stanford seniors who soon would receive their coveted Stanford degrees. Most in that audience probably were delighted with Jobs's message urging them to pursue their dreams—and equally delighted that they were buoyed by the experience, friendships, faculty and learning—and degree—on all counts that going to college at Stanford had made opportune. The Steve Jobs inspirational talk would have been more compelling as a "case against college" had he chosen to deliver it to 16-year-olds at, for example, Oakland Tech or another inner city high school which faces chronic low funding and other external crises and whose students probably won't have the option to enroll at Stanford or other prestigious colleges and universities. But he didn't—and for good reason.

Twenty-first century philanthropists such as Peter Thiel, Steve Jobs, and Bill Gates stand in sharp contrast to a major philanthropist from the late nineteenth century—Ezra Cornell. Cornell made a fortune in what was in the mid-nineteenth century the ultimate transformational high-tech field of its era—the telegraph. What was memorable about Ezra Cornell's biography and commitments was that he was from a very poor family and always regretted that he did not have the opportunity for much formal education. He especially lamented that he had neither the time, money, nor preparation to go to college. Hence, after having made his commercial fortune, his sustained commitment was to use his wealth for college building to assure that future generations of young Americans would have the educational opportunities that he did not have. Going to college, for Ezra Cornell, was not necessarily about making a future fortune or acquiring marketable skills. Higher education was about scholarly and intellectual exploration, as suggested by his motto associated with his namesake Cornell University: "I would found a college where anyone could study anything."[45]

The implication from such figures as Ezra Cornell of an earlier era or from a Peter Thiel or a Steve Jobs in the twenty-first century, is that whether in 1860 or 2014, the historical message is that there are good reasons to go—or not to go—to college. And, for potential philanthropists, there endure good reasons to give—or, not to give—to colleges and universities. And, given the diversity of American higher education, the choices are complicated by the options of where to go—such as two-year vocational vs. four-year liberal arts college or small campus versus large flagship state university—and what to study, and for what end—an associate degree, a bachelor's degree, or perhaps prelude to an advanced degree. We also have in the United States a long tradition of some professions such as performing arts and major league baseball where one need not first have a college education. The spate of current articles do not make *the* case against college—they make *a* case, or several cases, depending on an individual's situation and goals. A maxim of societal behavior is that strident advocacy makes a point and at the same time fosters alternative and counter points.

In sum, the fervent articles denigrating college unwittingly make indirect and direct cases of numerous good reasons to go to college. Why, of course, the exceptional genius does not need the delay of required courses. Partying by 20-year-olds is going to take place at sports bars quite apart from being enrolled in college. In fact, most accounts of Silicon Valley successful entrepreneurs suggest that unabashed partying is par for their course. So, why begrudge that or dismiss that as a nuisance and distraction linked exclusively to undergraduate life?

But even a wealthy high-tech entrepreneur such as Mark Zuckerberg did gain from going to Harvard by finding the name and inspiration for "Facebook"—not from Philosophy 101 but from the booklets distributed during freshman orientation week. How to calculate the net worth of that informal collegiate experience? And for the multitude of bright, talented committed high school graduates who were not selected for Peter Thiel's highly selective program, might not there be a thoughtful choice about college that just might provide some good learning and opportunities? The net result is that we do not have "The Case" against college—but the more subtle, provocative question of many cases for and against going to college as befits a complex, diverse, and credentialed American society. Maybe going to college is not such a great idea. Maybe *not* going to college is not such a great idea.[46]

Even though Peter Thiel's college alternative program probably will not prevail as a widespread alternative to the traditional college experience, especially for academically talented high school students, its real and symbolic importance today is that it sounds an alert against complacence among incumbent college officials. Foremost will be concern by parents and students about rising college costs and what some public criticisms describe as "college's diminishing returns rooted in cost and quality concerns."[47] All these intense questions, concerns and debates in the national press and within foundations are pertinent for philanthropy and support of higher education in the twenty-first century. A firm grounding in historical context suggests that these issues are not new. Nor are they resolved once and for all. Each generation of college and university leaders, trustees, staff, students, and alumni must explore and work through the complex implications to create both the ideals and realities of a sound model for higher education. It should be one that draws on the past to connect the present and future in a way that is thoughtful and educationally sound.

A convenient, conventional wisdom is that "Talk is cheap!" To the contrary, talk—especially informed and earnest talk among and across constituencies in a civil society—is *not* cheap at all. It is essential and imperative for defining issues about the missions and purposes of American colleges and universities, whether in 1636 or in 2014, especially if they are dependent on philanthropy defined as "voluntary support for the public good." Our hope is that our critical analysis contributes to the vitality of higher education for the institutional and national welfare of the United States.

An author's dream for the concluding paragraphs of a book is the opportunity to convey the message to readers, "All's well that ends well!" In the case of philanthropy and higher education fortune appears to have smiled. On February 12, 2014, the Council for Aid to Education released its annual "Voluntary Support of Education" survey and announced that "record giving to higher education is back." What this meant was that "America's colleges and universities took in $33.8 billion in charitable contributions during the 2013 fiscal year, nearly a 10-percent increase over 2012 and the biggest sum ever raised by the sector. The previous record for charitable gifts to colleges was $31.6 billion during the 2008 fiscal year, before the recession stifled donations."[48] This followed closely from the news a month earlier that college endowments had returned an average of 11.7 percent in 2013, due in large part to a rebounding stock market.

Higher education is distinctive in the nonprofit sector because of its reliance on—and ability to attract—big gifts. A breakdown of the sources of the $33.8 billion gifts in 2013 included $10-billion from foundations; $9 billion from college alumni; $6.2 billion from non-alumni individuals; and $5.1 billion from corporations. Data on alumni giving were complex and sent mixed signals. On the one hand, the short-term news was good for higher education, as alumni-giving increased 17 percent from 2012 to 2013. Furthermore, the average amount of an alumnus gift increased by more than 18 percent. On the other hand, even this resurgence was inadequate to reverse a quarter century trend of alumni donations as a declining percentage of all giving to colleges and universities.

At about the same time the Council for Aid to Education published its "Voluntary Support of Education" survey, the philanthropic and fund-raising consulting firm of Marts & Lundy released a special report with the big news of "The Big Gift Revival" for 2013 giving to higher education. The prelude noted, "The nonprofit world has been waiting to see tangible signs of true recovery, and 2013 clearly demonstrated that for the leading philanthropists it is time to give back and to give back in a significant way. Across the board, the mega- gifts that came to define campaigns in the early years of this century have now returned in a way that is in many ways even more powerful than what we saw before the Great Recession took hold."[49] Big gifts tended to go to large, established research universities, including Columbia, Stanford, and the University of Southern California—each of which reported having received "nine-figure gifts." The Marts & Lundy report authors emphasized, "As in the past, the preponderance of big gifts went to higher education, and we believe that higher education continues to be the engine that generates the big ideas that are essential for the generation of big gifts. Big donors want big impact, and American research universities in particular can legitimately claim to deal with the large challenges faced by our society in the twenty-first century."

The good news, then, is that higher education in the United States continues to maintain and perhaps enhance its tradition of being a source of innovation and ideas while also being the magnet for generous support from alumni, individuals, foundations, and corporations. Within the various tables of the recent favorable reports, however, are sources of concern. Most troubling is that there persists a "boom-and-bust" mentality among campus development offices and the national fund-raising consulting firms—a nervous resignation that follows the oscillations of the stock market as if development officers were on the floor of the New York Stock Exchange or Chicago Board of Trade during each late afternoon, watching the fluctuations of "The Big Board." It suggests a deep-rooted character among presidents and development offices that is reactive more than it is proactive in making the case for colleges and universities.

Development offices have tended to accept and acquiesce to what they hear are dominant trends at any given moment—such as the recent observations about the primacy and goodness of "big gifts to prestigious, established institutions." The report about record fund-raising for 2013 was not merely informational because it carried strong editorial endorsement that the good news also signified a healthy trend. What if the report for 2013 carried the news of an opposite profile—namely, that thousands of small individual donors, not big donors, had carried the day? Would the report authors then as a matter of course applaud this trend?

In other words, the report *endorsed* the giving trends and priorities. This means that organized advocates for philanthropy in higher education tend to increase, not ameliorate, differences among institutions, with the best getting better—and more! Successful and prestigious colleges and universities pull further and further ahead from the pack.

Perhaps this is a fitting sign that talent and innovation are rewarded. At the same time it is not an especially innovative or inspiring model because it suggests that philanthropy for higher education has crystallized into a fixed approach. There also is a need for the bittersweet realization that it is not a perfect arrangement. As Henry Rosovsky commented when he was Dean of Arts and Sciences at Harvard College, "To me, some parts of American higher education are one of the country's greatest glories. In fact, I make bold to say to our critics—and there are many these days—that fully two thirds to three quarters of the best universities in the world are located in the United States. (That we also are home to a large share of the world's worst colleges and universities is not now my concern.)"[50] Rosovsky's wry observation, although good natured, still sent a clear message: philanthropic support has reinforced its claim to providing a margin of national excellence—but it usually is skewed toward a small, select group that already was well served. The news about the increases in total giving to higher education is good news as a financial balance sheet. It says little about purposes for giving.

Dean Rosovsky was quite right in noting the polarities of the very good and the very weak colleges and universities. Yet this oversimplifies the diversity and the potential for varied educational contributions within this fascinating mix of thousands of degree-granting colleges and universities. In addition to the prestigious "steeples of excellence" there is a great deal of underappreciated teaching, learning, and service that takes place at colleges, public and independent, which have modest resources and lean endowments. Often the "value added" these colleges make in the lives of students suggest they are a wise, effective choice for a donor's dollars.[51] A question and challenge for systematic philanthropy and fund-raising is how to recognize and support the vitality marbled throughout many institutions in the large, diverse landscape of American higher education in the twenty-first century.

To answer that question and to come up with genuine new directions in philanthropy and higher education, one may wish to supplement the headline news (and self-congratulations) about the annual giving total of $34 billion and then turn an eye to innovations elsewhere on campus. A promising model comes from Princeton University where an experimental course, "FRS 157: Philanthropy," has been taught by Professor Stanley Katz of the Woodrow Wilson School. Freshmen learn over a semester "the basic foundations and historical context of philanthropy, and eventually get the chance to make actual donations using funds provided to the class."[52] The course is part of a nationwide project created by a Texas-based philanthropic organization, "Once Upon a Time Foundation." Its resultant course is part of the Philanthropy Lab and the aim of the project is "to provide students with practical experience in philanthropy and the opportunity to think consciously about giving back to society." Thirteen colleges and universities are participating in this project to provide philanthropy courses. According to Princeton's Professor Katz, "class discussions revolved around whose interests should be prioritized and why, which organizations to donate to within each interest group, whether to donate to long-term projects or short-term projects, and whether the students wanted to direct their money to specific projects or to leave the decision to experts in the field."

At the same time that the article about the Princeton philanthropy course and project was published, the University of Pennsylvania announced the launching of its Center for Minority Serving Institutions (MSIs). It is dedicated to understanding and empowering MSIs through applied research, providing tool kits for media relations and fund-raising, and for sponsoring a micro-giving campaign. Although the MSIs are far down on the annual tallies for donations received, these institutions enroll about 20 percent of the nation's college students. In short, they serve—but are themselves underserved.

The new ventures at Princeton and Penn suggest new potential for colleges and universities to be a philanthropy in the fullest sense beyond the balance sheet, and as more than just an institution that receives donations.[53] Along with such earlier innovations as service learning, these campus-based initiatives represent the kind of thoughtful commitment to the future of voluntary service for the public good where colleges and universities, through their educational programs, can leave the world a better place.

Notes

Introduction

1. Doreen Carvajal, "In Need, French Museums Turn to Masses, Chapeaux in Hand," *The New York Times* (December 24, 2012) pp. A1, A3.
2. James Howell Smith, *Honorable Beggars: The Middlemen of American Philanthropy* (Madison: University of Wisconsin PhD Dissertation, 1968).
3. Frank T. Rhodes, Informal Introductory Comments of 1996 address, with formal version published as "The University and Its Critics," in William G. Bowen and Harold T. Shapiro, Editors, *Universities and Their Leadership* (Princeton, NJ: Princeton University Press, 1998) pp. 3–14.
4. Kirk Semple, "Affluent Asians in U.S. Turning to Philanthropy," *The New York Times* (January 9, 2013) pp. A1, A20.
5. See, for example, Robert H. Bremner, *American Philanthropy* (Chicago: University of Chicago Press, second edition, 1988); and Merle Curti and Roderick Nash, *Philanthropy in the Shaping of American Higher Education* (New Brunswick, NJ: Rutgers University Press, 1965).
6. Tamar Lewin, "Maryland Renames Law School after Gift: $30 Million Grant and Big Ambitions," *The New York Times* (April 25, 2011) p. A14.
7. Allan Nevins, *The State Universities and Democracy* (Urbana: University of Illinois Press, 1962) p. 104.
8. "The Class of 1937," cover story for *Life* magazine (June 7, 1937).
9. Burton R. Clark, "Belief and Loyalty in College Organization," *The Journal of Higher Education* (June 1971) vol. 42, no. 16, pp. 499–515.
10. John R. Thelin, "Horizontal History and Higher Education," in Marybeth Gasman, Editor, *The History of U.S. Higher Education: Methods for Understanding the Past* (New York and London: Routledge, 2010) pp. 71–83.

1   Connecting Past and Present: Historical Background on Philanthropy and American Higher Education

1. Merle Curti and Roderick Nash, *Philanthropy in the Shaping of American Higher Education* (New Brunswick, NJ: Rutgers University Press, 1965).

Robert H. Bremner, *American Philanthropy* (Chicago and London: University of Chicago Press, second edition, 1988).

2. Tamar Lewin, "Report Says Stanford Is First University to Raise $1 Billion in a Single Year," *The New York Times* (February 21, 2013) p. A17.

3. Summary Figures as Published in "News Alert," *Harvard Crimson*, September 21, 2013).

4. "New England's First Fruits 1640," in *Collections of the Massachusetts Historical Society*, 1792, vol. 1, pp. 242–248.

5. *Charter of the College of Rhode Island of 1764*, as published in Walter C. Bronson, *The History of Brown University, 1764–1914* (Providence, RI: Brown University, 1914) pp. 500–507.

6. Jesse Brundage Sears, "Finances of the Early Colleges" in *Philanthropy in the History of American Higher* Education (Washington, D.C.: US Government Printing Office, 1922) pp. 16–19.

7. Margery Somers Foster, *Out of Smalle Beginnings…An Economic History of Harvard College in the Puritan Period* (Cambridge, Massachusetts: Belknap Press of Harvard University, 1962).

8. James Barron, "Book Published in 1640 Makes Record Sale at Auction," *The New York Times* (November 27, 2013) p. A19.

9. See, for example, the case of Dartmouth in James Axtell, "Dr. Wheelock's Little Red School," *The European and the Indian: Essay in the Ethnohistory of Colonial North America* (New York: Oxford University Press, 1981) Chapter 4, pp. 87–109.

10. George Keller, *Academic Strategy* (Baltimore and London: Johns Hopkins University Press, 1983).

11. Helen Lefkowitz Horowitz, *Campus Life: Undergraduate Cultures from the End of the Eighteenth Century to the Present* (Chicago: University of Chicago Press, 1987) pp. 57, 58, 61.

12. Daniel J. Boorstin, "The Booster College," *The Americans: The National Experience* (New York: Harper and Row, 1965) pp. 161–165.

13. John Whitehead, *The Separation of College and State* (New Haven, CT: Yale University Press, 1973).

14. Marybeth Gasman, *Envisioning Black Colleges: A History of the United Negro College Fund* (Baltimore, MD: Johns Hopkins University Press, 2007) pp. 11–14. Stephen J. Wright, "The Black Colleges and Universities: Historical Background and Future Prospects," *Virginia Foundation for the Humanities Newsletter* (Spring 1988) vol. 14, pp. 1–4.

15. Helen Lefkowitz Horowitz, *Alma Mater: Design and Experience in the Women's Colleges from Their Nineteenth-Century Beginnings to the 1930s* (New York: Knopf, 1984). See also, Andrea Walton, Editor, *Women and Philanthropy in Education* (Bloomington and Indianapolis: Indiana University Press, 2005).

16. Christopher Jencks and David Riesman, *The Academic Revolution* (Garden City, NY: Doubleday Anchor, 1968) pp. 314–320.

17. Frederick T. Gates, "Rules of Procedure" (Memorandum of May 26, 1890) as reprinted in James Howell Smith, *Honorable Beggars: The Middlemen of*

American Philanthropy (Madison: University of Wisconsin PhD Dissertation, 1968) pp. 256–265.

18. Bruce Kimball and Benjamin Ashby Johnson, "The Beginning of 'Free Money' Ideology in American Universities: Charles W. Eliot at Harvard, 1869–1909," *History of Education Quarterly* (2012) vol. 52, pp. 222–250 (Kimball, pp. 223–224).

19. John B. Boles, *University Builder: Edgar Odell Lovett and the Founding of the Rice Institute* (Baton Rouge: Louisiana State University Press, 2007).

20. Kimball and Johnson, "The Beginning of 'Free Money' Ideology."

21. Burton R. Clark, *The Distinctive College: Antioch, Reed & Swarthmore* (Chicago: Aldine Publishers, 1970).

22. Frederick Rudolph, "Counterrevolution," *The American College and University: A History* (New York: Alfred Knopf, 1962) pp. 440–461.

23. Robert F. Durden, "Building on Two Campuses: 'The Most…Beautiful Educational Plant in America,'" *The Launching of Duke University, 1924–1949* (Durham and London: Duke University Press, 1993) pp. 27–48.

24. Donald Fisher, *Fundamental Development of the Social Sciences: Rockefeller Philanthropy and the United States Social Science Research Council* (Ann Arbor: University of Michigan Press, 1993).

25. Curti and Nash, *Philanthropy in the Shaping*, p. 181. See also, John R. Thelin, "Small by Design: Resilience in an Era of Mass Higher Education," in *Meeting the Challenge: America's Independent Colleges and Universities since 1956* (Washington, D.C.: Council of Independent Colleges, 2006). See esp. pp. 3–36.

26. Bremner, "The Business of Benevolence and the Industry of Destruction," in *American Philanthropy*, pp. 116–135. See also, David M. Kennedy, "Don't Blame Hoover," *Stanford Magazine* (January/February 1999) pp. 44–51.

27. Rebecca Lowen, *Creating the Cold War University: The Transformation of Stanford* (Berkeley, LA; London: University of California Press, 1999).

28. John R. Thelin, *Games Colleges Play* (Baltimore and London: The Johns Hopkins University Press, 1994) pp. 77–83.

29. Thelin, *Games Colleges Play*, pp. 116–124.

30. Curti and Nash, *Philanthropy in the Shaping*, pp. 238–258.

31. James Piereson and Naomi Schaefer, "The Problem with Public Policy Schools," *The Washington Post* (December 6, 2013).

32. Emory University Student Verse as quoted in Nancy Diamond, "Catching Up: The Advance of Emory University Since World War II," in Roger L. Geiger with Susan Richardson, Editors, *History of Higher Education Annual 1999: Southern Higher Education in the Twentieth Century* (1999) vol. 19, pp. 149–183.

33. Waldemar A. Nielsen, "The Crisis of the Nonprofits," *Change* magazine (1980) vol. 12, no. 1, pp. 23–29.

34. Lewis B. Mayhew, *Surviving the Eighties: Strategies and Procedures for Solving Fiscal and Enrollment Problems* (San Francisco: Jossey-Bass, 1980) pp. 76–77.

35. Earl F. Cheit, *The New Depression in Higher Education: A Study of Financial Conditions at 41 Colleges and Universities* (New York: McGraw-Hill, 1973).

36. Carnegie Council on Policy Studies in Higher Education, *Three Thousand Futures: The Next Twenty Years for Higher Education* (San Francisco: Jossey-Bass, 1980). See also, Bruce B. Vladek, "The Over-Investment Crisis in Higher Education," *Change* (1979) vol. 10, no. 11, p. 39.

37. John R. Thelin, "Institutional History in Our Own Time," *The CASE International Journal of Educational Advancement* (June 2000) vol. 1, no. 1, pp. 9–23.

38. Charles T. Clotfelter, *Buying the Best: Cost Escalation in Elite Higher Education* (Princeton, NJ: Princeton University Press, 1996) (National Bureau of Economic Research Monograph).

39. Jacques S. Steinberg, "Harvard's $2.1 Billion Tops Colleges' Big Fund-Raising," *The New York Times* (October 7, 1999).

40. Mary B. Marcy, "Why Foundations Have Cut Back in Higher Education," *The Chronicle of Higher Education* (July 25, 2003).

41. Jencks and Riesman, *The Academic Revolution*.

42. Chester E. Finn, Jr., *Scholars, Dollars and Bureaucrats* (Washington, D.C.: Brookings Institution, 1978).

43. Ronald G. Ehrenberg, *Tuition Rising: Why College Costs So Much* (Cambridge, MA and London, England: Harvard University Press, 2000).

44. Robert S. Shepard, "How Can a University That Raises a Billion Dollars Have a Tight Budget?," *The Chronicle of Higher Education* (January 12, 1994) p. A48.

45. Arenson, Karen W., "Soaring Endowments Widen a Higher Education Gap," *The New York Times* (February 4, 2008) p. A14.

46. Joanne Barkan, "As Government Funds Dwindle, Giant Foundations Gain Too Much Power," *The Chronicle of Philanthropy* (October 20, 2013) p. A1. See also, John R. Thelin, "The Gates Foundation's Uncertain Legacy," *The Chronicle of Higher Education* (July 14, 2013).

2 Giving and Receiving: Major Philosophical Concepts and Theoretical Issues in Philanthropy

1. Uri Gneezy and John A. List, *The Why Axis: Hidden Motives and the Undiscovered Economics of Everyday Life* (New York: Public Affairs, 2013) p. 171.

2. Claire Gaudiani, *The Greater Good: How Philanthropy Drives the American Economy and Can Save Capitalism* (New York: Henry Holt, 2003) p. 2.

3. *Giving USA: The Annual Report on Philanthropy for the year 2012* (Chicago: Giving USA Foundation, 2013).

4. Merle Curti, "American Philanthropy and the National Character," *American Quarterly* (1958) vol. 10, pp. 420–437.

5. Robert H. Bremner, *American Philanthropy* (Chicago: University of Chicago Press, second edition, 1988) p. 3.

6. Robert A. Gross, "Giving in American: From Charity to Philanthropy," in Lawrence J. Friedman and Mark D. McGarvie, Editors, *Charity,*

Philanthropy, and Civility in American History (Cambridge: Cambridge University Press, 2003) p. 31.

7. Richard B. Gunderman, *We Make a Life by What We Give* (Bloomington: Indiana University Press, 2008) pp. 21–22.

8. Robert L. Payton, *Philanthropy: Voluntary Action for the Public Good* (New York: American Council on Education/Macmillan Publishing Company, 1988).

9. Friedman and McGarvie, *Charity, Philanthropy*, p. 2.

10. David C. Hammack, Editor, *Making the Nonprofit Sector in the United States* (Bloomington: Indiana University Press, 1998) pp. 6–8.

11. Jesse Brundage Sears, *Philanthropy in the History of American Higher Education* (Washington, D.C.: US Government Printing Office, 1922) p. 10.

12. *Giving USA: The Annual Report on Philanthropy for the Years 2000, 2005, and 2012* (Chicago: Giving USA Foundation, 2001, 2006, and 2013).

13. Payton, *Philanthropy: Voluntary Action*, p. xvi.

14. Ellen Condliffe Lagemann as quoted in Elizabeth M. Lynn and D. Susan Wesley, "Toward a Fourth Philanthropic Response: American Philanthropy and Its Public," in Amy A. Kass, Editor, *The Prefect Gift: the Philanthropic Imagination in Poetry and Prose* (Bloomington: Indiana University Press, 2002) p. 103.

15. Peter Frumkin, *Strategic Giving: The Art and Science of Philanthropy* (Chicago: The University of Chicago Press, 2006).

16. http://transcripts.cnn.com/TRANSCRIPPS/1312/15/hcsg.ol.html; (December18, 2013).

17. Steven Pinker, *The Better Angles of Our Nature* (New York: Penguin Books, 2011) p. 583.

18. Richard Dawkins *The Selfish Gene* (Oxford: Oxford University Press, 1976). Edward O. Wilson, *Sociobiology: The New Synthesis* (Cambridge, MA: Belknap Press of Harvard University Press, 2006). Edward O. Wilson, *The Social Conquest of Earth* (New York: Liveright Publishing Corporation, 2012).

19. Lee Alan Dugatkin, *The Altruism Equation: Seven Scientists Search for the Origins of Goodness* (Princeton: Princeton University Press, 2006). Owen Harman, *The Price of Altruism: George Price and the Search for the Origins of Kindness* (New York: W. W. Norton, 2010).

20. Peter Singer's many publications include *The Life You Can Save: How to Play Your Part in Ending World Poverty* (New York: Random House Trade Paperbacks, 2009).

21. Lewis Hyde, *The Gift: Imagination and the Erotic Life of Property* (New York: Vintage Books, 1983) pp. xi–xiv.

22. Ibid, pp. 41–55.

23. Marcel Mauss, *The Gift: The Form and Reason for Exchange in Archaic Societies* (New York: W. W. Norton, 1990).

24. Claude Levi-Strauss, *Introduction to the Work of Marcel Mauss* (London: Routledge, 1987) pp. 24–25.

25. Mary Douglas, "Foreword," in Mauss, *The Gift*, p. 12.

26. Mauss, *The Gift*, p. 18.
27. Hyde, *The Gift*, p. xiv.
28. Paul Veyne, *Bread and Circuses* (London: Penguin Books, 1992).
29. Natalie Zeman Davis, *The Gift in Sixteenth-Century France* (Madison: University of Wisconsin Press, 2000) p. 7.
30. Ibid., p. 11.
31. Anne Derbes and Mark Sandona, "Ave charitate plena': Variations on the Theme of Charity in the Arena Chapel," *Speculum* (2001) vol. 76, pp. 599–637, esp. p. 605.
32. Davis, *The Gift*, p. 12.
33. Ibid., p. 12.
34. Ibid., p. 13.
35. Ibid., p. 33.
36. Richard M. Titmuss, *The Gift Relationship: From Human Blood to Social Policy* (New York: New Press, 1997) p. 276.
37. Ibid., p. 11.
38. Ibid., p. 311.
39. Ibid., p. 306.
40. Kenneth E. Boulding, *The Economy of Love and Fear: A Preface to Grants Economics* (Belmont, CA: Wadsworth Publishing Company, 1973) p. 1.
41. Payton, *Philanthropy*, p. 47.
42. Boulding, *The Economy of Love*, p. 4.
43. Ibid., p. 26.
44. Ibid.
45. Michael P. Moody, *Pass It On: Serial Reciprocity as a Principle of Philanthropy* (Indianapolis: Indiana University Center on Philanthropy, 1998) p. 7.
46. Ibid., p. 3.
47. Bremner, *American Philanthropy*, p. 16.
48. Moody, *Pass It On*, p. 6.
49. Payton, *Philanthropy*, p. 53.
50. Michael P. Moody, "Reciprocity," *Learning to Give: An Action of the Heart, a Project for the Mind* (Electronic version retrieved July 10, 2006) p. 3.
51. Giving Till It Hurts," *The Wall Street Journal* (July 6, 2007) p. W1.
52. Erik H. Erikson and Joan M. Erikson, *The Life Cycle Completed* (New York: W. W. Norton, Extended Version, 1997) p. 126.
53. Claude Levi-Strauss, "Reciprocity, the Essence of Social Life," in Lewis A. Cosner, Editor, *The Pleasures of Sociology* (New York: New American Library, 1980) pp. 69–80.
54. Robert L. Payton and Michael P. Moody, *Understanding Philanthropy: Its Meaning and Mission* (Bloomington: Indiana University Press, 2008) p. 122.
55. Ibid., p. 123.
56. Ibid., p. 67.
57. Anna Faith Jones, "Doors and Mirrors," in H. Peter Karoff, Editor, *Just Money: A Critique of Contemporary American Philanthropy* (Boston, MA: TPI Editions, 2004) p. 54.

58. E. Bruce Heilman, chancellor and former president of the University of Richmond, was interviewed on the campus of that institution on November 10, 2003.

59. Merle Curti and Roderick Nash, *Philanthropy in the Shaping of American Higher Education* (New Brunswick, NJ: Rutgers University Press, 1965) pp. 263–264.

60. Kenneth Prewitt, "Foundations," in Walter A. Powell and Richard Steinberg, Editors, *The Nonprofit Sector: A Research Handbook* (New Haven, CT: Yale University Press, 2006) p. 367.

61. Frumkin, *Strategic Giving*, p. 12.

62. Peter Goldmark, "Before the Storm," in Karoff, *Just Money*, pp. 24–25.

63. Friedman and McGarvie, *Charity, Philanthropy*, p. 10.

64. Frumkin, *Strategic Giving*, pp. 177–187.

65. Paul G. Schervish, "Major Donors, Major Motives: The People and the Purpose Behind Major Gifts," in Lilya Wagner and Timothy L. Seiler, Editors, *Reprising Timeless Topics*, New Directions for Philanthropic Fundraising (San Francisco: Jossey-Bass, vol. 47, 2005) pp. 59–87.

66. Daniel H. Pink, *Drive: The Surprising Truth About What Motivates Us* (New York: Riverhead Books, 2009) pp. 1–11.

67. Ibid., p. 32.

68. Gregory L. Cascione, *Philanthropists in Higher Education: Institutional, Biographical, and Religious Motivations for Giving* (New York: Routledge Falmer, 2003) pp. 2–10.

69. Max Weber, *The Protestant Ethic and the Spirit of Capitalism* (Oxford: Oxford University Press, Revised 1920 Edition, 2011).

70. Cascione, *Philanthropists in Higher Education*, p. 85.

71. James R. Wood and James G. Houghland Jr., "The Role of Religion in Philanthropy," in J. Van Til and Associates, Editors, *Critical Issues in American Philanthropy* (San Francisco: Jossey Bass, 1990) pp. 99–132.

72. Gaudiani, *The Greater Good*, p. 7.

73. David H. Smith, "Introduction: Doing Good," in David H. Smith, Editor, *Good Intentions: Moral Obstacles & Opportunities* (Bloomington: Indiana University Press, 2005) p. 8.

74. Deni Elliott, *The Kindness of Strangers: Philanthropy and Higher Education* (New York: Rowman & Littlefield, 2006) p. 30.

75. Paul G. Schervish, "Inclination, Obligation, and Association: What We Know and What We Need to learn about Donor Motivation," in Dwight F. Burlingame, Editor, *Critical Issues in Fund Raising* (New York: John Wiley, 1997) p. 130.

76. James Andreoni, "Impure Altruism and Donations to Public Goods: A Theory of Warm-Glow Giving," *The Economic Journal* (June 1990), vol. 100, pp. 464–477.

77. Cascione, *Philanthropists in Higher Education*, p. 20.

78. Frumkin, *Strategic Giving*, p. 18.

79. Ibid., p. 19.

80. "Number of Nonprofits Edged up Slightly in 2012 due to Purge of IRS Rolls," *The Chronicle of Philanthropy* (April 11, 2013) p. 28.

81. Kathleen S. Kelly, "From Motivations to Mutual Understanding: Shifting the Domain of Donor Research," in Burlingame, *Critical Issues in Fund Raising*, p. 146.

82. Kelly, "From Motivations," p. 149.

83. Cascione, *Philanthropists in Higher Education*, p. 127.

84. Schervish, "Inclination, Obligation," p. 128.

85. Francie Ostrower, *Why the Wealthy Give: The Culture of Elite Philanthropy* (Princeton: Princeton University Press, 1995), p. 135.

86. Burton A. Weisbrod, *The Nonprofit Economy* (Cambridge, MA: Harvard University Press, 1988) pp. 1–6.

87. Harvey C. Mansfield and Delba Winthrop, Translators and Editors, *Alexis de Tocqueville: Democracy in America* (Chicago: University of Chicago Press, 2000).

88. Weisbrod, *The Nonprofit Economy*, pp. 20–22.

89. Kelly, "From Motivations," p. 147.

90. Stuart C. Mendel, "A Field of Its Own," *Stanford Social Innovation Review* (Winter 2014) vol. 12, no.1, pp. 61–62.

3   Philanthropists and Their Foundations

1. Jesse Brundage Sears, *Philanthropy in the History of American Higher Education* (Washington, D.C.: US Government Printing Office, 1922). Robert Bremner, *American Philanthropy* (Chicago: University of Chicago Press, 1960 and 1988). Merle Curti and Roderick Nash, *Philanthropy in the Shaping of American Higher Education* (New Brunswick, NJ: Rutgers University Press, 1965).

2. Joel L. Fleishman, J. Scott Kohler, and Steven Schindler, *Casebook for the Foundation: A Great American Secret—How Private Wealth is Changing the World* (New York: Public Affairs, 2007).

3. For detailed profiles on selected major foundations including the General Education Board, the Rosenwald Trust, and the Markey Trust see John R. Thelin and Richard W. Trollinger, *Time Is of the Essence* (Washington, D.C.: Aspen Institute Program on Philanthropy and Social Innovation, October 2009).

4. Waldemar A. Nielsen, *The Big Foundations* (New York and London: Columbia University Press, 1972).

5. Listings of total bequests to foundations as presented in Bruce A. Kimball and Benjamin Ashby Johnson, "The Beginning of 'Free Money' Ideology in American Universities: Charles W.Eliot at Harvard, 1869–1909," *History of Education Quarterly* (May 2012) vol. 52, no. 7, pp. 222–250.

6. Robert H. Wiebe, *The Search for Order, 1877 to 1920* (New York: Hill and Wang, 1967).

7. Barry D. Karl and Stanley N. Katz, "The American Private Philanthropic Foundation and the Public Sphere, 1890–1930," *Minerva* (March 1983) vol. 19 (1981), pp. 236–270.

8. Eric Anderson and Alfred Moss, *Dangerous Donations: Northern Philanthropy and Southern Black Education, 1902–1930* (Columbia: University of Missouri Press, 1999).

9. Ellen Condliffe Lagemann, *Private Power for the Public Good: A History of the Carnegie Foundation for the Advancement of Teaching* (Middletown, CT: Wesleyan University Press, 1983). For a detailed account of the larger, host foundation which eventually absorbed the CFAT see also Ellen Condliffe Lagemann, *The Politics of Knowledge: The Carnegie Corporation, Philanthropy, and Public Policy* (Chicago: University of Chicago Press, 1989).

10. Thomas Neville Bonner, *Iconoclast: Abraham Flexner and a Life in Learning* (Baltimore, MD and London: Johns Hopkins University Press, 2002).

11. Ellen Condliffe Lagemann, "Public Policy and Sociology: Gunnar Myrdal's *An American Dilemma,*" in *The Politics of Knowledge*, pp. 123–141.

12. James Howell Smith, "Frederick Taylor Gates: Fund Raiser and Businessman," in *Honorable Beggars: The Middlemen of American Philanthropy* (Madison: University of Wisconsin PhD dissertation, 1960) pp. 183–227. See also, Frederick T. Gates, *Chapters in My Life* (New York: 1977).

13. Raymond B. Fosdick, *Adventures in Giving: The Story of the General Education Board* (New York: Harper & Row, 1962).

14. James D. Anderson, *The Education of Blacks in the South, 1860–1935* (Chapel Hill: University of North Carolina Press, 1988).

15. Clyde W. Barrow, *Universities and the Capitalist State: Corporate Liberalism and the Reconstruction of American Higher Education, 1894–1928* (Madison: University of Wisconsin Press, 1990).

16. Ken Chernow, *Titan: The Life of John D. Rockefeller, Sr.* (New York: Random House, 1998). See also, Grant Segall, *John D. Rockefeller: Anointed with Oil* (Oxford and New York: Oxford University Press, 2001).

17. Anderson, *The Education of Blacks.*

18. Amy E. Wells, "Contested Ground: Howard Odum, the Southern Agrarians, and the Emerging University in the South During the 1930s," *History of Higher Education Annual* (2001) vol. 21, pp. 79–101.

19. Peter M. Ascoli, *Julius Rosenwald: The Man Who Built Sears, Roebuck and Advanced the Cause of Black Education in the American South* (Bloomington: Indiana University Press, 2006).

20. Edwin R. Embree, *Julius Rosenwald Fund: Review of Two Decades, 1917–1936* (Chicago: Julius Rosenwald Fund, 1936). Edwin R. Embree and Julia Waxman, *Investment in People: The Story of the Julius Rosenwald Fund* (New York: Harper, 1949).

21. Greg Grandin, *Fordlandia: The Rise and Fall of Henry Ford's Forgotten Jungle City* (New York: Metropolitan Books/ Henry Holt, 2009).

22. Dwight McDonald, *The Ford Foundation: The Men and the Millions* (New York: Reynal, 1956).

23. John R. Thelin, *A History of American Higher Education* (Baltimore, MD: Johns Hopkins University Press, 2011, second edition) p. 284.

24. Goldie Blumenstyk, "New Head of Ford Fund's Education Program Is Champion of Women and Minority Students," The *Chronicle of Higher Education* (December 9, 1992) pp. A27–A28.

25. K. Teltsch, "Derby Enthusiasts Will Set Big Trust for Medical Research," *The New York Times* (August 26, 1984). John H. Dickason and Dunan Neuhauser, "Spending Out, the Markey Way," *Foundation News & Commentary* (Sept/Oct 1999) vol. 40, no. 5.

26. National Research Council, 2004, *Bridging the Bed-Bench Gap: Contributions of the Markey Trust* (Washington, D.C.: The National Academies Press, 2004).

27. Julie L., Nicklin, "Markey Trust, Having Given $500-Million, Will Close This Year," *The Chronicle of Higher Education* (February 28, 1997).

28. Clark Kerr, *The Uses of the University* (Cambridge, MA: Harvard University Press, 1963).

29. Jon Cohen, "Philanthropy's Rising Tide Lifts Science," *Science* (October 8, 1999) vol. 286, no. 5438, pp. 214–223.

30. John R. Thelin, "The Gates Foundation's Uncertain Legacy," *The Chronicle of Higher Education* (July 13, 2013). In the analysis I present here I make a significant departure from the original article. Namely, I raise (and answer) the question about whether a major private foundation should be compared in terms of mission and financial resources to a major federal agency such as NSF or NIH. In contrast to my silence on this issue in my CHE article, my commentary here is that it is fair and appropriate to compare a large foundation to a federal research agency.

31. See the numerous articles in the Special Report on the Gates Foundation issue of *The Chronicle of Higher Education* (July 13, 2013).

32. Joanne Barkan, "As Government Funds Dwindle, Giant Foundations Gain Too Much Power," *The Chronicle of Philanthropy* (October 20, 2013) p. A1.

33. Waldemar A. Nielsen, *The Golden Donors: A New Anatomy of the Great Foundations* (New York: Truman Talley Books of E. P. Dutton, 1985). Ellen Condliffe, Lagemann, Editor, *Philanthropic Foundations: New Scholarship, New Possibilities* (Bloomington: Indiana University Press, 1999).

34. John W. Gardner, *Excellence: Can We Be Equal and Excellent Too?* (New York: W. W. Norton, 1961).

4   Endowments: Colleges and the Stewardship of Good Fortune

1. This chapter draws extensively from our article, "Forever Is a Long Time: Reconsidering Universities' Perpetual Endowment Policies in the Twenty-First Century," published originally in the journal, *History of Intellectual Culture* (2010/11) vol. 9, no. 1, pp.1–17. To confirm and reinforce our commentary in the "Acknowledgments" section, we thank editor P. J. Stortz for his kind permission to reprint the article here.

2. "College Endowments Over $250-Million, 2012," *The Chronicle of Higher Education Almanac, 2013–2014* (August 23, 2013) p. 56.

3. See the extended narrative of John D. Rockefeller's considerations in establishing the General Education Board as a limited-life foundation, in Raymond B. Fosdick, *Adventures in Giving: The Story of the General Education Board* (New York: Harper and Row, 1962). Chernow, Ron, *Titan: The Life of John D. Rockefeller, Sr.* (New York: Random House, 1998); and also, Grant Segall, *John D. Rockefeller: Anointed with Oil* (Oxford and New York: Oxford University Press, 2001).

4. Goldie Blumenstyk, "Pressure Builds on Wealthy Colleges to Spend More of Their Assets," *The Chronicle of Higher Education* (November 2, 2007) vol. 54, no. 10, pp. A1–A20, A21. J. J. Hermes, "Senators Weigh Idea of Requiring Payout Rates for Large University Endowments," *The Chronicle of Higher Education* (September 27, 2007). Stephanie Strom, "How Long Should Gifts Just Grow?: Trillions of Tax-Free Dollars Earning Double-Digit Returns are Inciting Calls to Speed Up Spending," *The New York Times* (Giving Section) (November 12, 2007) pp. H1, H30.

5. Endowment data presented in "Resources" section titled "Total Return on College Endowments" in *The Chronicle of Higher Education Almanac Issue for 2007–2008*, p. 33.

6. Howard Bowen, *The Costs of Higher Education: How Much Do Colleges and Universities Spend Per Student and How Much Should They Spend?* (San Francisco: Jossey-Bass, 1980), see esp. pp. 19–20.

7. Henry Hansmann, "Why Do Universities Have Endowments?," *Journal of Legal Studies* (January 1990) vol. 19, pp. 3–42.

8. David Riesman, *Constraint and Variety in American Education* (Garden City, NY: Doubleday Anchor, 1956).

9. Gaye Tuchman, *Wanna Be U: Inside the Corporate University* (Chicago: University of Chicago Press, 2009).

10. Endowment data presented in "Resources" section titled "College and University Endowments Over $200-Million, 2006" in *The Chronicle of Higher Education Almanac Issue for 2007–2008*, p. 32.

11. Robert H. Bremner, "Benevolent Trusts and Distrusts," in *American Philanthropy* (Chicago: University of Chicago Press, 1960) pp. 100–115.

12. Bowen, *The Costs of Higher Education*, see esp. pp. 19–20. See also, William F. Lasher and Deborah L. Greene, "College and University Budgeting: What Do We Know? What Do We Need to Know?" in Michael Paulsen and John Smart, Editors, *The Finance of Higher Education: Theory, Research, Policy and Practice* (New York: Agathon Press, 2001) pp. 501–542, esp. pp. 511–512.

13. Francie Ostrower, *Limited Life Foundations: Motivations, Experiences, and Strategies* (The Urban Institute: Center on Nonprofits and Philanthropy, February 2009). Francie Ostrower, "Foundation Life Spans: A Vexing Issue," *The Chronicle of Philanthropy* (May 19, 2009). John R. Thelin and Richard Trollinger, *Time is of the Essence: Foundations and the Policies of Limited Life and Endowment Spend-Down* (Washington, D.C.: Aspen Institute, 2009). Loren Renz and David Wolcheck, *Perpetuity or Limited Lifespan: How Do Family Foundations Decide?* (Washington, D.C.: Foundation Center with the Council on Foundations, 2009). An influential work preceding the studies published from 2005 to 2009 is Nielsen, Waldemar A., "The Pitfalls of Perpetuity," *Inside American Philanthropy: The Dramas*

of Donorship (Norman and London: University of Oklahoma Press, 1996) ch. 17, pp. 245–252.

14. As quoted in Hermes, "Senators Weigh Idea."
15. Strom, "How Long Should Gifts Just Grow?"
16. For a definitive statement of the tradition of academic institutions to resent and resist any federal regulation that would intrude on the autonomy of colleges and universities, see Derek C. Bok, "The Federal Government and the University," *The Public Interest* (Winter 1980) pp. 80–101.
17. See, for example, Karen W. Arenson, "Soaring Endowments Widen a Higher Education Gap" *The New York Times* (February 4, 2008) p. A14; and Blumenstyk, "Pressure Builds on Wealthy Colleges."
18. Hermes, "Senators Weigh Idea."; Strom, "How Long Should Gifts Just Grow?"; Arenson, "Soaring Endowments Widen"; and Blumenstyk, "Pressure Builds on Wealthy Colleges."
19. Nielsen, "The Pitfalls of Perpetuity." See also, Ostrower, "Foundation Life Spans."
20. Julie Nicklin, "Markey Trust, Having Given $500-Million, Will Close This Year," *The Chronicle of Higher Education* (February 28, 1997).
21. Diane Granat, "America's 'Give While You Live' Philanthropist," *APF Reporter* (2003) vol. 21.
22. Jesse Brundage Sears, "Development of a Theory of Philanthropy," *Philanthropy in the History of American Higher Education* (Washington, D.C.: US Government Printing Office, 1922) pp. 1–9.
23. Jesse Brundage Sears, "Summary and Conclusions," *Philanthropy in the History*, pp. 103–111.
24. For historical background on Harvard University's endowment and fundraising, see Carl A.Vigeland, *Great Good Fortune: How Harvard Makes Its Money* (New York: Houghton Mifflin, 1986).
25. Laurence M. Veysey, *The Emergence of the American University* (Chicago: University of Chicago Press, 1964) p. 63. John B. Boles, *University Builder: Edgar Odell Lovett and the Founding of The Rice Institute* (Baton Rouge: Louisiana State University Press, 2007).
26. John R. Thelin, "Access and Affordability," *A History of American Higher Education* (Baltimore, MD and London: Johns Hopkins University Press, 2004) pp. 168–171.
27. Ronald G. Ehrenberg, *Tuition Rising: Why College Costs So Much* (Cambridge, MA: Harvard University Press, 2000).
28. Charles T. Clotfelter, Jr., *Buying the Best: Cost Escalation in Elite Higher Education* (Princeton, NJ: Princeton University Press, 1996).
29. Brad Wolverton, "Senate Committee Examines Endowments," *The Chronicle of Higher Education* (June 8, 2007) vol. 53, no. 40, p. A25. Justin Pope, "Congress Eyes College Wealth: Endowments Tied to Tuition Concerns," Associated Press Article (October 15, 2007).
30. For a detailed account on this see Merle Curti and Roderick Nash, "For Alma Mater" and "Corporations and Higher Learning," in *Philanthropy and the Shaping of American Higher Education* (New Brunswick, NJ: Rutgers University Press, 1965) pp. 186–211 and 238–248.

31. An excellent summary of these frequent justifications of perpetual endowments that wealthy universities have invoked are provided—along with the
author's well-argued counters and refutations of these claims—in Hansmann,
"Why Do Universities Have Endowments?"

32. See, for example, Steve O. Michael, "Why Give to a College That Already
Has Enough?," *The Chronicle of Higher Education* (July 6, 2007). See
also, Richard Ekman, "Many Small Private Colleges Thrive With Modest
Endowments," *The Chronicle of Higher Education* (June 2, 2006).

33. Knight Commission on Intercollegiate Athletics, *Restoring the Balance:
Dollars, Values, and the Future of College Sports* (Miami, FL: The Knight
Foundation, 2010). This report and other data indicate that in a given year
only about 17 to 20 intercollegiate athletics programs are self-supporting,
even though the National Collegiate Athletic Association's categorical definition for big-time programs includes self-support as a characteristic. The
Knight Commission data also indicate that only about 7 to 8 programs, even
among highly commercialized athletics departments, show a sustained record
of self-support and operating in the black over five consecutive years.

34. Benjamin Ginsberg, *The Fall of the Faculty: The Rise of the All-Administrative
University and Why It Matters* (New York and London: Oxford University
Press, 2011).

35. Systematic documentation of the disproportionate shift in university spending away from academic and instructional programs is presented in Donna
M. Desrochers and Jane Wellman, *Where Does the Money Come From?
Where Does It Go? What Does It Buy?: Trends in College Spending, 1999–
2009* (Washington, D.C.: The Delta Cost Project, 2011).

36. See, for example, analysis of campus spending at well-endowed colleges and
universities in Andrew Hacker, "They'd Much Rather Be Rich," *The New
York Review of Books* (October 11, 2007).

37. Hansmann, "Why Do Universities Have Endowments?"

38. Jack A. Clarke, "Turgot's Critique of Perpetual Endowments," *French
Historical Studies* (Autumn 1964) vol. 3, no. 4, pp. 495–506.

39. Jesse Brundage Sears, "Place of Educational Foundations in Turgot's Social
Theory," *Philanthropy in the History of American Higher Education*
(Washington, D.C.: US Government Printing Office, 1922) pp. 1–3.

40. Eamon Duffy, *The Stripping of the Altars: Traditional Religion in England,
1400–1580* (New Haven, CT: Yale University Press, 1992). Geoffrey
Baskerville, *English Monks and the Suppression of the Monasteries* (New
Haven, CT: Yale University Press, 1937). A. G. Dickens, *The English
Reformation* (London: B. T. Batsford, 1989, second edition).

41. Quoted in Frederick Rudolph, "The Colonial College," *The American
College and University: A History* (New York: Knopf, 1962) p. 8.

42. Daniel Webster's statement has been attributed to his closing argument to the
Supreme Court in the case, *Trustees of Dartmouth College* v. *Woodward*
(1819). See esp. John Whitehead, "How to Think About the Dartmouth College
Case," *History of Education Quarterly* (Fall 1986) vol. 26, pp. 333–349.

43. Michelle York, "What's in a Name? Some Obscure Scholarships Often Go
Begging," *The New York Times* (January 3, 2006).

44. Example cited in Michelle York, "What's in a Name? Some Obscure Scholarships Often Go Begging," *The New York Times* (January 3, 2006).

45. Henry Hansmann, "Why Do Universities Have Endowments?" See esp. his discussion in Chapter XI "The Preferences of Donors," pp. 33–34.

46. Theodore H. Frank, "Class Action Watch: *Cy Pres* Settlements," *Inside* (March 2008) pp. 1, 21.

47. University Leadership Council, *Competing in the Era of Big Bets: Achieving Scale in Multidisciplinary Research* (Washington, D.C.: The Education Advisory Board, 2009).

48. Diane B. Henriques, "Madoff Scheme Kept Rippling Outward, Across Borders," *The New York Times* (December 19, 2008) p. A1.

49. Robert S. Shepard, "How Can a University That Raises a Billion Dollars Have a Tight Budget?," *The Chronicle of Higher Education* (January 12, 1994) p. A48.

50. Rhoula Khalaf, "Customized Accounting," *Forbes* Magazine (May 25, 1992) p. 50.

51. David F. Swensen, *Pioneering Portfolio Management: An Unconventional Approach to Institutional Investment* (New York: Free Press, 2000).

52. Andrew Delbanco, "The Universities in Trouble," *The New York Review of Books* (May 14, 2009) vol. 56, no. 8.

5   Government Relations and the Nonprofit Sector: Legislation and Policies in Philanthropy and Higher Education

1. Nathan Glazer, "Regulating Businesses and the Universities: One Problem or Two?," *The Public Interest* (Summer 1979) pp. 42–65. Burton A. Weisbrod, *The Nonprofit Economy* (Cambridge, MA and London, England: Harvard University Press, 1988).

2. John Whitehead, *The Separation of College and State* (New Haven, CT: Yale University Press, 1973). See also, John Whitehead, "How to Think About the Dartmouth College Case," *History of Education Quarterly* (Fall 1986) vol. 26, no. 3, pp. 333–349; and John R. Thelin, "The Dartmouth College Case: The Debate Over 'Private' and 'Public' Colleges," *A History of American Higher Education* (Baltimore, MD: Johns Hopkins University Press, 2011) pp. 70–73.

3. Derek C. Bok, "The Federal Government and the University," *The Public Interest* (Winter 1980) pp. 80–101. Carnegie Foundation for the Advancement of Teaching, *Control of the Campus: A Report on the Governance of Higher Education* (Carnegie Foundation for the Advancement of Teaching: Princeton, New Jersey, 1982). Glazer, "Regulating Businesses and the Universities."

4. Robert H. Bremner, "Benevolent Trusts and Distrusts," in *American Philanthropy* (Chicago and London: University of Chicago Press, 1988) pp. 100–115.

5. Bremner, "Looking Backward: 1980s–1960s," in *American Philanthropy*, pp. 177–188.

6. Chester E. Finn, Jr., *Scholars, Dollars, and Bureaucrats* (Washington, D.C.: Brookings Institution, 1978).

7. John R. Thelin, "Schools for Scandal, 1946 to 1960," in *Games Colleges Play: Scandal and Reform in Intercollegiate Athletics* (Baltimore and London: Johns Hopkins University Press, 1994) pp. 98–127.

8. Merle Curti and Roderick Nash, "Corporations and Higher Learning," in *Philanthropy in the Shaping of American Higher Education* (New Brunswick, NJ: Rutgers University Press, 1965) pp. 238–258. See also, John R. Thelin, "Small By Design: Resilience in an Era of Mass Higher Education," in *Meeting the Challenge: America's Independent Colleges and Universities Since 1956* (Washington, D.C.: Council of Independent Colleges, 2006) pp. 3–36, esp. pp. 11–15.

9. New Jersey Superior Judge Alfred P. Stein (1951) as quoted in Thelin, "Small By Design," p. 12.

10. Merle Curti and Roderick Nash, *Philanthropy in the Shaping of American Higher Education* (New Brunswick, NJ: Rutgers University Press, 1965).

11. Rob Reich, Lacey Dorn and Stefanie Sutton, *Any Thing Goes: Approval of Nonprofit Status by the IRS* (Stanford, California: Stanford University Center on Philanthropy and Civil Society, 2009) pp. 8–12.

12. Ibid.

13. Kentucky Utilities Community Service Announcement, *The Lexington (Ky.) Daily Herald* (December 12, 2013) p. B10.

14. Ginia Bellafante, "Bulk of Charitable Giving Is Not Earmarked for the Poor," *The New York Times* (September 9, 2012) p. 27.

15. Eric Lipton, "Fight Over Minimum Wage Illustrates Web of Industry Ties," *The New York Times* (February 10, 2014) pp. A1, A11.

16. Charles E. Shepard, "United Way Head Resigns Over Spending Habits," *The Washington Post* (February 28, 1992); Obituary, "William Aramay, United Way Leader Who Was Jailed for Fraud, Dies at 84," *The New York Times* (November 13, 2011).

17. Courtney Leatherman, "New York Regents Vote to Remove 18 of 19 Adelphi University Trustees," *The Chronicle of Higher Education* (February 21, 1997).

18. Stephanie Strom, "Nonprofits Fear Losing Tax Benefit," *The New York Times* (December 2, 2010).

19. Nannerl O. Keohane, "If a Handsome Income Is Your Goal in Life, You Should Be in Some Other Line of Work," *The Chronicle of Higher Education* (December 7, 1994).

20. Reliance on presidential base salary data is preferable to citing total compensation packages because the former category leans toward understatement. Compensation packages, in contrast, often include numerous benefits and individually negotiated provisions that drive up dollars and stretch credibility. For example, the highest annual compensation package for the president of a private college or university in 2011 exceeded $3 million. This strikes us as so high that it skews the general profile and probably warrants board

explanation to which we are not privy. In another instance, a state university president who was terminated had a compensation package surpassing $2.6 million for the year—but evidently this included buy-out clauses. Our intent is to avoid embellishment or exaggeration on the presidential incomes. However, some national data bases provide only compensation packages, not base salaries.

21. Tamar Lewin, "Pay for U.S. College Presidents Continues to Grow," *The New York Times* (December 15, 2013).

22. "Highest-Paid Chief Executives at Public Universities, 2011–12," *The Chronicle of Higher Education Almanac, 2013–14* (August 23, 2013) p. 8.

23. "Brandeis Paid Ex-President $4.9 Million This Month," *Inside Higher Ed* (January 24, 2014).

24. Ry Rivard, "Brandeis Changes Compensation Policies after $5 Million Payout to Ex-President," *Inside Higher Ed* (January 30, 2014).

25. William Yardley, "Coach Johnny Orr, 86; Improved Pay and Iowa State: Obituary," *The New York Times* (January 4, 2014) p. A15.

26. Donna M. Desrochers, Colleen M. Lenihan, and Jane Wellman, *Trends in College Spending, 1998–2008: Where Does the Money Come From? Where Does It Go? What Does It Buy?* (Washington, D.C.: Delta Cost Project, 2010).

27. Mark Schlabach, "The NCAA: Where Does the Money Go?," *ESPN Sports Center News Release* (July 12, 2011).

28. Alan Judd, "University of Georgia Foundations' Endowment Management Comes Under Scrutiny," *The Atlanta Journal Constitution* (November 24, 2003).

29. Julianne Basinger, "University of Georgia Regents Drop Foundation," *The Chronicle of Higher Education* (June 4, 2004).

30. Joshua Karlin-Resnick, "Georgia Regents Mend Fences with University's Fund-Raising Foundations," *The Chronicle of Higher Education* (August 13, 2004).

31. Stephanie Strom, "Fees and Trustees: Paying the Keepers of the Cash," *The New York Times* (July 10, 2003).

32. Mark Pitsch, "Foundation Releases Donor List: U of L Data Includes McConnell Center Gifts," *The Louisville Courier-Journal* (December 14, 2004) pp. A1, A10.

33. Stephanie Strom, "A Tax Benefit That Bypasses Idea of Charity," *The New York Times* (April 25, 2005) pp. A1, A15.

34. "Yale: 'F' in Ethics," Editorial in *The Indianapolis Star* (March 22, 1995) p. A10; Massimo Calbresi, "Education: How to Lose $20 Million," *Time* (March 27, 1995) p. 69.

35. Kathryn Masterson, "Judge Rules Fisk U. Can Sell O'Keeffe Art, But with Stipulations," *The Chronicle of Higher Education* (November 4, 2010).

36. Oliver Staley and Janet Frankston Lorin, "Princeton Settles Lawsuit Over $900 Million Endowment," *Bloomberg News Service* (December 10, 2008).

37. Katherine Mangan, "Descendent of 19th-Century Donor Sues Tulane Over Dissolution of Women's College," *The Chronicle of Higher Education* (August 20, 2008).

38. Lois Therrien, "Getting Joe College To Pay for City Services," *Business Week* (July 16, 1990) p. 37. Goldie Blumenstyk, "Town-Gown Battles Escalate as Beleaguered Cities Assail College Tax Exemptions," *The Chronicle of Higher Education* (June 29, 1988). Patrick Healy, "Colleges vs. Communities: Battles Intensify Over City Efforts to Win Payments from Tax-Exempt Institutions," *The Chronicle of Higher Education* (May 5, 1995) pp. A27, A32. "Boston May Ask Its Colleges to Pay More in Lieu of Taxes," *The Boston Globe* (April 6, 2010).

39. Elisabeth Rosenthal, "Benefits Questioned in Tax Breaks for Nonprofit Hospitals," *The New York Times* (December 16, 2013) pp. A12, A20.

40. Goldie Blumenstyk, "Princeton's Royalty Windfall Leads to Challenge of Tax-Exempt Status," *The Chronicle of Higher Education* (July 8, 2013). James Piereson and Naomi Schaefer Riley," Why Shouldn't Princeton Pay Taxes?," *The Wall Street Journal* (August 20, 2013) p. A15. David Vezacos and Susan Decker, "Princeton Drug Royalties Spark Suit Over Tax Exemption," *Bloomberg News Service* (September 4, 2013).

41. Scott Jaschik, "Extensive IRS Audits Find Many Colleges Are Violating Tax Laws," *The Chronicle of Higher Education* (January 20, 1995) p. A18. Eric Frazier, "IRS Steps Up Scrutiny of Colleges and Other Nonprofit Groups," *The Chronicle of Higher Education* (December 20, 2010).

42. Bok, "The Federal Government and the University."

43. Glazer, "Regulating Businesses and the Universities."

44. Steve Eder, "For ESPN, Millions to Remain in Connecticut," *The New York Times* (December 27, 2013) pp. A1, B12–B13.

45. Arthur Levine, "Higher Education's New Status as a Mature Industry," *The Chronicle of Higher Education* (January 31, 1997) p. A48.

46. Suzanne Perry, "Charities Get Tough Questions on Tax Breaks—and Can Expect More," *The Chronicle of Higher Education* (February 14, 2013).

6   Professionalization of Philanthropy: Fund-Raising and Development

1. Merle Curti and Roderick Nash, *Philanthropy in the Shaping of American Higher Education* (New Brunswick, NJ: Rutgers University Press, 1965) p. 55.

2. James Howell Smith, *Honorable Beggars: The Middlemen of American Philanthropy* (Madison: University of Wisconsin PhD Dissertation, 1968).

3. Scott M. Cutlip, *Fund Raising in the United States: It's Role in America's Philanthropy* (New Brunswick, NJ: Transaction Publishers, 1965, 1990) p. 3.

4. Mark J. Drozdowski, *A Peculiar Calling: Confessions of a College Fund Raiser* (New York: Universe, 2008).

5. Dominic J. Brewer, Susan M. Gates, and Charles A. Goldman, *In Pursuit of Prestige: Strategy and Competition in U.S. Higher Education* (New Brunswick, NJ: Transaction Publishers, 2002).*The New Institutionalism in Organizational Analysis* is the title of a 1991 book edited by Walter W. Powell

and Paul J. DiMaggio. This volume contains their famous 1983 essay, "The Iron Cage Revisited: Institutional Isomorphism and Collective Rationality in Organizational Fields," which is credited with stimulating renewed interest in institutionalism.

6. *Giving USA 2013: The Annual Report on Philanthropy for the Year 2013* (Chicago: Giving USA Foundation, 2013).

7. Don Troop, "Gifts to Colleges Hit $33.8 Billion, Topping Pre-Recession Levels," http://chronicle.com/article/gifts-to-Colleges-Hit/144707//cid=at.

8. Merle Curti, "American Philanthropy and the National Character," *American Quarterly* (1958) vol. 10, no. 4, pp. 420–437.

9. John R. Thelin, *A History of American Higher Education* (Baltimore, MD: Johns Hopkins University Press, 2004).

10. Frederick Rudolph, *The American College & University: A History* (Athens: University of Georgia Press, 1962,1990) p. 47.

11. Ron Chernow, *Titan: The Life of John D. Rockefeller, Sr.* (New York: Random House, 1998).

12. Smith, *Honorable Beggars*, p. 21.

13. Olivier Zunz, *Philanthropy in America: A History* (Princeton, NJ: Princeton University Press, 2012) p. 3.

14. Curti and Nash, *Philanthropy in the Shaping*, pp. 201–202.

15. Ibid, p. 201.

16. Cutlip, *Fund Raising in the United States*, p. 54.

17. Ibid.

18. Zunz, *Philanthropy in America*, p. 2.

19. Cutlip, *Fund Raising in the United States*, p. 44.

20. Ibid., p. 42.

21. Michael J. Worth and James W. Asp II, *The Development Officer in Higher Education: Toward an Understanding of the Role* (Washington, D.C.: George Washington University, Graduate School of Education and Human Development, ASHE-ERTC Higher Education Report No. 4, 1994) p. 8.

22. Barbara J. Brittingham and Thomas R. Pezzullo, *The Campus Green: Fund Raising in Higher Education* (Washington, D.C.: School of Education and Human Development, The George Washington University, ASHE-ERIC Higher Education Report No. 1, 1990) p. 12.

23. Ibid., p. 13.

24. In 2006, the American Association of Fundraising Counsel, (AAFRC) changed its name to the Giving Institute: Leading Consultants to Non-Profits. In part, the change reflects the fact that some of the members firms offer services beyond fund-raising. The new name also reflects the organization's annual publication, *Giving USA*, which it has published since 1957.

25. Zunz, *Philanthropy in America*, p. 68.

26. Harlow J. Heneman, "Foreword," in John W. Leslie, *Focus on Understanding and Support: A Study in College Management* (Washington, D.C.: American College Public Relations Association, 1969) pp. ix–xii.

27. R. L. Stuhr would later become a principal in the Chicago-based consulting firm of Gonser, Gerber, Tinker, and Stuhr.

28. Worth and Asp II, *The Development Officer in Higher Education*, pp. 4–5.
29. Harold J. Seymour, *Designs for Fund-Raising: Principles, Patterns, Techniques* (New York: McGraw-Hill Book Company, 1966) p. 115.
30. Worth and Asp II, *The Development Officer in Higher Education*, p. 9
31. Curti and Nash, *Philanthropy in the Shaping*, p. 208.
32. Leslie, *Focus on Understanding*, pp. 17–18.
33. Ibid., p. 1.
34. A. Westley Rowland, General Editor, *Handbook of Institutional Advancement: A Modern Guide to Executive Management, Institutional Relations, Fund-Raising, Alumni Administration, Government Relations, Publications, Periodicals, and Enrollment Management.* (San Francisco: Jossey-Bass Inc., second edition, 1986) p. xiii.
35. According to Drezner, Michael J. Worth identified the same three major trends. In Noah D. Drezner, *Philanthropy and Fundraising in American Higher Education* (Hoboken, NJ: Wiley Periodicals, ASHE Higher Education Report, vol. 37, no. 2, 2011) pp. 25–26.
36. Michael Barbaro, "$1.1 Billion in Thanks from Bloomberg to John Hopkins," *The New York Times*, January 26, 2013. http://www.nytimes./com/2013/01/27/nyregion/at-1-1-billion-bloomber.
37. Curti and Nash, *Philanthropy in the Shaping*, p. 242.
38. Ibid., p. 246.
39. *Giving USA: The Annual Report on Philanthropy for the Year 2012* (Chicago: Giving USA Foundation) p. 136.
40. *Giving USA 1970*, p. 24; *Giving USA 1981*, p. 15; *Giving USA 2001*, pp. 72–73.
41. *Giving USA 2013*, p. 91.
42. Curti and Nash, *Philanthropy in the Shaping*, p. 210
43. Gregory L. Cascione, *Philanthropists in Higher Education: Institutional, Biographical, and Religious Motivations for Giving* (New York: Routledge Falmer, 2003) p. 2.
44. J. Mercer, "The Fund Raiser as President," *The Chronicle of Higher Education* (vol. 42, no. 3, September 15, 1995) pp. A35–36.
45. Drezner, *Philanthropy and Fundraising*, pp. 14–15.

7   Colleges and Their Constituencies: New Directions in Philanthropy

1. Robert Putnam, *Bowling Alone: The Collapse and Revival of American Community* (New York: Simon and Schuster, 2000).
2. See, for example, Harvey C. Mansfield and Delba Winthrop, Translators and Editors, *Alexis de Tocqueville: Democracy in America* (Chicago: University of Chicago Press, 2000).
3. Allison Schneider, "Empty Tables at the Faculty Club Worry Some Academics," *Chronicle of Higher Education* (June 13, 1997) p. A12.

4. Peter Dobkin Hall, *Inventing the Nonprofit Sector* (Baltimore and London: Johns Hopkins University Press, 1992).

5. Ian Lovett, "Lasting Tributes Meet Early End in Bankruptcy," *The New York Times* (September 6, 2013) pp. A11, A13.

6. Andrew Martin, "Degrees of Debt—a Reckoning for Colleges: Building a Showcase Campus, Using an I.O.U.," *The New York Times* (December 14, 2012) pp. A1, B4.

7. University of Southern California: The Campaign for the University, "A Historic $50 Million Gift establishes the USC Michelson Center for Convergent Bioscience," paid full page advertisement, *The New York Times* (January 14, 2014) p. A13.

8. Scott Jaschik on "Rich Harvard, Poor Harvard" (2013) *Inside Higher Ed* (November 11, 2013).

9. See, for example, Andrea Walton and Marybeth Gasman, Editors, *Philanthropy, Volunteerism & Fundraising in Higher Education* (Boston: Pearson Publishing, 2008) (Association for the Study of Higher Education, ASHE Reader Series).

10. Don Troop, "The Secrets of 'Million-Dollar Ready' Colleges," *Inside Higher Ed* (December 11, 2013). See also earlier work: Jerold Panas, *Mega Gifts: Who Gives Them, Who Gets Them.* (Medford, MA: Emerson & Church Publishers, second edition, 2005); and, Gary A. Tobin and Aryeh K. Weinberg, *Mega-Gifts in American Philanthropy: Giving Patterns, 2001–2003* (San Francisco: Institute for Jewish & Community Research, 2007).

11. Jon Swartz, "Band of Billionaires Pledge to Give: Buffett, Gateses Call on Wealthy to Donate Up to Half of Their Fortunes," *USA Today* (August 5, 2010) p. B1.

12. George Soros, "My Philanthropy," *The New York Review of Books* (June 23, 2011).

13. Michael Barbaro, "Bloomberg to Johns Hopkins: Thanks a Billion (Well, $1.1 Billion)," *The New York Times* (January 27, 2013) pp. 1, 16.

14. Ann E. Kaplan, Editor, "Philanthropy in 1992: The Numbers," *Giving USA: The Annual Report on Philanthropy for the Year 1992* (New York: AAFRC Trust for Philanthropy, 1993) pp. 9–46.

15. For a provocative analysis of universities' failure to heed signals of change, see Andrew Delbanco, "The Universities in Trouble," *The New York Review of Books* (May 14, 2009) vol. 56, no. 8.

16. "Berkeley Undergraduate Profile," Office of Planning, University of California, Berkeley (2014).

17. We are indebted to high education scholar Noah D. Drezner who brought our attention to this Hebrew word for "charity."

18. Noah D. Drezner, "Arguing for a Different View: Deaf-Serving Institutions as Minority-Serving," in Marybeth Gasman, Benjamin Baez, and Caroline Sotello Vierennes Turner, Editors, *Understanding Minority Serving Institutions* (Albany, NY: State University Press at Albany, 2008) pp. 57–69.

19. Mary B. Marcy, "Why Foundations Have Cut Back in Higher Education," *The Chronicle of Higher Education* (July 25, 2003).

20. Gasman, Baez and Turner, *Understanding Minority Serving Institutions*.
21. Marybeth Gasman, *Envisioning Black Colleges: A History of the United Negro College Fund* (Baltimore, MD: Johns Hopkins University Press, 2007).
22. Marybeth Gasman and Noah D. Drezner, "A Maverick in the Field: The Oram Group and Fundraising in the Black College Community During the 1970s," *History of Education Quarterly* (November 2009) vol. 49, no. 4, pp. 465–506.
23. Andrea Walton, Editor, *Women and Philanthropy in Education* (Bloomington and Indianapolis: Indiana University Press, 2005).
24. Marybeth Gasman, "Sisters in Service: African American Sororities and Philanthropic Support of Education," in Walton, *Women and Philanthropy in Education*, pp. 194–214.
25. Sarah Henry Lederman, "Philanthropy and Social Casework: Mary E. Richmond and the Russell Sage Foundation, 1909–1928," in Walton, *Women and Philanthropy in Education*, pp. 60–80.
26. Amy E. Wells, "Considering Her Influence: Sydnor H. Walker and Rockefeller Support for Social Work, Social Scientists, and Universities in the South," in Walton, *Women and Philanthropy in Education*, pp. 127–147.
27. "Student Demographics," *The Chronicle of Higher Education Almanac Issue, 2011–2012* (August 26, 2011) vol. 58, no. 1, p. 32.
28. J. Travis McDearmon, "Hail to Thee, Our Alma Mater: Alumni Role Identity and the Relationship to Institutional Support Behaviors," *Research in Higher Education* (2013) vol. 54, pp. 288–302.
29. Paul Sullivan, "Among Young Inheritors, An Urge to Redistribute," *The New York Times* (March 26, 2013) p. F3.
30. Richard Perez-Pena, "Facebook Founder to Donate $100 Million to Remake Newark Schools," *The New York Times* (September 22, 2010).
31. John R. Thelin and Lawrence L. Wiseman, *The Old College Try: Balancing Academics and Athletics* (Washington, D.C.: ASHE-ERIC Research Reports, 1989).
32. This model (and modest) proposal may appear to be grounded in fiction or wishful thinking. It is, however, based on the creative, persuasive conversation that took place at The College of William and Mary in Virginia in the early 1990s. The provost thanked alumnus donor and prosperous entrepreneur for a $5 million gift that was a wonderful contribution to intercollegiate sports—and would qualify for renaming the stadium in the donor's honor. And, explained the Provost, a matching gift for academic programs would truly demonstrate the donor as an alumnus having equal commitment to educational excellence. The result was a win-win for the generous and loyal alumnus and Alma Mater!
33. Associated Press, "University of Illinois to Drop Controversial 'Chief Illiwinek' Mascot," (February 16, 2007) syndicated article.
34. John D. Columbo and Mark A. Hall, *The Charitable Tax Exemption* (Boulder, Colorado: Westview Press, 2005).
35. "Blue Grass Community Foundation: We're In It For Good!," "About Us" section, website (January 10, 2013).

36. Linda B. Blackford, "Joe Craft Donated 'Majority' of Money for New Rupp Arena Locker Rooms," *The Lexington (Ky.) Daily Herald* (January 8, 2013) p. A1.

37. Peter Singer, "Good Charity, Bad Charity," *The New York Times* (August 11, 2013) Sunday Review, p. 6.

38. Ken Stern, "The Charity Swindle," *The New York Times* (November 26, 2013) p. A21.

39. Ray D. Madoff, "How the Government Gives," *The New York Times* (December 7, 2013) p. A19.

40. Lawrence Rosen, "Have Colleges Flouted the Prudent-Investor Rule?," *The Chronicle of Higher Education* (August 8, 2010).

41. Peter Buffett, "The Charitable-Industrial Complex," *The New York Times* (July 26, 2013) p. A23.

42. John Hawks, *For a Good Cause?: How Charitable Institutions Become Powerful Economic Bullies* (Secaucus, NJ: Carol Publishing Group, 1997).

43. Ben Wieder, "Thiel Fellowships Pay 24 Talented Students $100,000 Not to Attend College," *Inside Higher Ed* (May 25, 2011).

44. Steven Jobs, "You've Got To Find What You Love," Commencement Speech at Stanford University (Stanford, CA: June 12, 2005).

45. Carl Becker, *Cornell University: Founders and Founding* (Ithaca, NY: Cornell University Press, 1943).

46. John R. Thelin, "Parsing the Case Against College," *Inside Higher Ed* (January 11, 2013).

47. Kathleen Parker, "College's Diminishing Returns Rooted in Cost, Quality Concerns," syndicated column published in *The Lexington (Kentucky) Herald-Leader* (January 29, 2014) p. A15. For broader context and detailed informed debate on this issue see John R.Thelin, *The Rising Costs of Higher Education: A Reference Handbook* (Santa Barbara, CA; Denver, CO; and Oxford, England: ABC-CLIO Publishers, 2013).

48. Don Troop, "Gifts to Colleges Hit $33.8-Billion, Topping Pre-Recession Levels," *The Chronicle of Higher Education* (February 12, 2014).

49. Marts & Lundy, *Special Report: 2013 Giving to Higher Education: The Big Gift Revival* (New York: Marts & Lundy, February 2014).

50. Henry Rosovsky, *The University: An Owner's Manual* (New York and London: W. W. Norton and Company, 1990) p. 29.

51. Steve O. Michael, "Why Give to a College That Already Has Enough?," *Chronicle of Higher Education* (July 6, 2007). See also, Richard Ekman, "Many Small Private Colleges Thrive With Modest Endowments," *The Chronicle of Higher Education* (June 2, 2006).

52. Do-Hyeong Myeong, "Freshman Seminar Donates $25,000 at End of Course to Charitable Organizations," *The Daily Princetonian* (February 11, 2014).

53. Dick Merriman, "The College as a Philanthropy. Yes, a Philanthropy," *The Chronicle of Higher Education* (October 31, 2010).

Bibliography

The sources listed in the first section below represent major scholarly works dealing with social, historical, and policy analyses of significant philanthropic issues. Following this categorical listing of scholarly sources is a second section with citations for selected, illustrative articles published in such media as *The Chronicle of Higher Education*, *The Chronicle of Philanthropy*, *Inside Higher Ed*, and *The New York Times*. The net aim is to provide readers with readily available sources that convey diverse perspectives combined with a fusion of past and present episodes in understanding philanthropy and higher education. Specific, full citations also are provided for pertinent articles, documents, and books in the endnotes for each chapter.

Major Scholarly Works

Anderson, Eric and Alfred A. Moss, *Dangerous Donations: Northern Philanthropy and Southern Black Education, 1902–1930* (Columbia: University of Missouri Press, 2003).

Anderson, James D., *The Education of Blacks in the South, 1860–1935* (Chapel Hill: University of North Carolina Press, 1988).

Andreoni, James, "Impure Altruism and Donations to Public Goods: A Theory of Warm-Glow Giving," *The Economic Journal* (June 1990) vol. 100, pp. 464–477.

Ascoli, Peter M., *Julius Rosenwald: The Man Who Built Sears, Roebuck and Advanced the Cause of Black Education in the American South* (Bloomington: Indiana University Press, 2006).

Associated Press, "University of Illinois to Drop Controversial 'Chief Illiwinek' Mascot" (February 16, 2007) syndicated article.

Axtell, James, "Dr. Wheelock's Little Red School," *The European and the Indian: Essay in the Ethnohistory of Colonial North America* (New York: Oxford University Press, 1981) Chapter 4, pp. 87–109.

Barron, James, "Book Published in 1640 Makes Record Sale at Auction," *The New York Times* (November 27, 2013) p. A19.

Barrow, Clyde W., *Universities and the Capitalist State: Corporate Liberalism and the Reconstruction of American Higher Education, 1894–1928* (Madison: University of Wisconsin Press, 1990).

Basinger, Julianne, "University of Georgia Regents Drop Foundation," *The Chronicle of Higher Education* (June 4, 2004).

Baskerville, Geoffrey, *English Monks and the Suppression of the Monasteries* (New Haven, CT: Yale University Press, 1937).

Becker, Carl, *Cornell University: Founders and Founding* (Ithaca, NY: Cornell University Press, 1943).

Bellafante, Ginia, "Bulk of Charitable Giving Is Not Earmarked for the Poor," *The New York Times* (September 9, 2012) p. 27.

Bok, Derek C., "The Federal Government and the University," *The Public Interest* (Winter 1980) pp. 80–101.

Boles, John B., *University Builder: Edgar Odell Lovett and the Founding of The Rice Institute* (Baton Rouge: Louisiana State University Press, 2007).

Bonner, Thomas Neville, *Iconoclast: Abraham Flexner and a Life in Learning* (Baltimore, MD: Johns Hopkins University Press, 2002).

Boorstin, Daniel J., "The Booster College," in *The Americans: The National Experience* (New York: Harper and Row, 1965) pp. 161–165.

"Boston May Ask Its Colleges to Pay More in Lieu of Taxes," *The Boston Globe* (April 6, 2010).

Boulding, Kenneth E., *The Economy of Love and Fear: A Preface to Grants Economics* (Belmont, CA: Wadsworth Publishing Company, 1973).

Bowen, Howard R., *The Costs of Higher Education: How Much Do Colleges and Universities Spend Per Student and How Much Should They Spend?* (San Francisco: Jossey-Bass, 1980).

Bremner, Robert H., *American Philanthropy* (Chicago: University of Chicago Press, second edition, 1988).

——— *Giving: Charity and Philanthropy in History* (New Brunswick, NJ: Transaction Publishers, 1996).

Brewer, Dominic J., Susan M. Gates, and Charles A. Goldman, *In Pursuit of Prestige: Strategy and Competition in U.S. Higher Education* (New Brunswick, NJ: Transaction Publishers, 2002).

Brilliant, Eleanor L., *Private Charity and Public Inquiry: A History of the Filer and Peterson Commissions* (Bloomington: Indiana University Press, 2000).

Brittingham, Barbara and Thomas Pezzullo, *The Campus Green: Fund Raising in Higher Education* (Washington, D.C.: ASHE ERIC, 1990).

Burlingame, Dwight F., Editor, *Critical Issues in Fund Raising* (New York: John Wiley, 1997) p. 146.

——— *The Responsibilities of Wealth* (Bloomington: Indiana University Press, 1992).

Burlingame, Dwight F. and Lamont J. Hulse, Editors, *Taking Fund Raising Seriously: Advancing the Profession and Practice of Raising Money* (San Francisco: Jossey-Bass Publishers, 1992).

Calbresi, Massimo, "Education: How to Lose $20 Million," *Time* (March 27, 1995) p. 69.

Carnegie Council on Policy Studies in Higher Education, *Three Thousand Futures: The Next Twenty Years for Higher Education* (San Francisco: Jossey-Bass, 1980).

Carnegie Foundation for the Advancement of Teaching, *The Control of the Campus: A Report on the Governance of Higher Education* (Princeton, NJ: Princeton University Press, 1982).

Cascione, Gregory L., *Philanthropists in Higher Education: Institutional, Biographical, and Religious Motivations for Giving* (New York: Routledge Falmer, 2003).

Charter of the College of Rhode Island of 1764, as published in Walter C. Bronson, *The History of Brown University, 1764–1914* (Providence, RI: Brown University, 1914) pp. 500–507.

Cheit, Earl F., *The New Depression in Higher Education: A Study of Financial Conditions at 41 Colleges and Universities* (New York: McGraw-Hill, 1973).

Chernow, Ron, *Titan: The Life of John D. Rockefeller, Sr.* (New York: Random House, 1998).

Clark, Burton R., "Belief and Loyalty in College Organization," *The Journal of Higher Education* (June 1971) vol. 42, no. 16, pp. 499–515.

——— *The Distinctive College: Antioch, Reed & Swarthmore* (Chicago: Aldine, 1970).

Clarke, Jack A., "Turgot's Critique of Perpetual Endowments," *French Historical Studies* (Autumn 1964) vol. 3, no. 4, pp. 495–506.

"The Class of 1937," cover story for *Life* magazine (June 7, 1937).

Clotfelter, Charles T., *Buying the Best: Cost Escalation in Elite Higher Education* (Princeton, NJ: Princeton University Press, 1996) (National Bureau of Economic Research Monograph).

Clotfelter, Charles T., Ronald G. Ehrenberg, Malcolm Getz, and John J. Siegried, Editors, *Economic Challenges in Higher Education* (Chicago and London: University of Chicago Press, 1992) (National Bureau of Economic Research Monograph).

Clotfelter, Charles T., and Thomas Ehrlich, Editors, *Philanthropy and the Nonprofit Sector in a Changing America* (Bloomington: Indiana University Press, 1999).

Cohen, Jon, "Philanthropy's Rising Tide Lifts Science," *Science* (October 8, 1999) vol. 286, no. 5438, pp. 214–223.

Colombo, John D. and Mark A. Hall, *The Charitable Tax Exemption* (Boulder, CO: Westview Press, 2005).

Curti, Merle, "American Philanthropy and the National Character," *American Quarterly* (1958) vol. 10, pp. 420–437.

Curti, Merle and Roderick Nash, *Philanthropy in the Shaping of American Higher Education* (New Brunswick, NJ: Rutgers University Press, 1965).

Cutlip, Scott M., *Fund Raising in the United States: Its Role in America's Philanthropy* (New Brunswick, NJ: Transaction Publishers, 1965, 1990).

Davis, Natalie Zeman, *The Gift in Sixteenth-Century France* (Madison: The University of Wisconsin Press, 2000).

Dawkins, Richard, *The Selfish Gene* (Oxford: Oxford University Press, 1976).

Delbanco, Andrew, "The Universities in Trouble," *The New York Review of Books* (May 14, 2009) vol. 56, no. 8, pp. 33–37.

Derbes, Anne and Mark Sandona, "Ave charitate plena': Variations on the Theme of Charity in the Arena Chapel," *Speculum* (2001) vol. 76, pp. 599–637.

Desrochers, Donna M. and Jane Wellman, *Where Does the Money Come From? Where Does It Go? What Does It Buy?: Trends in College Spending, 1999–2009* (Washington, D.C.: The Delta Cost Project, 2010).

Diamond, Nancy, "Catching Up: The Advance of Emory University Since World War II," in Roger L. Geiger with Susan Richardson, Editors, *History of Higher Education Annual 1999: Southern Higher Education in the Twentieth Century* (1999) vol. 19, pp. 149–183.

Dickason, John H. and Dunan Neuhauser, "Spending Out, the Markey Way," *Foundation News & Commentary* (Sept/Oct 1999) vol. 40, no. 5.

Dickens, A. G., *The English Reformation* (London: B. T. Batsford, 1989, second edition).

Drezner, Noah D., *Philanthropy and Fundraising in American Higher Education* (Hoboken, NJ: Wiley Periodicals, Inc. ASHE Higher Education Report, vol. 37, no. 2, 2011) pp. 25–26.

Drozdowski, Mark J., *A Peculiar Calling: Confessions of a College Fund Raiser* (New York: Universe, Inc., 2008).

Duffy, Eamon, *The Stripping of the Altars: Traditional Religion in England, 1400–1580* (New Haven, CT: Yale University Press, 1992).

Dugatkin, Lee A., *The Altruism Equation: Seven Scientists Search for the Origins of Goodness* (Princeton, NJ: Princeton University Press, 2006).

Durden, Robert F., *The Launching of Duke University, 1924–1949* (Durham and London: Duke University Press, 1993).

Eder, Steve, "For ESPN, Millions to Remain in Connecticut," *The New York Times* (December 27, 2013) pp. A1, B12–B13.

Ehrenberg, Ronald G., *Tuition Rising: Why College Costs So Much* (Cambridge, MA: Harvard University Press, 2000).

Elliott, Deni, *The Kindness of Strangers: Philanthropy and Higher Education* (New York: Rowman & Littlefield, 2006).

Embree, Edwin R., *Julius Rosenwald Fund: Review of Two Decades, 1917–1936* (Chicago: The Julius Rosenwald Fund, 1936).

Embree, Edwin R. and Julia Waxman, *Investment in People: The Story of the Julius Rosenwald Fund* (New York: Harper, 1949).

Erikson, Erik H. and Joan M. Erikson, *The Life Cycle Completed* (New York: W. W. Norton, Extended Version, 1997).

Finn, Chester E. Jr., *Scholars, Dollars and Bureaucrats* (Washington, D.C.: Brookings Institution, 1978).

Fisher, Donald. *Fundamental Development of the Social Sciences: Rockefeller Philanthropy and the United States Social Science Research Council* (Ann Arbor: University of Michigan Press, 1993).

Fleishman, Joel L., Kohler, J. Scott, and Steven Schindler, *Casebook for The Foundation: A Great American Secret—How Private Wealth is Changing the World* (New York: Public Affairs, 2007).

Fosdick, Raymond B., *Adventures in Giving: The Story of the General Education Board* (New York: Harper & Row, 1962).

Foster, Margery Somers, *Out of Smalle Beginnings... An Economic History of Harvard College in the Puritan Period* (Cambridge, MA: Belknap Press of Harvard University, 1962).

Frank, Theodore H., "Class Action Watch: *Cy Pres* Settlements," *Inside* (March 2008) pp. 1, 21.

Friedman, Lawrence J. and Mark D. McGarvie, Editors, *Charity, Philanthropy, and Civility in American History* (Cambridge: Cambridge University Press, 2003).

Frumkin, Peter, *Strategic giving: The Art and Science of Philanthropy* (Chicago: University of Chicago Press, 2006).

Gardner, John W., *Excellence: Can We Be Equal and Excellent Too?* (New York: W. W. Norton, 1961).

Gasman, Marybeth, *Envisioning Black Colleges: A History of the United Negro College Fund* (Baltimore, MD: Johns Hopkins University Press, 2007).

Gasman, Marybeth, Benjamin Baez, and Caroline Sotello Vierennes Turner, Editors, *Understanding Minority Serving Institutions* (Albany, NY: State University Press at Albany, 2008).

Gasman, Marybeth and Noah D. Drezner, "A Maverick in the Field: The Oram Group and Fundraising in the Black College Community During the 1970s," *History of Education Quarterly* (November 2009) vol. 49, no. 4, pp. 465–506.

Gates, Frederick T., *Chapters in My Life* (New York: Free Press, 1977).

Gaudiani, Claire, *The Greater Good: How Philanthropy Drives the American Economy and Can Save Capitalism* (New York: Henry Holt, 2003).

Ginsberg, Benjamin, *The Fall of the Faculty: The Rise of the All-Administrative University and Why It Matters* (New York and London: Oxford University Press, 2011).

Glazer, Nathan, "Regulating Businesses and the Universities: One Problem or Two?," *The Public Interest* (Summer 1979) pp. 42–65.

Gneezy, Uri and John A., List, *The Why Axis: Hidden Motives and the Undiscovered Economics of Everyday Life* (New York: Public Affairs, 2013) p. 171.

Goldmark, Peter, "Before the Storm," in H. Peter Karoff, Editor, *Just Money: A Critique of Contemporary American Philanthropy* (Boston: TPI Editions, 2004) pp. 24–25.

Grace, Kay Sprinkel, *Beyond Fund Raising: New Strategies for Nonprofit Innovation and Investment* (New York: John Wiley, 1997).

Grace, Kay Sprinkel and Alan L. Wendroff, *High Impact Philanthropy: How Donors, Boards, and Nonprofit Organizations can Transform Communities* (New York: John Wiley, 2001).

Granat, Diane, "America's 'Give While You Live' Philanthropist," *APF Reporter* (2003) vol. 21.

Grandin, Greg, *Fordlandia: The Rise and Fall of Henry Ford's Forgotten Jungle City* (New York: Metropolitan Books/ Henry Holt, 2009).

Gunderman, Richard B., *We Make A A Life by What We Give* (Bloomington: Indiana University Press, 2008) pp. 21–22.

Hacker, Andrew, "They'd Much Rather Be Rich," *The New York Review of Books* (October 11, 2007).

Hall, Margaret Rooney, *The Dean's Role in Fund Raising* (Baltimore, MD and London: Johns Hopkins University Press, 1993).

Hall, Peter D., *Inventing the Nonprofit Sector: And Other Essays on Philanthropy, Voluntarism, and Nonprofit Organizations* (Baltimore, MD: Johns Hopkins University Press, 1992).

Hammack, David C., Editor, *Making the Nonprofit Sector in the United States* (Bloomington: Indiana University Press, 1998) pp. 6–8.

Hansmann, Henry, "Why Do Universities Have Endowments?" *Journal of Legal Studies* (January 1990) vol. 19, pp. 3–42.

Harman, *The Price of Altruism: George Price and the Search for the Origins of Kindness* (New York: W. W. Norton, 2010).

Hawks, John, *For a Good Cause?: How Charitable Institutions Become Powerful Economic Bullies* (Secaucus, NJ: Carol Publishing Group, 1997).

Henriques, Diane B., "Madoff Scheme Kept Rippling Outward, Across Borders," *The New York Times* (December 19, 2008) p. A1.

Hermes, J. J., "Senators Weigh Idea of Requiring Payout Rates for Large University Endowments," *The Chronicle of Higher Education* (September 27, 2007).

Horowitz, Helen Lekfowitz, *Alma Mater: Design and Experience in the Women's Colleges from Their Nineteenth-Century Beginnings to the 1930s* (New York: Knopf, 1984).

—— *Campus Life: Undergraduate Cultures from the End of the Eighteenth Century to the Present* (Chicago: University of Chicago Press, 1987).

Hyde, Lewis *The Gift: Imagination and the Erotic Life of Property* (New York: Vintage Books, 1983).

Jencks, Christopher and David Riesman, *The Academic Revolution* (Garden City, NY: Doubleday Anchor, 1968).

Jobs, Steven, "You've Got To Find What You Love," Commencement Speech at Stanford University (Stanford, CA: June 12, 2005).

Judd, Alan, "University of Georgia Foundations' Endowment Management Comes Under Scrutiny," *The Atlanta Journal Constitution* (November 24, 2003).

Kaplan, Ann E., Editor, *Giving USA: The Annual Report on Philanthropy for the Years 1992, 2000, 2005, and 2012* (New York: AAFRC Trust for Philanthropy, 1993, et al.).

Karl, Barry D. and Katz, Stanley N., "The American Private Philanthropic Foundation and the Public Sphere, 1890–1930," *Minerva* (March 1981) vol. 19, pp. 236–270.

Karlin-Resnick, Joshua, "Georgia Regents Mend Fences with University's Fund-Raising Foundations," *The Chronicle of Higher Education* (August 13, 2004).

Karoff, H. Peter, *The World We Want: New Dimensions in Philanthropy and Social Change* (New York: Altamira Press, 2007).

Karoff, H. Peter, Editor, *Just Money: A Critique of Contemporary American Philanthropy* (Boston: TPI Editions, 2004).

Kass, Amy A., Editor, *The Perfect Gift: The Philanthropic Imagination in Poetry and Prose* (Bloomington: Indiana University Press, 2002).

Keller, George, *Academic Strategy: The Management Revolution in American Higher Education* (Baltimore, MD and London: Johns Hopkins University Press, 1983).

Kennedy, David M., "Don't Blame Hoover," *Stanford Magazine* (January/February 1999) pp. 44–51.

Kerr, Clark, *The Uses of the University* (Cambridge, MA: Harvard University Press, 1963).

Kimball, Bruce with Benjamin A. Johnson, "The Beginning of 'Free Money' Ideology in American Universities: Charles W. Eliot at Harvard, 1869–1909," *History of Education Quarterly* (2012) vol. 52, pp. 222–250.

Krass, Peter, *Carnegie* (New York: John Wiley, 2002).

Lagemann, Ellen Condliffe, *The Politics of Knowledge: The Carnegie Corporation, Philanthropy, and Public Policy* (Chicago: University of Chicago Press, 1989).

———*Private Power for the Public Good: A History of the Carnegie Foundation for the Advancement of Teaching* (Middletown, CT: Wesleyan University Press, 1983).

Lagemann, Ellen Condliffe, Editor, *Philanthropic Foundations: New Scholarship, New Possibilities* (Bloomington: Indiana University Press, 1999).

Lasher, William F. and Deborah L. Greene, "College and University Budgeting: What Do We Know? What Do We Need to Know?," in Michael Paulsen and John Smart, Editors, *The Finance of Higher Education: Theory, Research, Policy and Practice* (New York: Agathon Press, 2001) pp. 501–542.

Leatherman, Courtney, "New York Regents Vote to Remove 18 of 19 Adelphi University Trustees," *The Chronicle of Higher Education* (February 21, 1997).

Leslie, John W., *Focus on Understanding and Support: A Study in College Management* (Washington, D.C.: American College Public Relations Association, 1969).

Levi-Strauss, Claude, "Reciprocity, the Essence of Social Life," in Lewis A. Cosner, Editor, *The Pleasures of Sociology* (New York: New American Library, 1980) pp. 69–80.

Lewin, Tamar, "Pay for U.S. College Presidents Continues to Grow," *The New York Times* (December 15, 2013).

———"Report Says Stanford Is First University to Raise $1 Billion in a Single Year," *The New York Times* (February 21, 2013) p. A17.

Liebersahn, Harry, *The Return of the Gift: European History of a Global Idea* (Cambridge University Press, 2011).

Lombardi, John, *How Universities Work* (Baltimore, MD and London: Johns Hopkins University Press, 2013).

Lowen, Rebecca, *Creating the Cold War University: The Transformation of Stanford* (Berkeley; London: University of California Press, 1999).

Lowenstein, Ralph, *Pragmatic Fund Raising for College Administrators and Fund Raisers* (Gainesville, Tallahassee, Tampa, Boca Raton, Jacksonville, Pensacola, Orland, and Miami: University Press of Florida, 1997).

Mangan, Katherine, "Descendent of 19th-Century Donor Sues Tulane Over Dissolution of Women's College," *The Chronicle of Higher Education* (August 20, 2008).

Mansfield, Harvey C. and Delba Winthrop, Translators and Editors, *Alexis de Tocqueville: Democracy in America* (Chicago: University of Chicago Press, 2000).

Marts & Lundy, *Special Report: 2013 Giving to Higher Education: The Big Gift Revival* (New York: Marts & Lundy, February 2014).

Masterson, Kathryn, "Judge Rules Fisk U. Can Sell O'Keeffe Art, But With Stipulations," *The Chronicle of Higher Education* (November 4, 2010).

Matthews, William H., *Adventures in Giving: The Story of the Rockefeller General Education Board* (New York: Dodd, Mead & Company, 1939).

Mauss, Marcel, *The Gift: The Form and Reason for Exchange in Archaic Societies*. Translated by W. D. Halls (New York: W. W. Norton, 1990).

Mayhew, Lewis B., *Surviving the Eighties: Strategies and Procedures for Solving Fiscal and Enrollment Problems* (San Francisco: Jossey-Bass, 1980).

McDearmon, J. Travis, "Hail to Thee, Our Alma Mater: Alumni Role Identity and the Relationship to Institutional Support Behaviors," *Research in Higher Education* (2013) vol. 54, pp. 288–302.

McDonald, Dwight, *The Ford Foundation: The Men and the Millions* (New York: Reynal, 1956).

Mendel, Stuart C., "A Field of Its Own," *Stanford Social Innovation Review* (Winter 2014) vol. 12, no.1, pp. 61–62.

Moody, Michael P., *Pass it On: Serial Reciprocity as a Principle of Philanthropy* (Indianapolis: Indiana University Center on Philanthropy, 1998).

——— "Reciprocity," *Learning to Give: An Action of the Heart, A Project for the Mind* (Electronic version retrieved July 10, 2006) p. 3.

National Research Council, 2004, *Bridging the Bed-Bench Gap: Contributions of the Markey Trust* (Washington, D.C.: The National Academies Press, 2004).

Nevins, Allan, *The State Universities and Democracy* (Urbana: University of Illinois Press, 1962) p. 82.

"New England's First Fruits 1640" in *Collections of the Massachusetts Historical Society*, 1792, vol. 1, pp. 242–248.

Nielsen, Waldemar A., *The Big Foundations* (New York and London: Columbia University Press, 1972).

——— "The Crisis of the Nonprofits," *Change* (1980) vol. 12, no. 1, pp. 23–29.

——— *The Golden Donors: A New Anatomy of the Great Foundations* (New York: Truman Talley Books of E. P. Dutton, 1985).

——— "The Pitfalls of Perpetuity," *Inside American Philanthropy: The Dramas of Donorship* (Norman and London: University of Oklahoma Press, 1996) ch. 17, pp. 245–252.

Ostrower, Francie, "Foundation Life Spans: A Vexing Issue," *The Chronicle of Philanthropy* (May 19, 2009).

———— *Limited Life Foundations: Motivations, Experiences, and Strategies* (Washington, D.C., The Urban Institute: Center on Nonprofits and Philanthropy, February 2009).

———— *Why The Wealthy Give: The Culture of Elite Philanthropy* (Princeton, NJ: Princeton University Press, 1995).

Panas, Jerold, *Mega Gifts: Who Gives Them, Who Gets Them.* (Medford, MA: Emerson & Church Publishers, second edition, 2005).

Payton, Robert L., *Philanthropy: Voluntary Action for the Public Good* (New York: American Council on Education/Macmillan Publishing Company, 1988).

Payton, Robert L. and Michael P. Moody, *Understanding Philanthropy: Its Meaning and Mission* (Bloomington: Indiana University Press, 2008).

Perez-Pena, Richard, "Facebook Founder to Donate $100 Million to Remake Newark Schools," *The New York Times* (September 22, 2010).

Perry, Suzanne, "Charities Get Tough Questions on Tax Breaks—and Can Expect More," *The Chronicle of Higher Education* (February 14, 2013).

Piereson, James and Naomi Schaefer, "The Problem with Public Policy Schools," *The Washington Post* (December 6, 2013).

Pink, Daniel H., *Drive: The Surprising Truth About What Motivates Us* (New York: Riverhead Books, 2009).

Pinker, Steven, *The Better Angles of Our Nature* (New York: Penguin Books, 2011).

Pitsch, Mark, "Foundation Releases Donor List: U of L Data Includes McConnell Center Gifts," *The Louisville Courier-Journal* (December 14, 2004) pp. A1, A10.

Pray, Francis C., General Editor, *Handbook for Educational Fund Raising: A Guide to Successful Principles and Practices for Colleges, Universities, and Schools* (San Francisco: Jossey-Bass Publishers, 1981).

Prewitt, Kenneth, "Foundations," in Walter A. Powell and Richard Steinberg, Editors, *The Nonprofit Sector: A Research Handbook* (New Haven, CT: Yale University Press, 2006) p. 367.

Prince, Russ A. and Karen M. File, *The Seven Faces of Philanthropy: A New Approach to Cultivating Major Donors* (San Francisco: Jossey-Bass Publishers, 1994).

Putnam, Robert, *Bowling Alone: The Collapse and Revival of American Community* (New York: Simon and Schuster, 2000).

Reich, Rob, Lacey Dorn and Stefanie Sutton, *Any Thing Goes: Approval of Nonprofit Status by the IRS* (Stanford, CA: Stanford University Center on Philanthropy and Civil Society, 2009).

Renz, Loren and David Wolcheck, *Perpetuity or Limited Lifespan: How Do Family Foundations Decide?* (Washington, D.C.: Foundation Center with the Council on Foundations, 2009).

Rhodes, Frank T., "The University and Its Critics," in William G. Bowen & Harold T. Shapiro, Editors, *Universities and Their Leadership* (Princeton, NJ: Princeton University Press, 1998) pp. 3–14.

Rhodes, Frank T., Editor, *Successful Fund Raising for Higher Education: The Advancement of Learning* (Washington, D.C.: American Council on Education and Oryx Press sponsored by Council for Advancement and Support of Education, 1997) (Series on Higher Education).

Riesman, David, *Constraint and Variety in American Education* (Garden City, NY: Doubleday Anchor, 1956).

Rivard, Ry, "Brandeis Changes Compensation Policies after $5 Million Payout to Ex-President," *Inside Higher Ed* (January 30, 2014).

Rosovsky, Henry, *The University: An Owner's Manual* (New York and London: W.W. Norton Publishers, 1990).

Rothschild, Michael, "Philanthropy and American Higher Education," in Charles T. Clotfelter and Thomas Ehrlich, Editors, *Philanthropy and the Nonprofit Sector in a Changing America* (Bloomington: Indiana University Press, 1999) pp. 413–427.

Rowland, A. Wesley, General Editor, *Handbook of Institutional Advancement: A Modern Guide to Executive Management, Institutional Relations, Fund-Raising, Alumni Administration, Government Relations, Publications, Periodicals, and Enrollment Management.* (San Francisco: Jossey-Bass, second edition, 1986).

Rudolph, Frederick, *The American College and University: A History* (New York: Alfred Knopf, 1962).

Schervish, Paul G., "Major Donors, Major Motives: The People and the Purpose Behind Major Gifts," in Lilya Wagner and Timothy L. Seiler, Editors, *Reprising Timeless Topics*, New Directions for Philanthropic Fundraising (San Francisco: Jossey-Bass, vol. 47, 2005) pp. 59–87.

Schlabach, Mark, "The NCAA: Where Does the Money Go?," *ESPN Sports Center News Release* (July 12, 2011).

Schneewind, J. B., Editor: *Giving: Western Ideas of Philanthropy* (Bloomington: Indiana University press, 1996).

Sears, Jesse Brundage, *Philanthropy in the History of American Higher Education* (Washington, D.C.: US Government Printing Office, 1922).

Segall, Grant, *John D. Rockefeller: Anointed with Oil* (Oxford and New York: Oxford University Press, 2001).

Seymour, Harold J., *Designs for Fund-Raising: Principles, Patterns, Techniques* (New York: McGraw-Hill, 1966)

Slosson, Edwin E., *Great American Universities* (New York: Macmillan Publishers, 1910).

Smith, David H., Editor, *Good Intentions: Moral Obstacles & Opportunities* (Bloomington: Indiana University Press, 2005).

Smith, James Howell, *Honorable Beggars: The Middlemen of American Philanthropy* (Madison: University of Wisconsin PhD Dissertation, 1968).

Soros, George, "My Philanthropy," *New York Review of Books* (June 23, 2011).

Staley, Oliver and Janet Frankston Lorin, "Princeton Settles Lawsuit Over $900 Million Endowment," *Bloomberg News Service* (December 10, 2008).

Strom, Stephanie, "Fees and Trustees: Paying the Keepers of the Cash," *The New York Times* (July 10, 2003).

—— "How Long Should Gifts Just Grow?: Trillions of Tax-Free Dollars Earning Double-Digit Returns are Inciting Calls to Speed Up Spending," *The New York Times* (Giving Section) (November 12, 2007) pp. H1, H30.

—— "A Tax Benefit That Bypasses Idea of Charity," *The New York Times* (April 25, 2005) pp. A1, A15.

Sturtevant, William T., *The Artful Journey: Cultivating and Soliciting the Major Gift* (Chicago: Bonus Books, 1997).

Swensen, David F., *Pioneering Portfolio Management: An Unconventional Approach to Institutional Investment* (New York: Free Press, 2000).

Thelin, John R., *Games Colleges Play: Scandal and Reform in College Sports* (Baltimore, MD and London: Johns Hopkins University Press, 1994).

—— *A History of American Higher Education* (Baltimore, MD and London: Johns Hopkins University Press, 2011, second edition).

—— "Horizontal History and Higher Education," in Marybeth Gasman, Editor, *The History of U.S. Higher Education: Methods for Understanding the Past* (New York and London: Routledge, 2010) pp. 71–83.

—— "Institutional History in Our Own Time: Higher Education's Shift from Managerial Revolution to Enterprising Evolution," *The CASE International Journal of Educational Advancement* (June 2000) vol. 1, no. 1, pp. 9–23.

—— *The Rising Costs of Higher Education: A Reference Handbook* (Santa Barbara, CA; Denver, CO; and Oxford, England: ABC-CLIO Publishers, 2013).

—— "Small by Design: Resilience in an Era of Mass Higher Education," in *Meeting the Challenge: America's Independent Colleges and Universities since 1956* (Washington, D.C.: Council of Independent Colleges, 2006).

Thelin, John R. and Lawrence L. Wiseman, *The Old College Try: Balancing Academics and Athletics in Higher Education* (Washington, D.C.: ASHE-ERIC Series on Higher Education, 1989).

Thelin, John R. and Richard W. Trollinger, "Forever Is a Long Time: Reconsidering Universities' Perpetual Endowment Policies in the Twenty-First Century," *History of Intellectual Culture* (2010/2011) vol. 9, no. 1, pp. 1–17.

—— *Time is of the Essence: Foundations and the Policies of Limited Life and Endowment Spend-Down* (Washington, D.C.: Aspen Institute Program on Philanthropy and Social Innovation, 2009).

Titmuss, Richard M. *The Gift Relationship: From Human Blood to Social Policy* (New York: The New Press, 1997).

Tobin, Gary A. and Aryeh K. Weinberg, *Mega-Gifts in American Philanthropy: Giving Patterns, 2001–2003* (San Francisco: Institute for Jewish & Community Research, 2007).

Trollinger, Richard W., *Philanthropy and Transformation in American Higher Education* (Lexington: University of Kentucky PhD Dissertation, 2009).

Tuchman, Gaye, *Wanna Be U: Inside the Corporate University* (Chicago: University of Chicago Press, 2009).

University Leadership Council, *Competing in the Era of Big Bets: Achieving Scale in Multidisciplinary Research* (Washington, D.C.: The Education Advisory Board, 2009).

Veysey, Laurence M., *The Emergence of the American University* (Chicago: University of Chicago Press, 1964).

Vezacos, David and Susan Decker, "Princeton Drug Royalties Spark Suit Over Tax Exemption," *Bloomberg News Service* (September 4, 2013).

Vigeland, Carl A., *Great Good Fortune: How Harvard Makes Its Money* (New York: Houghton Mifflin, 1986).

Vladek, Bruce B., "The Over-Investment Crisis in Higher Education," *Change* (1979) vol. 10, no. 11, p. 39.

Walton, Andrea, Editor, *Women and Philanthropy in Education* (Bloomington and Indianapolis: Indiana University Press, 2005).

Walton, Andrea and Marybeth Gasman, Editors, *Philanthropy, Volunteerism & Fundraising in Higher Education* (Boston: Pearson Publishing, 2008) (Association for the Study of Higher Education, ASHE Reader Series).

Weber, Max, *The Protestant Ethic and the Spirit of Capitalism* (Oxford: Oxford University Press, the Revised 1920 Edition, 2011).

Weisbrod, Burton A., *The Nonprofit Economy* (Cambridge, MA: Harvard University Press, 1988).

Welch, Patrice A., Editor, *Increasing Annual Giving* in *New Directions for Institutional Advancement* (San Francisco: Jossey Bass, 1980) (no. 7).

Wells, Amy E., "Contested Ground: Howard Odum, the Southern Agrarians, and the Emerging University in the South During the 1930s," *History of Higher Education Annual* (2001) vol. 21, pp. 79–101.

Whitehead, John, "How to Think about the Dartmouth College Case," *History of Education Quarterly* (Fall 1986) vol. 26, no. 3, pp. 333–349.

—— *The Separation of College and State* (New Haven, CT: Yale University Press, 1973).

Wilson, Edward O., *The Social Conquest of Earth* (New York: Liveright, 2012).

—— *Sociobiology: The New Synthesis* (Cambridge, MA: The Belknap Press of Harvard University Press, 2006).

Wood, James R. and James G. Houghland Jr., "The Role of Religion in Philanthropy," in J. Van Til and Associates, Editors, *Critical Issues in American Philanthropy* (San Francisco: Jossey Bass, 1990) pp. 99–132.

Worth, Michael and James W. Asp, *The Development Officer in Higher Education: Toward an Understanding of the Role* (Washington, D.C.: ASHE ERIC, 1994).

Worth, Michael J., Editor, *New Strategies for Educational Fund Raising* (Westport, CT: Praeger with American Council on Education, 2002).

Wright, Stephen J., "The Black Colleges and Universities: Historical Background and Future Prospects," *Virginia Foundation for the Humanities Newsletter* (Spring 1988) vol. 14, pp. 1–4.

"Yale: 'F' in Ethics," Editorial in *The Indianapolis Star* (March 22, 1995) p. A10;

Yardley, William, "Coach Johnny Orr, 86; Improved Pay and Iowa State: Obituary," *The New York Times* (January 4, 2014) p. A15.

York, Michelle, "What's in a Name? Some Obscure Scholarships Often Go Begging," *The New York Times* (January 3, 2006).

Zunz, Olivier, *Philanthropy in America: A History* (Princeton, NJ: Princeton University Press, 2011).

Articles

Philanthropy and higher education is a newsworthy topic in the public forum. Those who take its issues and policies seriously have had the benefit of the topic being covered by excellent writers and reporters in a variety of publications, including *The Chronicle of Higher Education*, *Inside Higher Ed*, *The Chronicle of Philanthropy*, and *The New York Times*. The following selected list of citations is illustrative of outstanding investigative reporting and journalism whose information and findings have been integral to this book.

Altschuler, Glenn, "Endowment Payout Rates Are Too Stingy," *The Chronicle of Higher Education* (March 31, 2000) p. B8.

Arenson, Karen W., "Soaring Endowments Widen a Higher Education Gap," *The New York Times* (February 4, 2008) p. A14.

Auletta, Ken, "Get Rich U.: Annals of Higher Education," *The New Yorker* (April 30, 2012) pp. 38–47.

Barbaro, Michael, "Bloomberg to Johns Hopkins: Thanks a Billion (Well, $1.1 Billion)," *The New York Times* (January 27, 2013) pp. A1, A16.

Barkan, Joanne, "As Government Funds Dwindle, Giant Foundations Gain Too Much Power," *The Chronicle of Philanthropy* (October 20, 2013) p. A1.

Barron, James, "Yale Will Pay $2.6 Billion to New Haven," *The New York Times* (April 3, 1990) pp. B1, B6.

Blackford, Linda B., "Joe Craft Donated 'Majority' of Money for New Rupp Arena Locker Rooms," *The Lexington (Kentucky) Herald-Leader* (January 8, 2013) p. A1.

Blumenstyk, Goldie, "New Head of Ford Fund's Education Program is Champion of Women and Minority Students," *The Chronicle of Higher Education* (December 9, 1991) pp. A27–A28.

——— "Pressure Builds on Wealthy Colleges to Spend More of Their Assets," *The Chronicle of Higher Education* (November 2, 2007) vol. 54, no. 10, pp. A1–A20, A21.

——— "Princeton's Royalty Windfall Leads to Challenge of Tax-Exempt Status," *The Chronicle of Higher Education* (July 8, 2013).

——— "Town-Gown Battles Escalate as Beleaguered Cities Assail College Tax Exemptions," *The Chronicle of Higher Education* (June 29, 1988).

Buffett, Peter, "The Charitable-Industrial Complex," *The New York Times* (July 26, 2013) p. A23.

Carvajal, Doreen, "In Need, French Museums Turn to Masses, Chapeaux in Hand," *The New York Times* (December 24, 2012) pp. A1, A3.

"College Endowments Over $250-Million, 2012," *The Chronicle of Higher Education Almanac, 2013–2014* (August 23, 2013) p. 56.

Eisenberg, Pablo, "Foundations' Failure to Give More is Inexcusable" *The Chronicle of Philanthropy* (November 27, 2008) pp. 26–27.

Ekman, Richard, "Many Small Private Colleges Thrive With Modest Endowments," *The Chronicle of Higher Education* (June 2, 2006).

Frazier, Eric, "IRS Steps Up Scrutiny of Colleges and Other Nonprofit Groups," *The Chronicle of Higher Education* (December 20, 2010).

Gibbons, Vera, "An Embarrassment of Riches," *Smart Money* (October 1998) pp. 138–143.

"Giving Till It Hurts," *The Wall Street Journal* (July 6, 2007) p. W1.

Healy, Patrick, "Colleges vs. Communities: Battles Intensify Over City Efforts to Win Payments from Tax-Exempt Institutions," *The Chronicle of Higher Education* (May 5, 1995) pp. A27, A32.

Jaschik, Scott, "Extensive IRS Audits Find Many Colleges are Violating Tax Laws," *The Chronicle of Higher Education* (January 20, 1995) p. A18.

———"Rich Harvard, Poor Harvard," *Inside Higher Ed* (November 11, 2013).

Keohane, Nannerl O., "If a Handsome Income Is Your Goal in Life, You Should Be in Some Other line of Work," *The Chronicle of Higher Education* (December 7, 1994).

Khalaf, Rhoula, "Customized Accounting," *Forbes* Magazine (May 25, 1992) p. 50.

Kolmerten, Carol, "What Professors Can Teach Fund Raisers—and Vice Versa," *The Chronicle of Higher Education* (December 5, 2003) p. B5.

Levine, Arthur, "Higher Education's New Status as a Mature Industry," *The Chronicle of Higher Education* (January 31, 1997) p. A48.

Levi-Strauss, Claude, *Introduction to the Work of Marcel Mauss* (London: Routledge, 1987).

Lewin, Tamar, "Maryland Renames Law School After Gift: $30 Million Grant and Big Ambitions," *The New York Times* (April 25, 2011) p. A14.

Lipton, Eric, "Fight Over Minimum Wage Illustrates Web of Industry Ties," *The New York Times* (February 9, 2014) pp. A1, A11.

Lovett, Ian, "Lasting Tributes Meet Early End in Bankruptcy: Memorials Are Removed as Church Changes Hands," *The New York Times* (September 6, 2013) pp. A11, A13.

Madoff, Ray D., "How Government Gives," *The New York Times* (December 7, 2013) p. A19.

Mangan, Katherine S., "An Unfair 'Tax'?: Law and Business Schools Object to Bailing Out Medical Centers," *The Chronicle of Higher Education* (May 15, 1998) pp. A43–A44.

Marcy, Mary B., "Why Foundations Have Cut Back in Higher Education," *The Chronicle of Higher Education* (July 25, 2003).

Martin, Andrew, "Degrees of Debt—a Reckoning for Colleges: Building a Showcase Campus, Using an I.O.U.," *The New York Times* (December 14, 2012) pp. A1, B4.

Mercer, J., "The Fund Raiser as President," *The Chronicle of Higher Education* (September 15, 1995) vol. 42, no. 3, pp. A35–36.

Merriman, Dick, "The College as a Philanthropy. Yes, a Philanthropy," *The Chronicle of Higher Education* (October 31, 2010).

Michael, Stephen O., "Why Give to a College That Already Has Enough?," *The Chronicle of Higher Education* (July 6, 2007).

Moody, Michael P., *Pass It On: Serial Reciprocity as a Principle of Philanthropy* (Indianapolis, Indiana: Indiana University Center on Philanthropy, 1998).

Myeong, Do-Hyeong, "Freshman Seminar Donates $25,000 at End of Course to Charitable Organizations," *The Daily Princetonian* (February 11, 2014).

Nicklin, Julie L., "Markey Trust, Having Given $500-Million, Will Close This Year," *The Chronicle of Higher Education* (February 28, 1997).

—— "Whitaker Foundation Seeks to Meet Goals and Go Out of Business," *The Chronicle of Higher Education* (February 28, 1997).

Parker, Kathleen, "College's Diminishing Returns Rooted in Cost, Quality Concerns," syndicated column published in *The Lexington (Kentucky) Herald-Leader* (January 29, 2014) p. A15.

Piereson, James and Naomi Schaefer Riley, "Why Shouldn't Princeton Pay Taxes?," *The Wall Street Journal* (August 20, 2013) p. A15.

Pope, Justin, "Congress Eyes College Wealth: Endowments Tied to Tuition Concerns," Associated Press Article (October 15, 2007).

Rosen, Lawrence, "Have Colleges Flouted the Prudent-Investor Rule?," *The Chronicle of Higher Education* (August 8, 2010).

Rosenthal, Elisabeth, "Benefits Questioned in Tax Breaks for Nonprofit Hospitals," *The New York Times* (December 16, 2013) pp. A12, A20.

Schneider, Allison, "Empty Tables at the Faculty Club Worry Some Academics," *The Chronicle of Higher Education* (June 13, 1997) p. A12.

Semple, Kirk, "Affluent Asians in U.S. Turning to Philanthropy," *The New York Times* (January 9, 2013) pp. A1, A20.

Shepard, Robert S., "How Can a University That Raises a Billion Dollars Have a Tight Budget?," *The Chronicle of Higher Education* (January 12, 1994) p. A48.

—— "United Way Head Resigns over Spending Habits," *The Washington Post* (February 28, 1992).

Singer, Peter, "Good Charity, Bad Charity," *The New York Times Sunday Review* (August 11, 2013) p. SR5.

—— *The Life You Can Save: How to Play Your Part in Ending World Poverty* (New York: Random House Trade Paperbacks, 2009).

Steinberg, Jacques, "Harvard's $2.1 Billion Taps Colleges' Big Fund Raising," *The New York Times* (October 7, 1999).

Stern, Ken, "The Charity Swindle," *The New York Times* (November 26, 2013) p. A21.

Strom, Stephanie, "Nonprofits Fear Losing Tax Benefit," *The New York Times* (December 2, 2010).

"Student Demographics," *The Chronicle of Higher Education Almanac Issue, 2011–2012* (August 26, 2011) vol. 58, no. 1, p. 32.

Sullivan, Paul, "Among Young Inheritors, An Urge to Redistribute," *The New York Times* (March 26, 2013) p. F3.

Swartz, Jon, "Band of Billionaires Pledge to Give: Buffett, Gateses Call on Wealthy to Donate Up to Half Their Fortunes," *USA Today* (August 5, 2010) p. B1.

Swiatek, Jeff, "A Chance to Eat, Drink and Be Silly," *The Indianapolis Star* (January 22, 1994) pp. C1, C2.

Teltsch, K. "Derby Enthusiasts will Set Big Trust for Medical Research," *The New York Times* (August 26, 1984).

Thelin, John R., "The Gates Foundation's Uncertain Legacy," *The Chronicle of Higher Education* (July 14, 2013).

—— "Parsing the Case Against College," *Inside Higher Ed* (January 11, 2013).

Therrien, Lois, "Getting Joe College to Pay for City Services," *Business Week* (July 16, 1990) p. 37.

Troop, Don, "Gifts to Colleges Hit $33.8-Billion, Topping Pre-Recession Levels," *The Chronicle of Higher Education* (February 12, 2014).

———— "The Secrets of 'Million-dollar Ready' Colleges," *Inside Higher Ed* (December 11, 2013).

Veyne, Paul, *Bread and Circuses* (London: Penguin Books, 1992).

Wiebe, Robert H., *The Search for Order, 1877 to 1920* (New York: Hill and Wang, 1967).

Wieder, Ben, "Thiel Fellowships Pay 24 Talented Students $100,000 Not To Attend College," *The Chronicle of Higher Education* (May 25, 2011).

Wolverton, Brad, "Senate Committee Examines Endowments," *The Chronicle of Higher Education* (June 8, 2007) vol. 53, no. 40, p. A25.

Index

Abrams, Frank and independent
    colleges, 123–4
altruism
    defined, 42–4
    effective, 44–6
    in nature, 43
    relationship to philanthropy, 42–6,
        60–1
alumni associations, 25, 154
American Education Society, 16–17
Andreoni, James, 61
annual giving, 160–1
appropriations from state
    governments, 16
architecture
    as a campaign tool, 4
    as an indicator of status, 3–4
athletics
    creation of independent
        associations, 27–8
    funding for, 27–8
    money generated by, 134–5
    as recipients of philanthropic gifts,
        177–80

Bayh-Dole Act of 1980, 141
Berea College, 23
Bernstein, Allison, 83
Bill and Melinda Gates Foundation,
    86–9
Bloomberg, Michael, 172–3
Bok, Derek, 141
books as donations, 13–14
Boston University, 30

Boulding, Kenneth, 51–3
Bowen, Howard, 98, 102
Boyle, Sir Robert, 15
Bremner, Robert, 37
Brown University. See The College
    of Rhode Island and Providence
    Plantations
Buffett, Peter, 183–4

campaign fund-raising, 164–5
Carey, William Polk, 3
Carnegie, Andrew, 21
Carnegie Foundation for the
    Advancement of Teaching
    (CFAT), 71–3
change theories, 55–8
charity differentiated from
    philanthropy, 37–8
Cheit, Earl F., 30
Christmas Seals campaign, 150
church affiliations and colleges, 19
Civil War, 17–18
Clark, Burton C., 23
Clark University, 20
Clotfelter, Charles, 102
Coca-Cola Corporation, 30
college agents. See fund raising:
    origins of
College of Rhode Island and
    Providence Plantations, 11
College of William and Mary, 108, 175
college presidents
    compensation paid to, 132–3
    role as fund raisers, 22–3

college towns and local government
relations. *See* Town and Gown
relations
colonial era
enrollments in, 15
philanthropy in, 10–16
compensation
paid to college coaches, 133
paid to college presidents, 132–3
conditions placed upon gifts, 14–15
corporate giving, 161–2
corporations' right to donate to higher
education, 123–4
Council for Advancement and Support
of Education (CASE), 143, 146, 155
Council for Financial Aid to Education,
28–9, 125–6, 162, 166
cy pres, doctrine of, 111

Dartmouth College v. *Woodward*
(1819), 109, 120
"dead hand" of endowments, 106–7,
110–11, 117
Deep Springs College, 23–4
Delta Cost Project, 134
development
creation and growth as a field, 153–5
as distinct from fund-raising, 153–4
elements common to comprehensive
programs, 159–65
development offices, 157–65
development personnel
differences by institutional type, 158
professional organizations for, 146,
152, 153–5, 157
donor motivation. *See* motivation
donors
attaching strings to gifts, 14–15
recognition of, 161
rights of, 137–9
Douglas, Mary, 48–50
Drezner, Noah, 174–5
Duke University, 24–5

Effective Altruism, 44–6.
See also altruism
Ehrenberg, Ronald G., 32

eleemosynary organizations, 109, 120
Eliot, Charles, 22
Emory University, 30
endowed professorships, 14
endowments, 95–117
decentralization of, 111–13
highest gross, 95
highest per capita by student, 95–6
legislation regarding, 96–7, 99–100,
103
perpetual endowments versus
limited life, 99–101, 103, 116–17
scholarship, 110–11
spending from, 96
tax benefits bestowed upon, 103

federal government support for higher
education, 32, 126. *See also* Bok,
Derek; Glazer, Nathan
federal regulations, absence of, 69
financial aid, 28–9, 32
"First Fruits" (Harvard College), 10
Fisk University, 138
Flexner, Abraham, 71–2
Ford Foundation, 28, 80–3
foundation relations, 162–3
foundations
private, 67–93
public resentment toward, 121–2
France, philanthropy in, 1
Frick, Henry C., 20
Frumkin, Peter, 56–7
fund raising
goals as measures of prestige, 159
origins and growth of, 145, 147–57
strategies for, 22–3

Gasman, Marybeth, 174–5
Gates Foundation. *See* Bill and
Melinda Gates Foundation
Gates, Frederick T., 19, 74–5, 148–9
General Education Board (GEB), 73–8
gifts
core beliefs about, 49–50
defined, 47–8, 51–2
in kind, 12–13, 14
reciprocity and the giving of, 48–54

Glazer, Nathan, 141
"Golden Age of Philanthropy," 31
Government relation to nonprofits, 119–43
Greenbrier Conference of 1958, 154–5
Grenville, George, 107–8
Gross, Robert, 37

Hansmann, Henry, 97, 106, 111
Harkness, Edward S., 24
Harvard College, 10, 14
Harvard, John, 10
Harvard University, 9, 22, 103–4, 170
Hearst family, 4
Henry VIII, 107
Hewlett Foundation. See William and Flora Hewlett Foundation
Hollis, Thomas, 14–15
"Honorable beggars," 1, 19
Hoover, Herbert, 26
Hopkins, Johns, 20
horizontal institutions, 6
Hyde, Lewis, 47–8

independent colleges and universities, donations to and tax exemptions, 123–4
Indiana University, 4
institutional advancement, 155
institutions, vertical and horizontal, 6

Jobs, Steve, 185–6

Karl, Barry D., 69
Katz, Stanley, 69
Keohane, Nannerl and nonprofit professional service, 131–3
Kimball, Bruce, 22

Life magazine, 4
Lilly family, 4
limited-life philanthropy. See General Education Board; Lucille P. Markey Charitable Trust; Rosenwald Fund
Lucille P. Markey Charitable Trust, 83–6

major gifts, 165
Markey Trust. See Lucille P. Markey Charitable Trust
Marts & Lundy, 188–9
Mauss, Marcel, 48–9
McDearmon, J. Travis, 176
McDonald, Dwight. See Ford Foundation
McGarvie and Friedman, 38–9
meliorism, 55
memorial stadium building boom, 26
morality (giving as a moral act), 44–6
Morrill Act, 18
motivation
    extrinsic versus intrinsic, 59
    Schervish's mobilizing factors, 58–64

namesake colleges, 20
National Collegiate Athletic Association (NCAA), 134
Native Americans, 15
Nevins, Allan, 3–4
Nielsen, Waldemar A., 90, 101
non-governmental organizations (NGOs). See nonprofit organizations
non-monetary donations. See gifts: in kind
nonprofit organizations
    ethical conduct of, 130–1
    perceived role of, 128–9
    relationship to business interests, 129–30
    as subsidiary units within universities, 135, 136
nonprofit sector, 64–6
Northwestern University, 153
Nunn, L. L., 24. See also Deep Springs College

Payton, Robert, 38
philanthropy
    by alumni, 25
    by Asian immigrants, 1–2
    defined, 36–41
    as differentiated from charity, 37–8
    dual nature of, 41

philanthropy—*Continued*
  as a family endeavor, 3, 4
  as a field of inquiry, 35
  from the perspective of public
    policy, 39–40
  integral role of women in, 175–6
  misuses of, 182–3
  teaching undergraduates about, 191
  unintended consequences of, 183–4
Pink, Daniel, 59
Pinker, Steven, 43
planned giving, 163–4
presidents. *See* college presidents
Princeton University, 138–9, 140–1
Putnam, Robert, 167

relief organizations, 17–18
religion as a motivation for giving,
    59–60
Rice, William Marsh, 21
Rockefeller Foundation, 25
Rockefeller, Sr., John D., 20, 75–6
Rockefeller University, 70
Rosenwald Fund, 78–80

Savage, Howard J., 71
Schervish, Paul. *See* motivation:
    Schervish's mobilizing factors
scholarships
  to promote certain professions, 16–17
  restrictions placed upon, 110
Scripps, Ellen Browning, 176
Sears, Jesse Brundage, 12, 40, 101
Section 501(c)(3) organizations,
    39–40, 119
  lax IRS oversight of, 127–8
serial reciprocity, 52–4. *See also* gifts:
    reciprocity and the giving of
Seymour, Harold J., 153
Singer, Peter, 181–2
Soros, George, 172
Sparks, Frank, 124–5
Sproul, Robert G., 27
Stanford, Leland and Jane, 20–1
Stanford University, 9, 26
Statute of Charitable Uses (1601), 40
Sterling bequest (Yale), 20
Stuhr, R. L., 153

subscriptions, 13
Swensen, David, 115

tax deductions as incentives for
    giving, 46, 58
tax exemptions, fairness of for higher
    education, 140–4
Tax Reform Act of 1969, 155–6
Thiel, Peter, 185
three great motivations of classical
    philosophy, 39, 51
TIAA-CREF, 71
Titmuss, Richard, 50–1
Town and Gown relations, 139–41
Tulane University, 139
Turgot, A. J., 106–7. *See also* "dead
    hand" of endowments

UBIT (Unrelated Business Income Tax),
    141
United States Postal Service, 2
university foundations, 28
University of California, Berkeley, 4
University of Georgia, 135–6
University of Pittsburgh Medical
    Center, 140
University of Southern California,
    169–70
university research foundations (URF),
    135

Vanderbilt, Commodore, 21
vertical institutions, 6
volunteer associations, 26

Walton, Andrea, 175
"Ward method," 151
Wells, Herman B, 4
Whitehead, John, 17
William and Flora Hewlett
    Foundation, 31, 86
windfall donations, 20
women
  education of, 18
  See also philanthropy: integral
    role of women in

Yale University, 137–8

CPSIA information can be obtained
at www.ICGtesting.com
Printed in the USA
LVOW01*0715220217

525056LV00011B/45/P

9 781137 319968